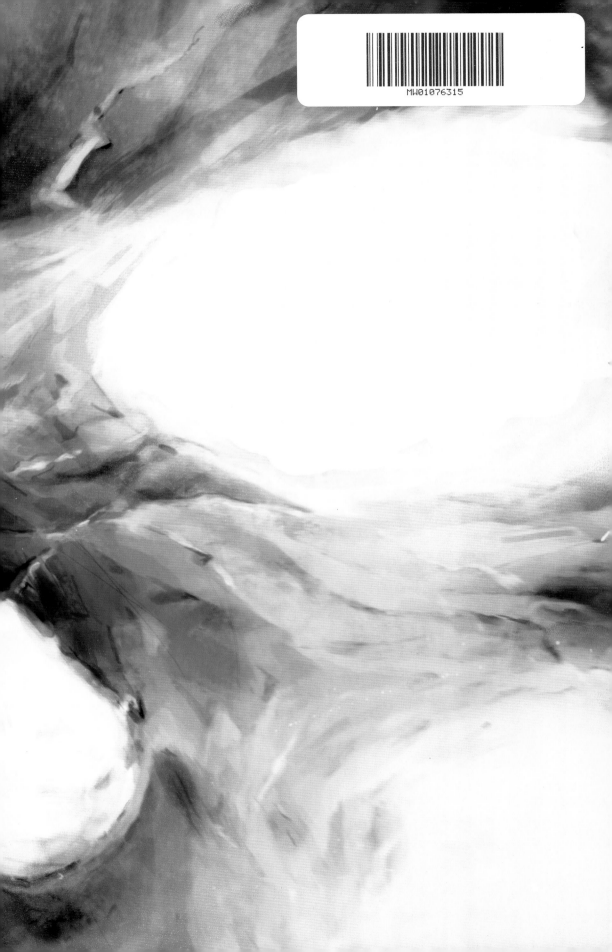

script
SAM SARKAR

art
GARRIE GASTONNY

color
SAKTI YUWONO

lettering
BEBE GIRAFFE

cover
BAGUS HUTOMO

co-developed & edited
DAVE ELLIOTT

pr & marketing
GIANLUCA GLAZER

ISBN: 978-1-60706-485-5

THE VAULT, Volume 1.
First Printing.
Published by Image Comics, Inc.
Office of publication: 2134 Allston Way,
2nd Floor, Berkeley, CA 94704. Copyright
© 2012 Sam Sarkar. All rights reserved.
Originally published in single magazine form
as THE VAULT #1-3. THE VAULT™ (including all
prominent characters featured herein), its logo and
all character likenesses are trademarks of Sam Sarkar,
unless otherwise noted. Image Comics® and its logos
are registered trademarks and copyrights of Image Comics,
Inc. All rights reserved. No part of this publication may be
reproduced or transmitted, in any form or by any means (except
for short excerpts for review purposes) without the express
written permission of Image Comics, Inc. All names, characters,
events and locales in this publication are entirely fictional. Any
resemblance to actual persons (living or dead), events or places,
without satiric intent, is coincidental. PRINTED IN KOREA.

International Rights Representative:
Christine Meyer (christine@gfloystudio.com).

IMAGE COMICS, INC.
Robert Kirkman - chief operating officer
Erik Larsen - chief financial officer
Todd McFarlane - president
Marc Silvestri - chief executive officer
Jim Valentino - vice-president

Eric Stephenson - publisher
Todd Martinez - sales & licensing coordinator
Sarah deLaine - pr & marketing coordinator
Branwyn Bigglestone - accounts manager
Emily Miller - administrative assistant
Jamie Parreno - marketing assistant
Kevin Yuen - digital rights coordinator
Tyler Shainline - production manager
Drew Gill - art director
Jonathan Chan - senior production artist
Monica Garcia - production artist
Vincent Kukua - production artist
Jana Cook - production artist
www.imagecomics.com

The VAULT

INTRODUCTION

Growing up in Nova Scotia, I was always fascinated by the mystery of the Oak Island Money Pit. First discovered by a teenager named Daniel McGinnis in 1795, the Money Pit remains one of the most famous treasure hunts in the world. Protected by an elaborate series of platforms and a specially dug flood channel, the Money Pit was always a nightmare of a dig.

Now over two hundred feet deep, the pit has claimed a number of lives over the history of its excavation and has been rumored to contain anything ranging from Captain Kidd's hoard, the treasure of the Knight's Templar to the Holy Grail. It has cost different backers several fortunes in attempts to raise treasure but the only things that have been found in it have only served to deepen its mystery, among them a large stone etched with mysterious symbols.

There are many theories on the Pit and more than a few point out the similarity of the pit's architecture and the engineering inside the Great Pyramid.

That lead me to the idea that perhaps the Money Pit was never intended for hiding treasure but was instead, a burial vault for something that was not made to be uncovered.

- Sam Sarkar

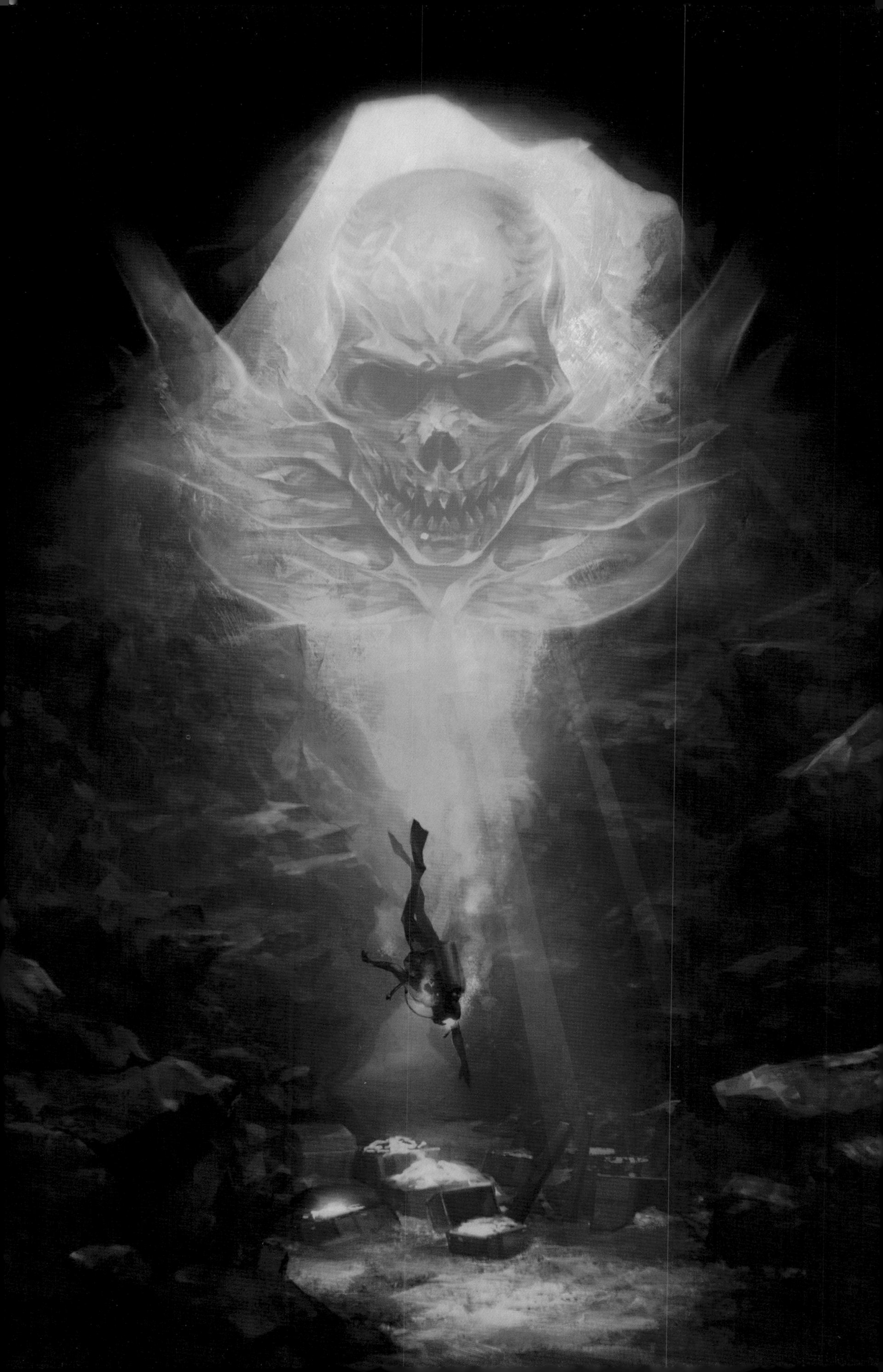

"This is the beginning
of how it all ends."

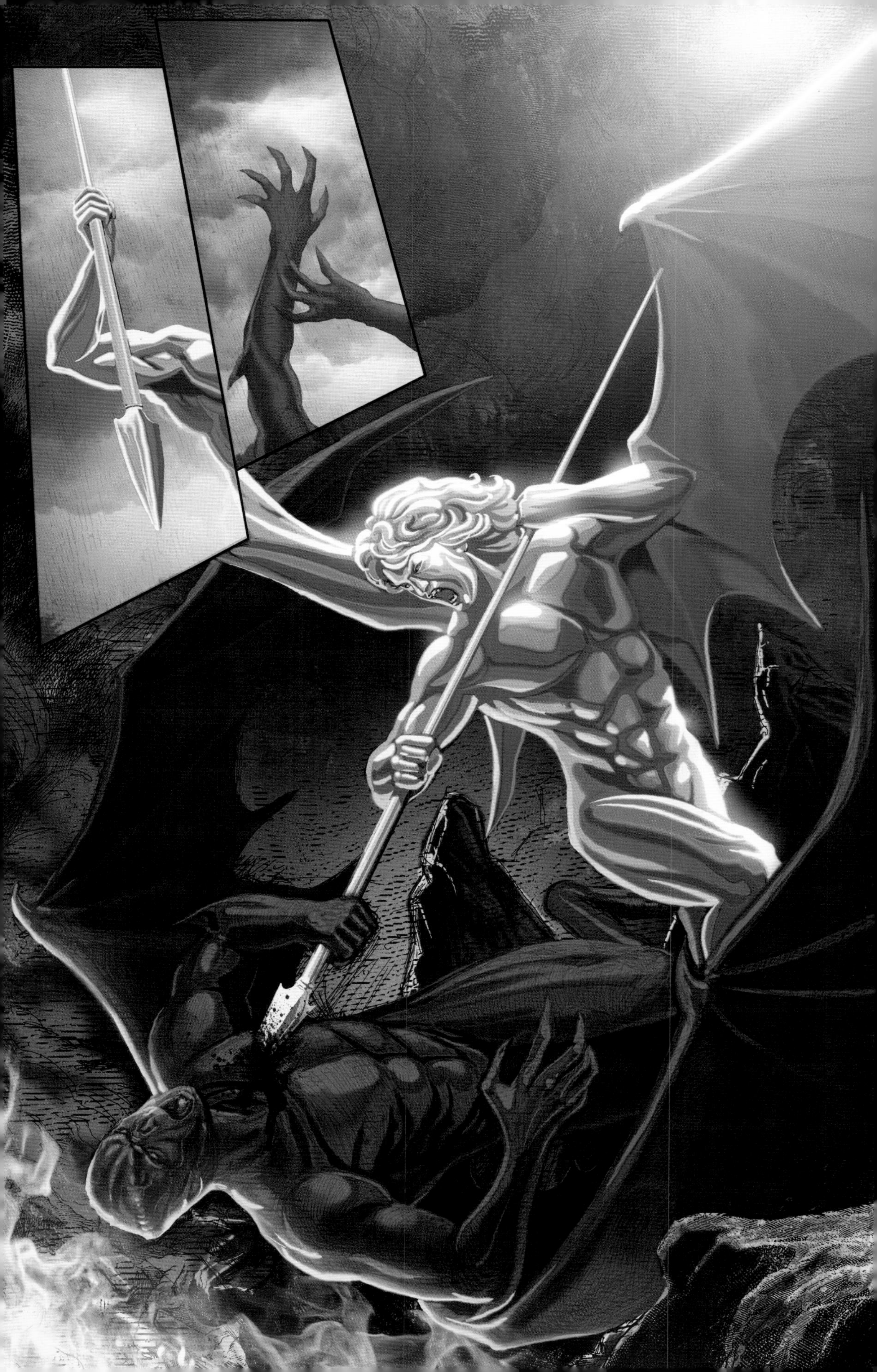

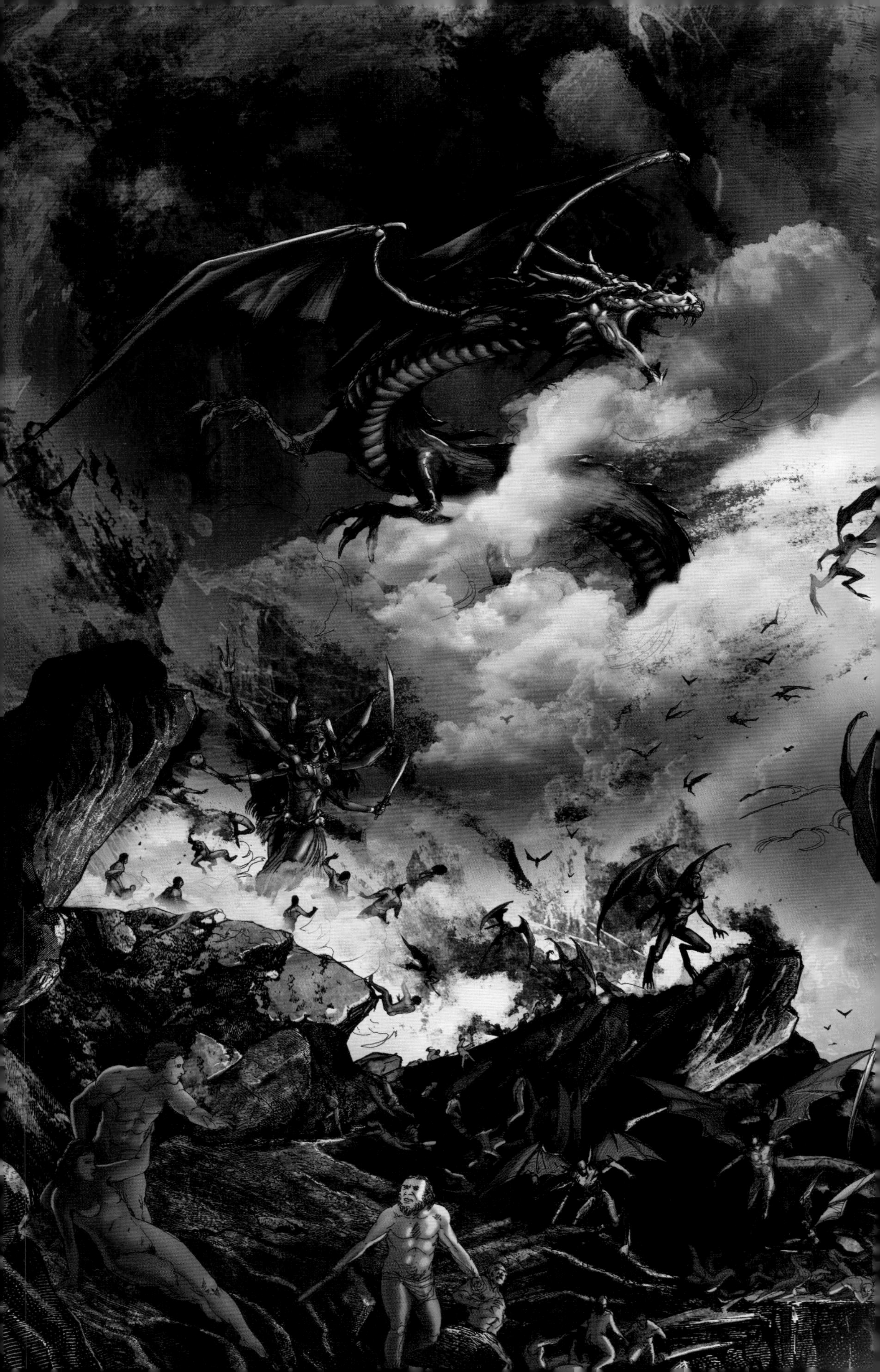

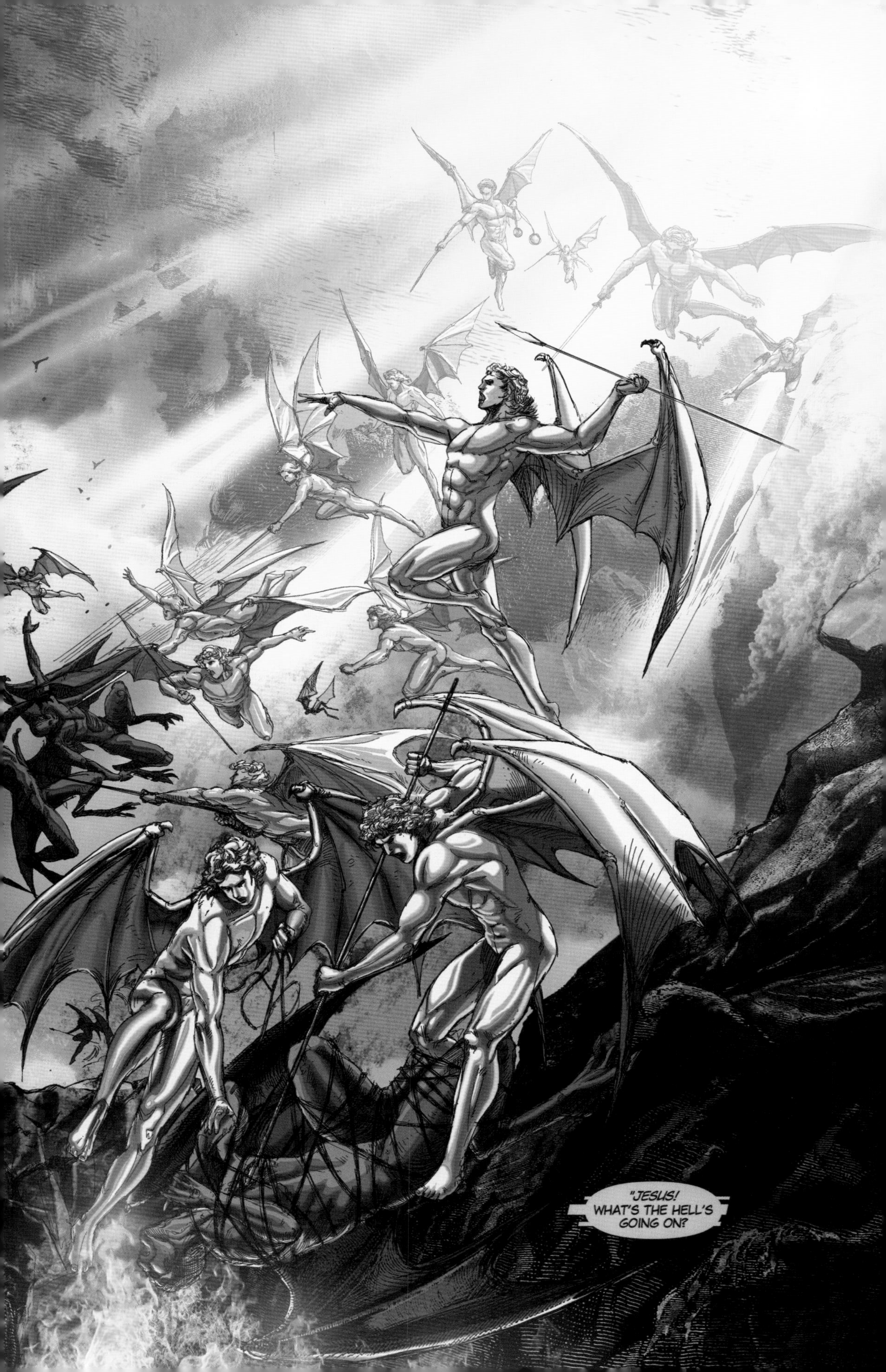
"JESUS!
WHAT'S THE HELL'S
GOING ON?

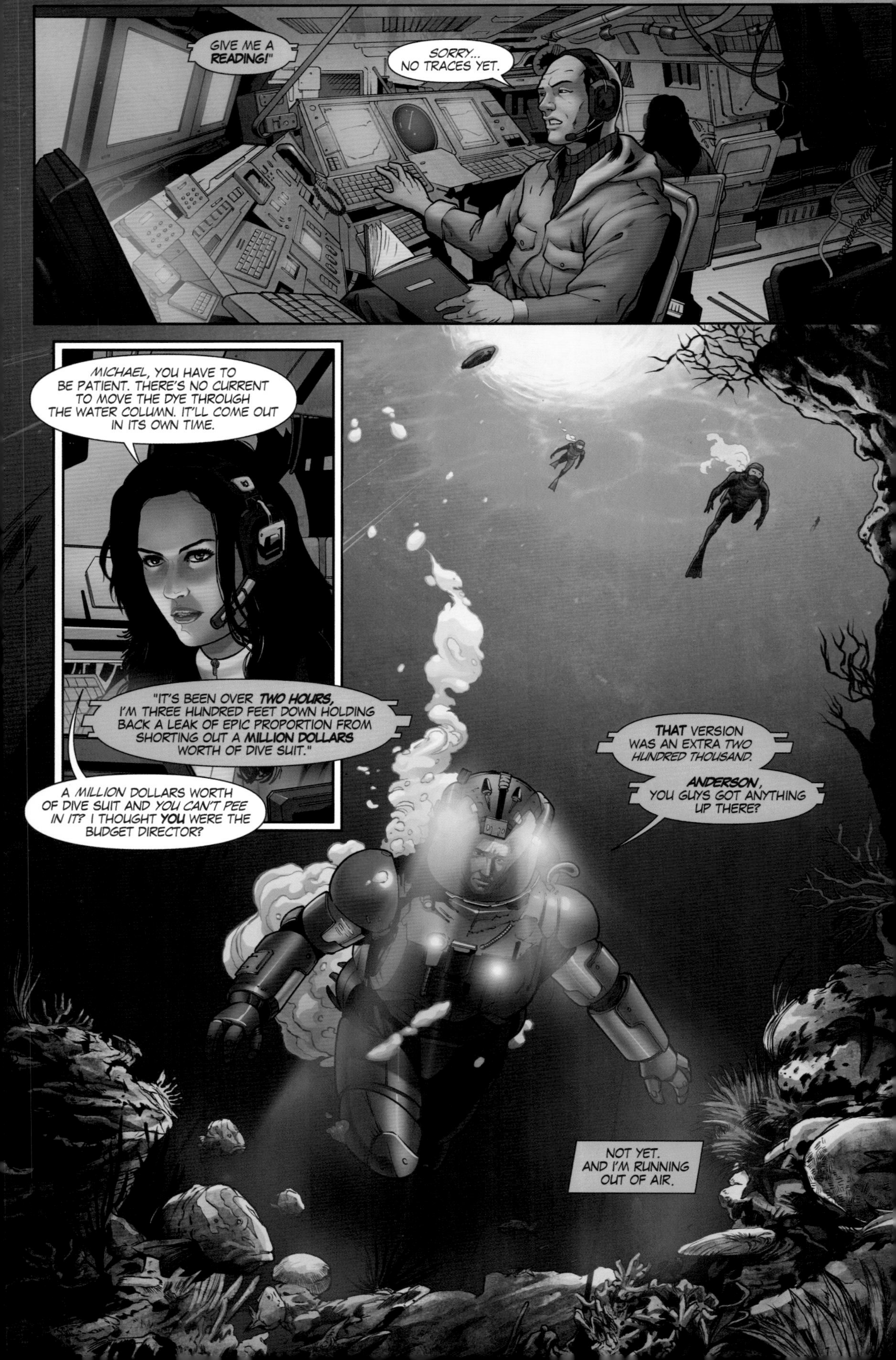
GIVE ME A READING!"
SORRY... NO TRACES YET.
MICHAEL, YOU HAVE TO BE PATIENT. THERE'S NO CURRENT TO MOVE THE DYE THROUGH THE WATER COLUMN. IT'LL COME OUT IN ITS OWN TIME.
"IT'S BEEN OVER TWO HOURS, I'M THREE HUNDRED FEET DOWN HOLDING BACK A LEAK OF EPIC PROPORTION FROM SHORTING OUT A MILLION DOLLARS WORTH OF DIVE SUIT."
A MILLION DOLLARS WORTH OF DIVE SUIT AND YOU CAN'T PEE IN IT? I THOUGHT YOU WERE THE BUDGET DIRECTOR?
THAT VERSION WAS AN EXTRA TWO HUNDRED THOUSAND.
ANDERSON, YOU GUYS GOT ANYTHING UP THERE?
NOT YET. AND I'M RUNNING OUT OF AIR.

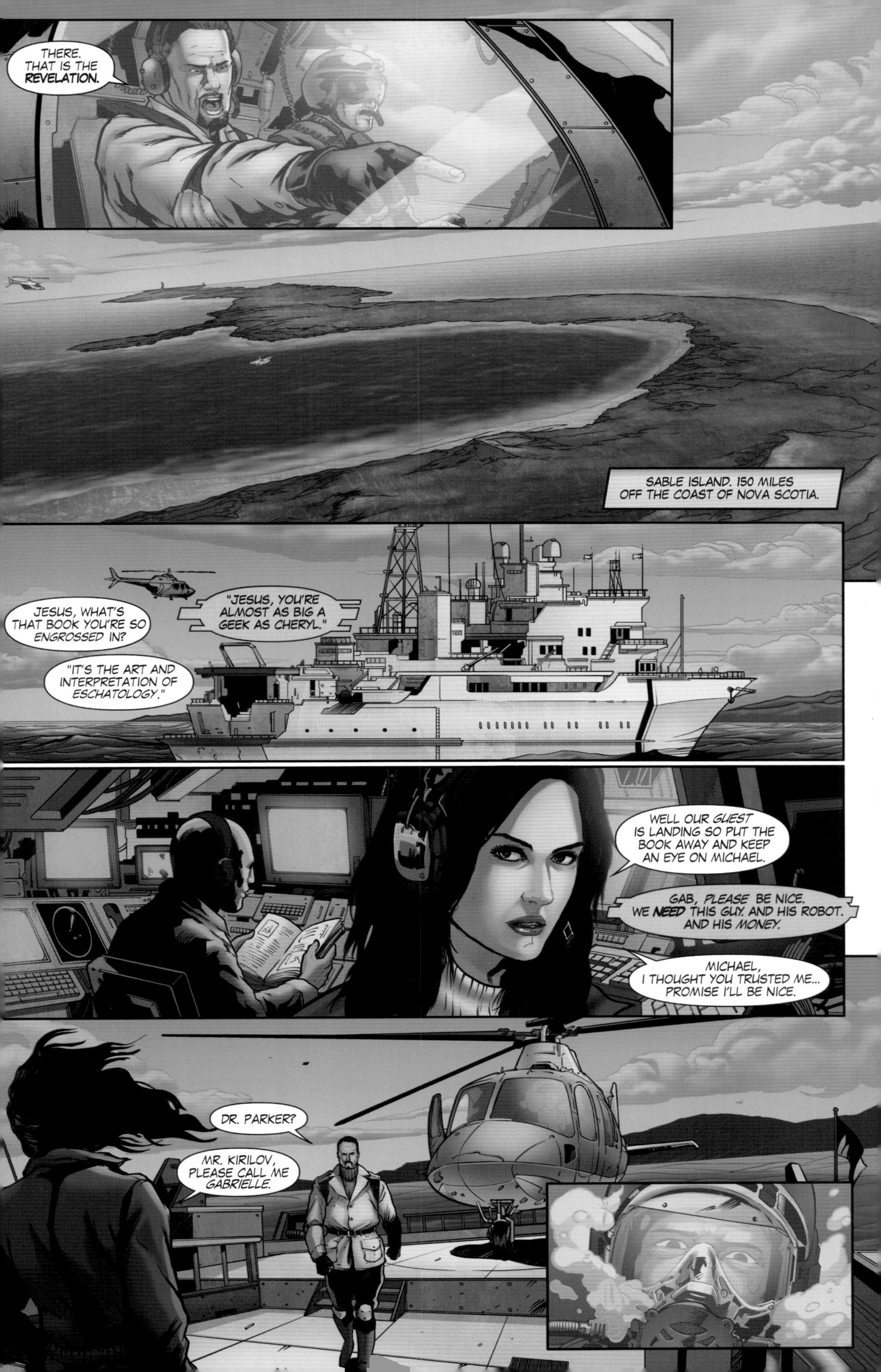
THERE. THAT IS THE REVELATION.
SABLE ISLAND. 150 MILES OFF THE COAST OF NOVA SCOTIA.
JESUS, WHAT'S THAT BOOK YOU'RE SO ENGROSSED IN?
"IT'S THE ART AND INTERPRETATION OF ESCHATOLOGY."
"JESUS, YOU'RE ALMOST AS BIG A GEEK AS CHERYL."
WELL OUR GUEST IS LANDING SO PUT THE BOOK AWAY AND KEEP AN EYE ON MICHAEL.
GAB, PLEASE BE NICE. WE NEED THIS GUY. AND HIS ROBOT. AND HIS MONEY.
MICHAEL, I THOUGHT YOU TRUSTED ME... PROMISE I'LL BE NICE.
DR. PARKER?
MR. KIRILOV, PLEASE CALL ME GABRIELLE.

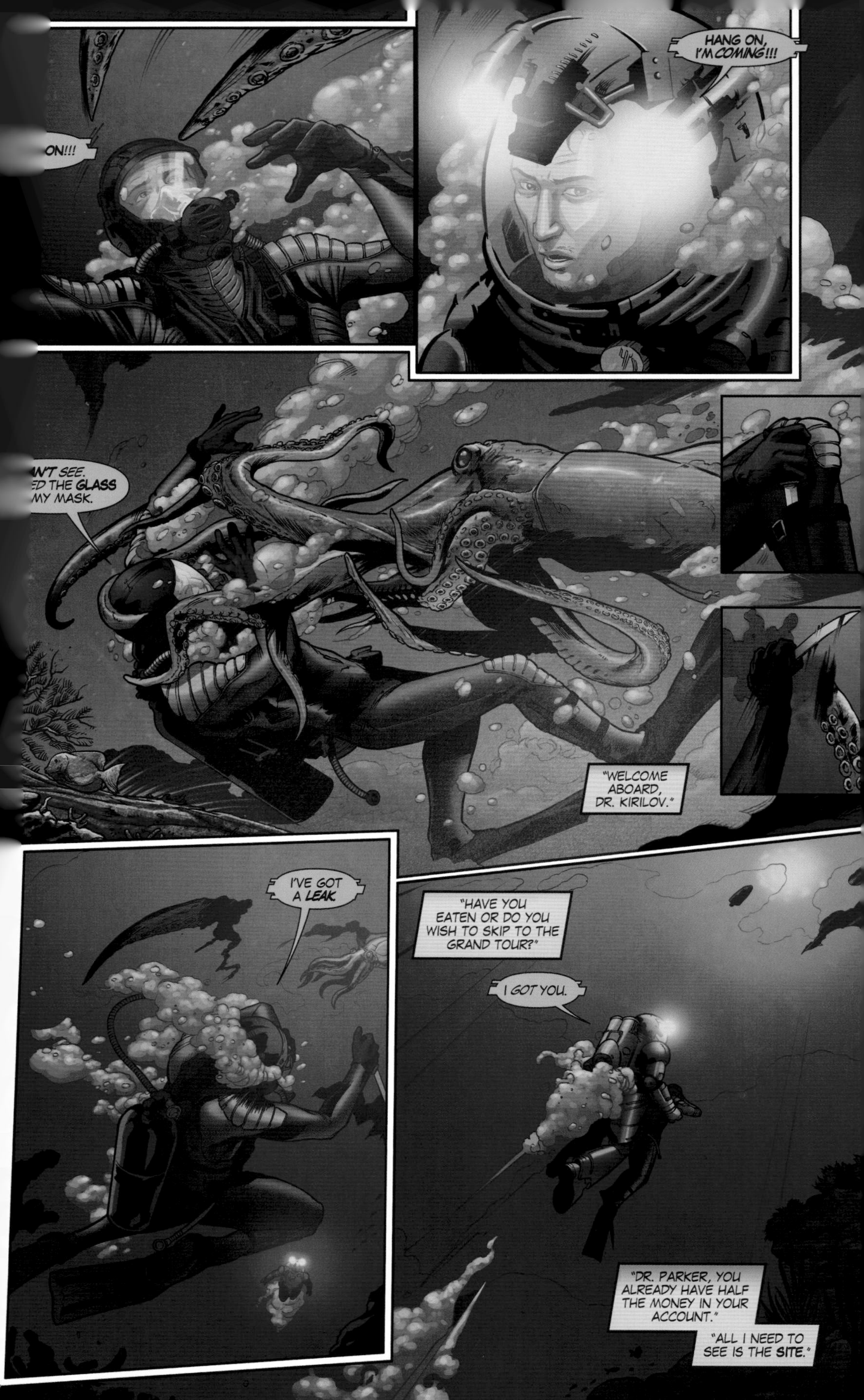

ON!!!
HANG ON, I'M COMING!!!
N'T SEE. ED THE GLASS MY MASK.
"WELCOME ABOARD, DR. KIRILOV."
I'VE GOT A LEAK.
"HAVE YOU EATEN OR DO YOU WISH TO SKIP TO THE GRAND TOUR?"
I GOT YOU.
"DR. PARKER, YOU ALREADY HAVE HALF THE MONEY IN YOUR ACCOUNT."
"ALL I NEED TO SEE IS THE SITE."

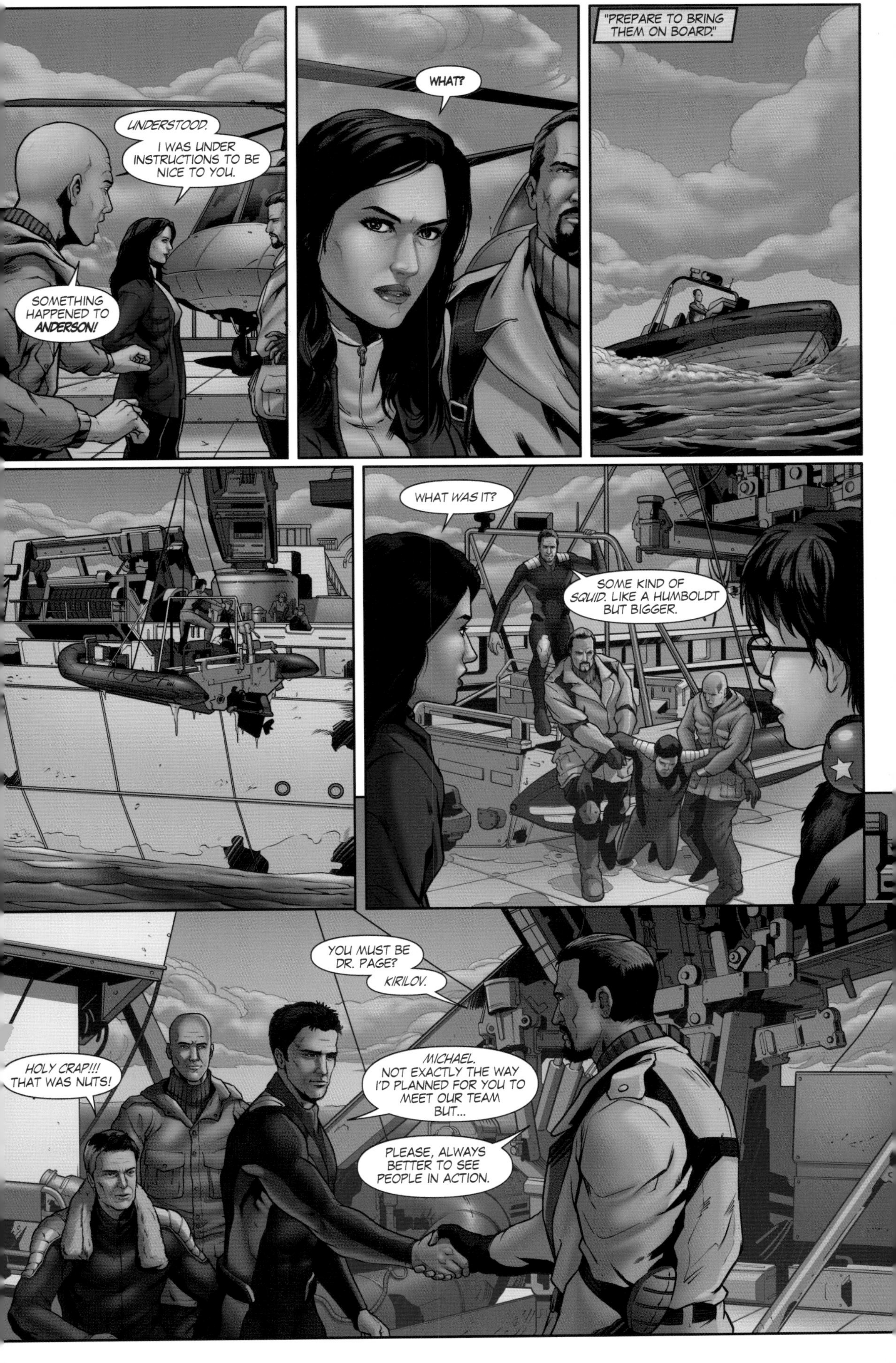
UNDERSTOOD.
I WAS UNDER INSTRUCTIONS TO BE NICE TO YOU.
SOMETHING HAPPENED TO ANDERSON!
WHAT?
"PREPARE TO BRING THEM ON BOARD."
WHAT WAS IT?
SOME KIND OF SQUID. LIKE A HUMBOLDT BUT BIGGER.
YOU MUST BE DR. PAGE?
KIRILOV.
HOLY CRAP!!! THAT WAS NUTS!
MICHAEL. NOT EXACTLY THE WAY I'D PLANNED FOR YOU TO MEET OUR TEAM BUT...
PLEASE, ALWAYS BETTER TO SEE PEOPLE IN ACTION.

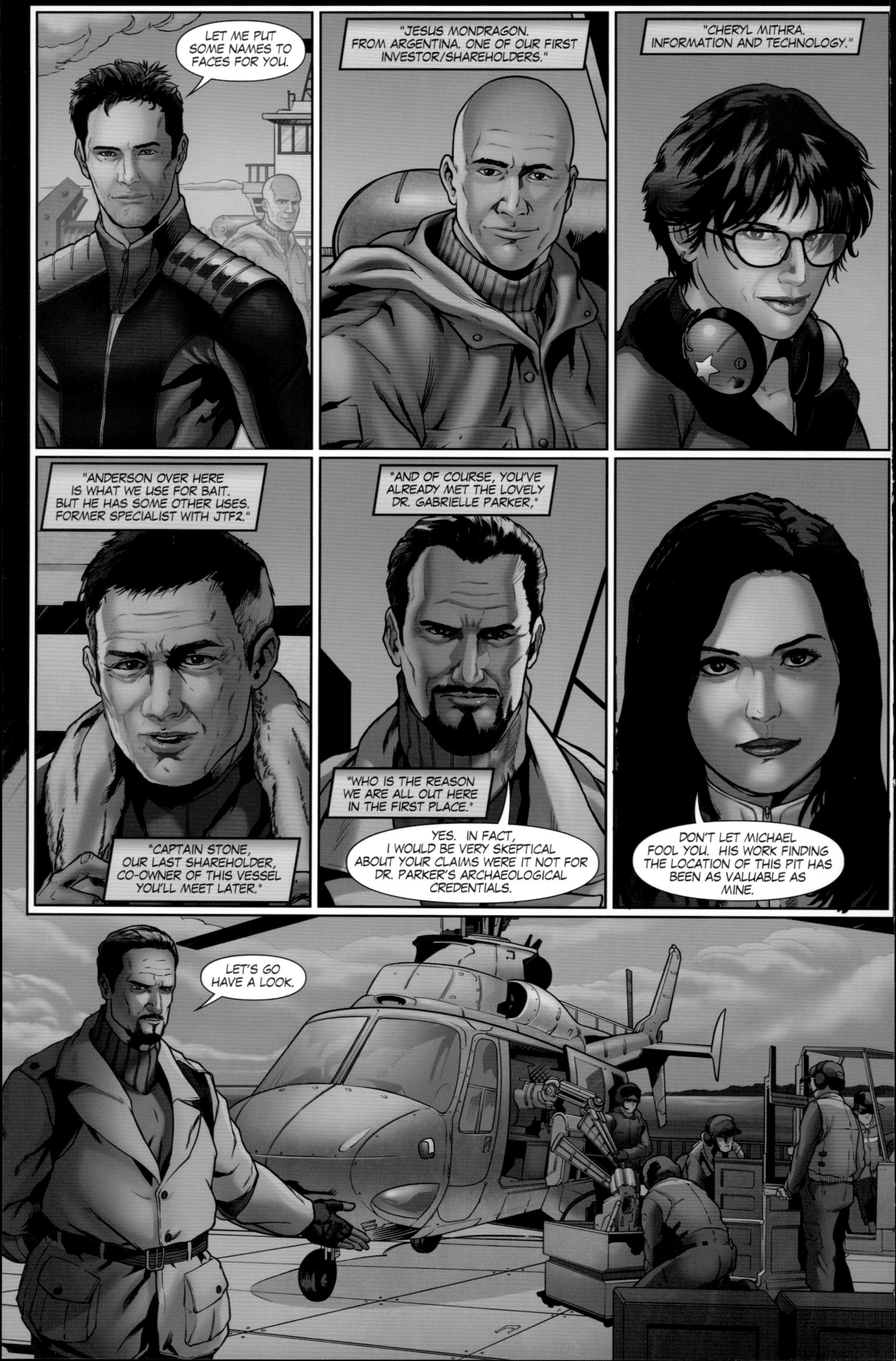
LET ME PUT SOME NAMES TO FACES FOR YOU.
"JESUS MONDRAGON. FROM ARGENTINA. ONE OF OUR FIRST INVESTOR/SHAREHOLDERS."
"CHERYL MITHRA. INFORMATION AND TECHNOLOGY."
"ANDERSON OVER HERE IS WHAT WE USE FOR BAIT. BUT HE HAS SOME OTHER USES. FORMER SPECIALIST WITH JTF2."
"CAPTAIN STONE, OUR LAST SHAREHOLDER, CO-OWNER OF THIS VESSEL YOU'LL MEET LATER."
"AND OF COURSE, YOU'VE ALREADY MET THE LOVELY DR. GABRIELLE PARKER,"
"WHO IS THE REASON WE ARE ALL OUT HERE IN THE FIRST PLACE."
YES. IN FACT, I WOULD BE VERY SKEPTICAL ABOUT YOUR CLAIMS WERE IT NOT FOR DR. PARKER'S ARCHAEOLOGICAL CREDENTIALS.
DON'T LET MICHAEL FOOL YOU. HIS WORK FINDING THE LOCATION OF THIS PIT HAS BEEN AS VALUABLE AS MINE.
LET'S GO HAVE A LOOK.

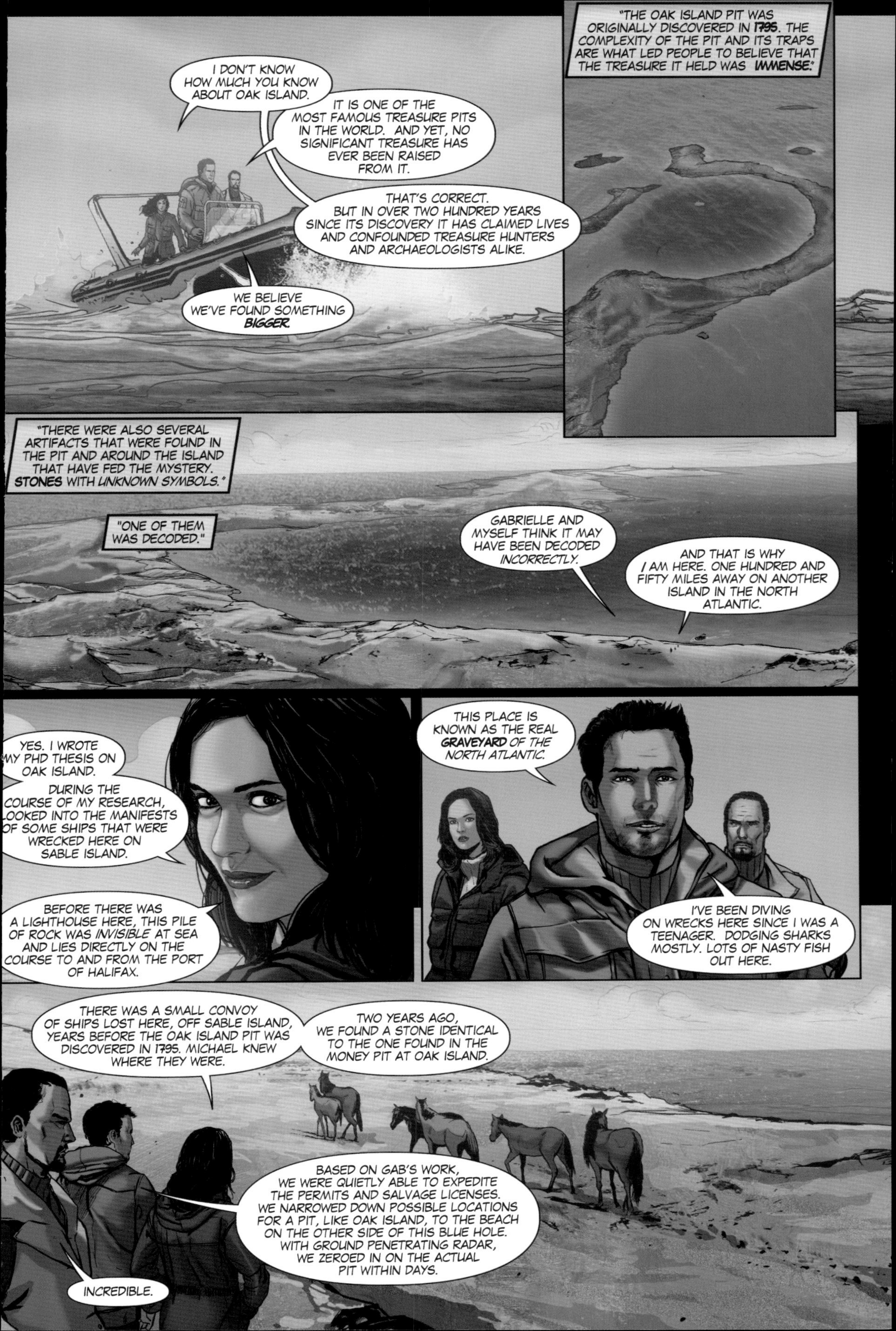
I DON'T KNOW HOW MUCH YOU KNOW ABOUT OAK ISLAND.
IT IS ONE OF THE MOST FAMOUS TREASURE PITS IN THE WORLD. AND YET, NO SIGNIFICANT TREASURE HAS EVER BEEN RAISED FROM IT.
THAT'S CORRECT. BUT IN OVER TWO HUNDRED YEARS SINCE ITS DISCOVERY IT HAS CLAIMED LIVES AND CONFOUNDED TREASURE HUNTERS AND ARCHAEOLOGISTS ALIKE.
WE BELIEVE WE'VE FOUND SOMETHING **BIGGER**.
"THE OAK ISLAND PIT WAS ORIGINALLY DISCOVERED IN **1795**. THE COMPLEXITY OF THE PIT AND ITS TRAPS ARE WHAT LED PEOPLE TO BELIEVE THAT THE TREASURE IT HELD WAS **IMMENSE**."
"THERE WERE ALSO SEVERAL ARTIFACTS THAT WERE FOUND IN THE PIT AND AROUND THE ISLAND THAT HAVE FED THE MYSTERY. **STONES** WITH *UNKNOWN SYMBOLS*."
"ONE OF THEM WAS DECODED."
GABRIELLE AND MYSELF THINK IT MAY HAVE BEEN DECODED *INCORRECTLY*.
AND THAT IS WHY *I* AM HERE. ONE HUNDRED AND FIFTY MILES AWAY ON ANOTHER ISLAND IN THE NORTH ATLANTIC.
YES. I WROTE MY PHD THESIS ON OAK ISLAND.
DURING THE COURSE OF MY RESEARCH, LOOKED INTO THE MANIFESTS OF SOME SHIPS THAT WERE WRECKED HERE ON SABLE ISLAND.
BEFORE THERE WAS A LIGHTHOUSE HERE, THIS PILE OF ROCK WAS *INVISIBLE* AT SEA AND LIES DIRECTLY ON THE COURSE TO AND FROM THE PORT OF HALIFAX.
THIS PLACE IS KNOWN AS THE REAL **GRAVEYARD** *OF THE NORTH ATLANTIC*.
I'VE BEEN DIVING ON WRECKS HERE SINCE I WAS A TEENAGER. DODGING SHARKS MOSTLY. LOTS OF NASTY FISH OUT HERE.
THERE WAS A SMALL CONVOY OF SHIPS LOST HERE, OFF SABLE ISLAND, YEARS BEFORE THE OAK ISLAND PIT WAS DISCOVERED IN 1795. MICHAEL KNEW WHERE THEY WERE.
TWO YEARS AGO, WE FOUND A STONE IDENTICAL TO THE ONE FOUND IN THE MONEY PIT AT OAK ISLAND.
BASED ON GAB'S WORK, WE WERE QUIETLY ABLE TO EXPEDITE THE PERMITS AND SALVAGE LICENSES. WE NARROWED DOWN POSSIBLE LOCATIONS FOR A PIT, LIKE OAK ISLAND, TO THE BEACH ON THE OTHER SIDE OF THIS BLUE HOLE. WITH GROUND PENETRATING RADAR, WE ZEROED IN ON THE ACTUAL PIT WITHIN DAYS.
INCREDIBLE.

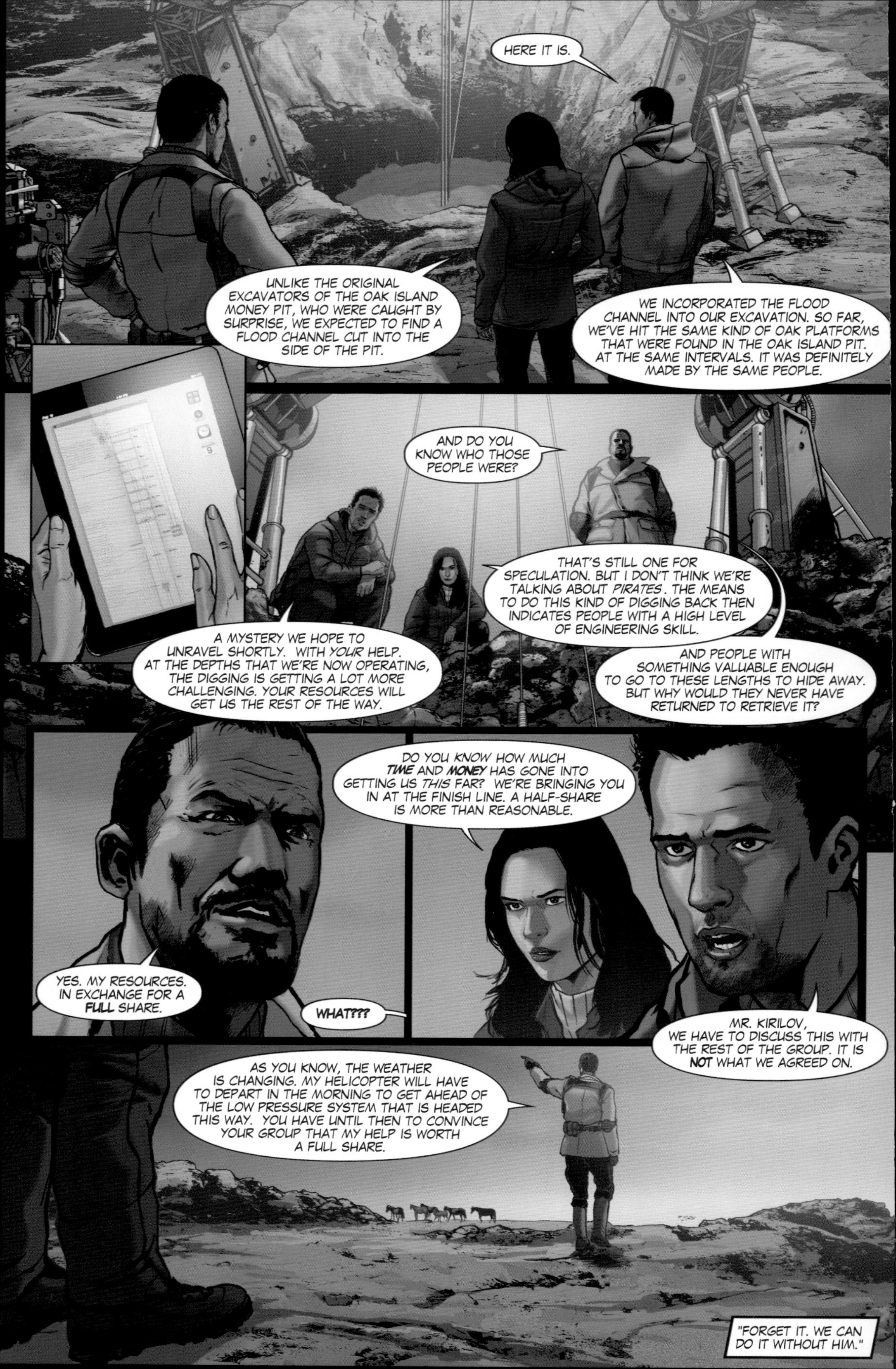
HERE IT IS.
UNLIKE THE ORIGINAL EXCAVATORS OF THE OAK ISLAND MONEY PIT, WHO WERE CAUGHT BY SURPRISE, WE EXPECTED TO FIND A FLOOD CHANNEL CUT INTO THE SIDE OF THE PIT.
WE INCORPORATED THE FLOOD CHANNEL INTO OUR EXCAVATION. SO FAR, WE'VE HIT THE SAME KIND OF OAK PLATFORMS THAT WERE FOUND IN THE OAK ISLAND PIT. AT THE SAME INTERVALS. IT WAS DEFINITELY MADE BY THE SAME PEOPLE.
AND DO YOU KNOW WHO THOSE PEOPLE WERE?
THAT'S STILL ONE FOR SPECULATION. BUT I DON'T THINK WE'RE TALKING ABOUT *PIRATES*. THE MEANS TO DO THIS KIND OF DIGGING BACK THEN INDICATES PEOPLE WITH A HIGH LEVEL OF ENGINEERING SKILL.
A MYSTERY WE HOPE TO UNRAVEL SHORTLY. WITH *YOUR* HELP. AT THE DEPTHS THAT WE'RE NOW OPERATING, THE DIGGING IS GETTING A LOT MORE CHALLENGING. YOUR RESOURCES WILL GET US THE REST OF THE WAY.
AND PEOPLE WITH SOMETHING VALUABLE ENOUGH TO GO TO THESE LENGTHS TO HIDE AWAY. BUT WHY WOULD THEY NEVER HAVE RETURNED TO RETRIEVE IT?
YES. MY RESOURCES. IN EXCHANGE FOR A **FULL** SHARE.
WHAT???
DO YOU *KNOW* HOW MUCH ***TIME*** AND ***MONEY*** HAS GONE INTO GETTING US *THIS* FAR? WE'RE BRINGING YOU IN AT THE FINISH LINE. A HALF-SHARE IS MORE THAN REASONABLE.
MR. KIRILOV, WE HAVE TO DISCUSS THIS WITH THE REST OF THE GROUP. IT IS **NOT** WHAT WE AGREED ON.
AS YOU KNOW, THE WEATHER IS CHANGING. MY HELICOPTER WILL HAVE TO DEPART IN THE MORNING TO GET AHEAD OF THE LOW PRESSURE SYSTEM THAT IS HEADED THIS WAY. YOU HAVE UNTIL THEN TO CONVINCE YOUR GROUP THAT MY HELP IS WORTH A FULL SHARE.
"FORGET IT. WE CAN DO IT WITHOUT HIM."

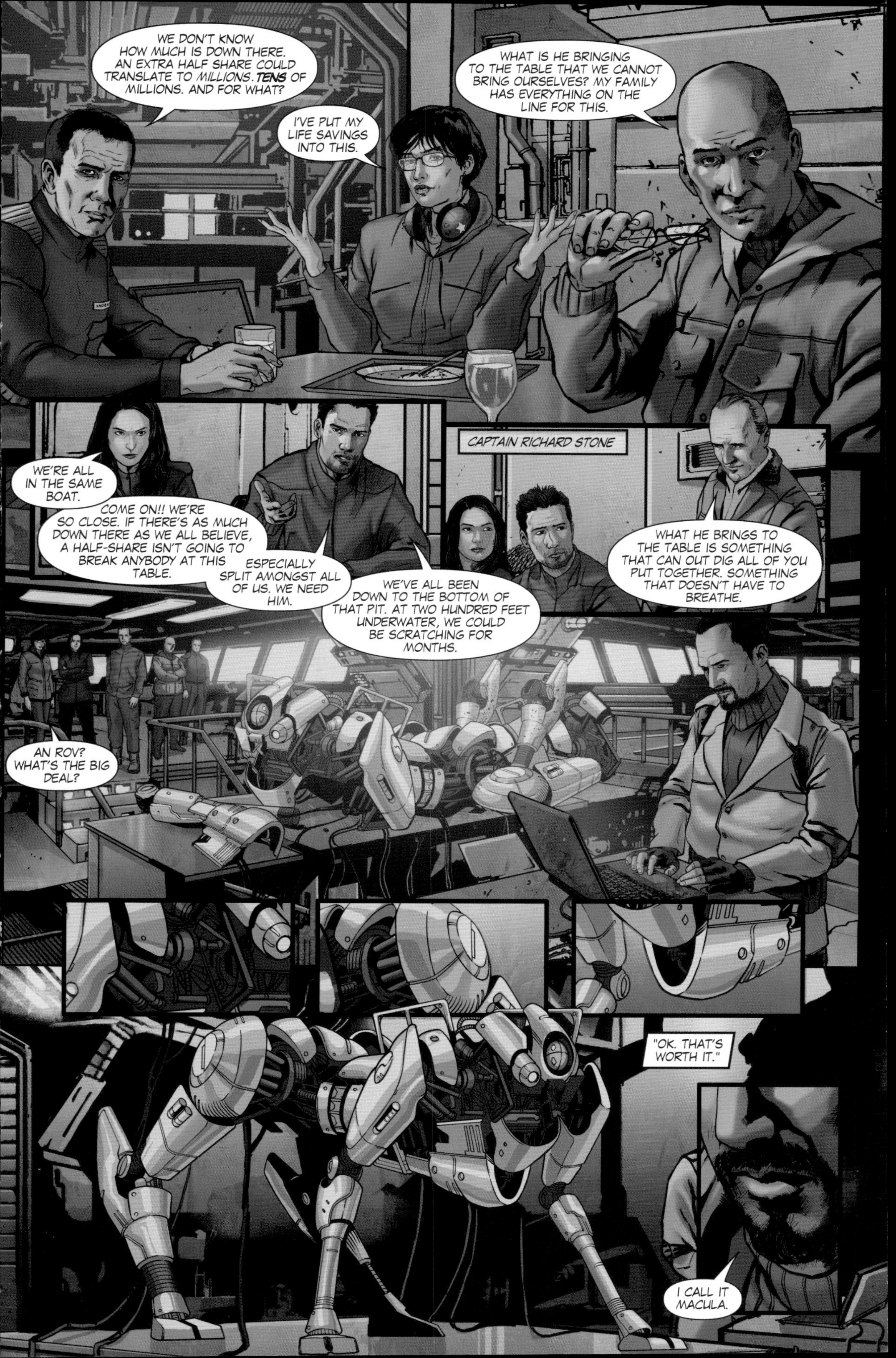
WE DON'T KNOW HOW MUCH IS DOWN THERE. AN EXTRA HALF SHARE COULD TRANSLATE TO MILLIONS. TENS OF MILLIONS. AND FOR WHAT?
I'VE PUT MY LIFE SAVINGS INTO THIS.
WHAT IS HE BRINGING TO THE TABLE THAT WE CANNOT BRING OURSELVES? MY FAMILY HAS EVERYTHING ON THE LINE FOR THIS.
WE'RE ALL IN THE SAME BOAT.
COME ON!! WE'RE SO CLOSE. IF THERE'S AS MUCH DOWN THERE AS WE ALL BELIEVE, A HALF-SHARE ISN'T GOING TO BREAK ANYBODY AT THIS TABLE.
ESPECIALLY SPLIT AMONGST ALL OF US. WE NEED HIM.
WE'VE ALL BEEN DOWN TO THE BOTTOM OF THAT PIT. AT TWO HUNDRED FEET UNDERWATER, WE COULD BE SCRATCHING FOR MONTHS.
CAPTAIN RICHARD STONE
WHAT HE BRINGS TO THE TABLE IS SOMETHING THAT CAN OUT DIG ALL OF YOU PUT TOGETHER. SOMETHING THAT DOESN'T HAVE TO BREATHE.
AN ROV? WHAT'S THE BIG DEAL?
"OK. THAT'S WORTH IT."
I CALL IT MACULA.

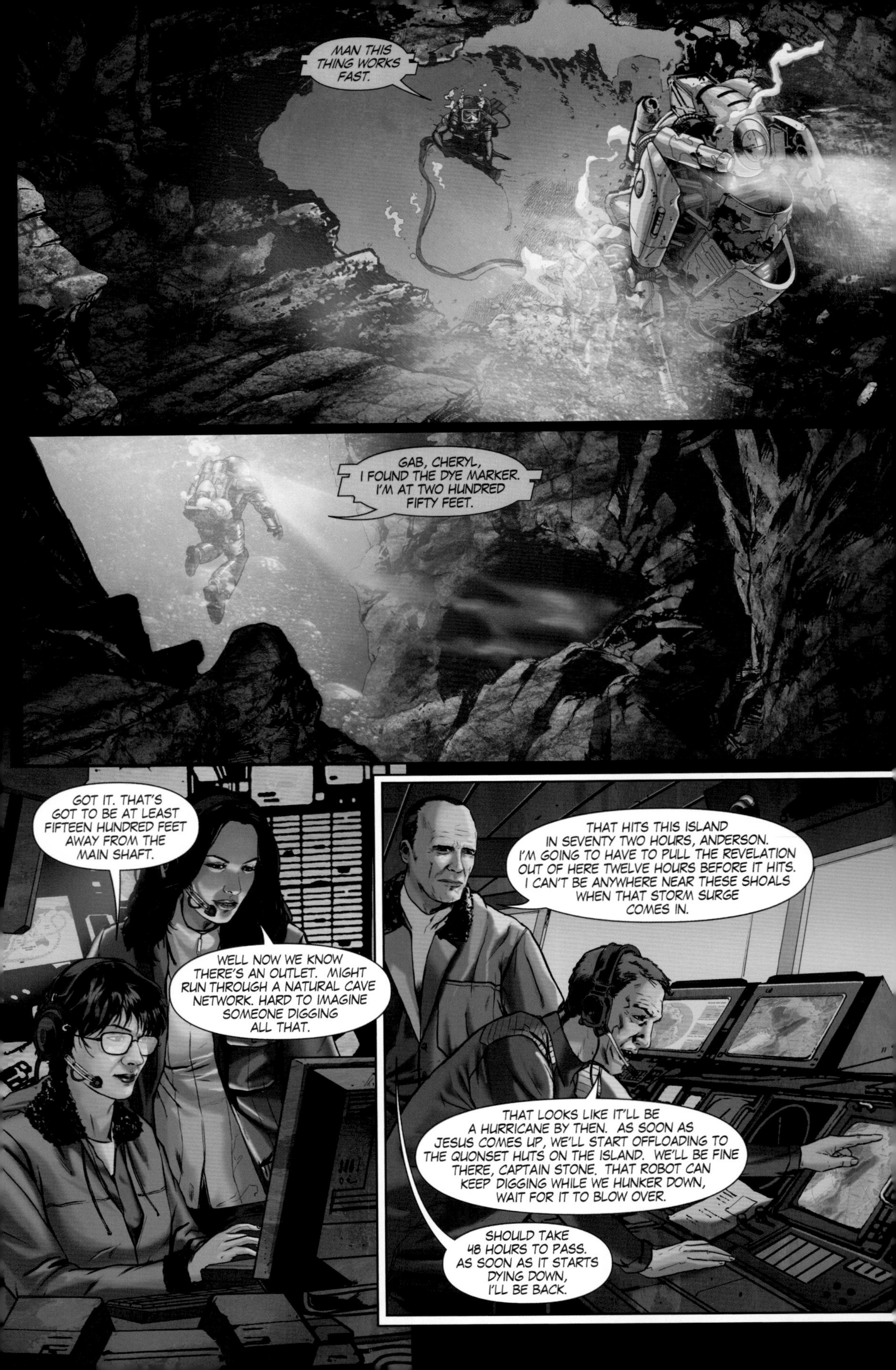
MAN THIS THING WORKS FAST.
GAB, CHERYL, I FOUND THE DYE MARKER. I'M AT TWO HUNDRED FIFTY FEET.
GOT IT. THAT'S GOT TO BE AT LEAST FIFTEEN HUNDRED FEET AWAY FROM THE MAIN SHAFT.
WELL NOW WE KNOW THERE'S AN OUTLET. MIGHT RUN THROUGH A NATURAL CAVE NETWORK. HARD TO IMAGINE SOMEONE DIGGING ALL THAT.
THAT HITS THIS ISLAND IN SEVENTY TWO HOURS, ANDERSON. I'M GOING TO HAVE TO PULL THE REVELATION OUT OF HERE TWELVE HOURS BEFORE IT HITS. I CAN'T BE ANYWHERE NEAR THESE SHOALS WHEN THAT STORM SURGE COMES IN.
THAT LOOKS LIKE IT'LL BE A HURRICANE BY THEN. AS SOON AS JESUS COMES UP, WE'LL START OFFLOADING TO THE QUONSET HUTS ON THE ISLAND. WE'LL BE FINE THERE, CAPTAIN STONE. THAT ROBOT CAN KEEP DIGGING WHILE WE HUNKER DOWN, WAIT FOR IT TO BLOW OVER.
SHOULD TAKE 48 HOURS TO PASS. AS SOON AS IT STARTS DYING DOWN, I'LL BE BACK.

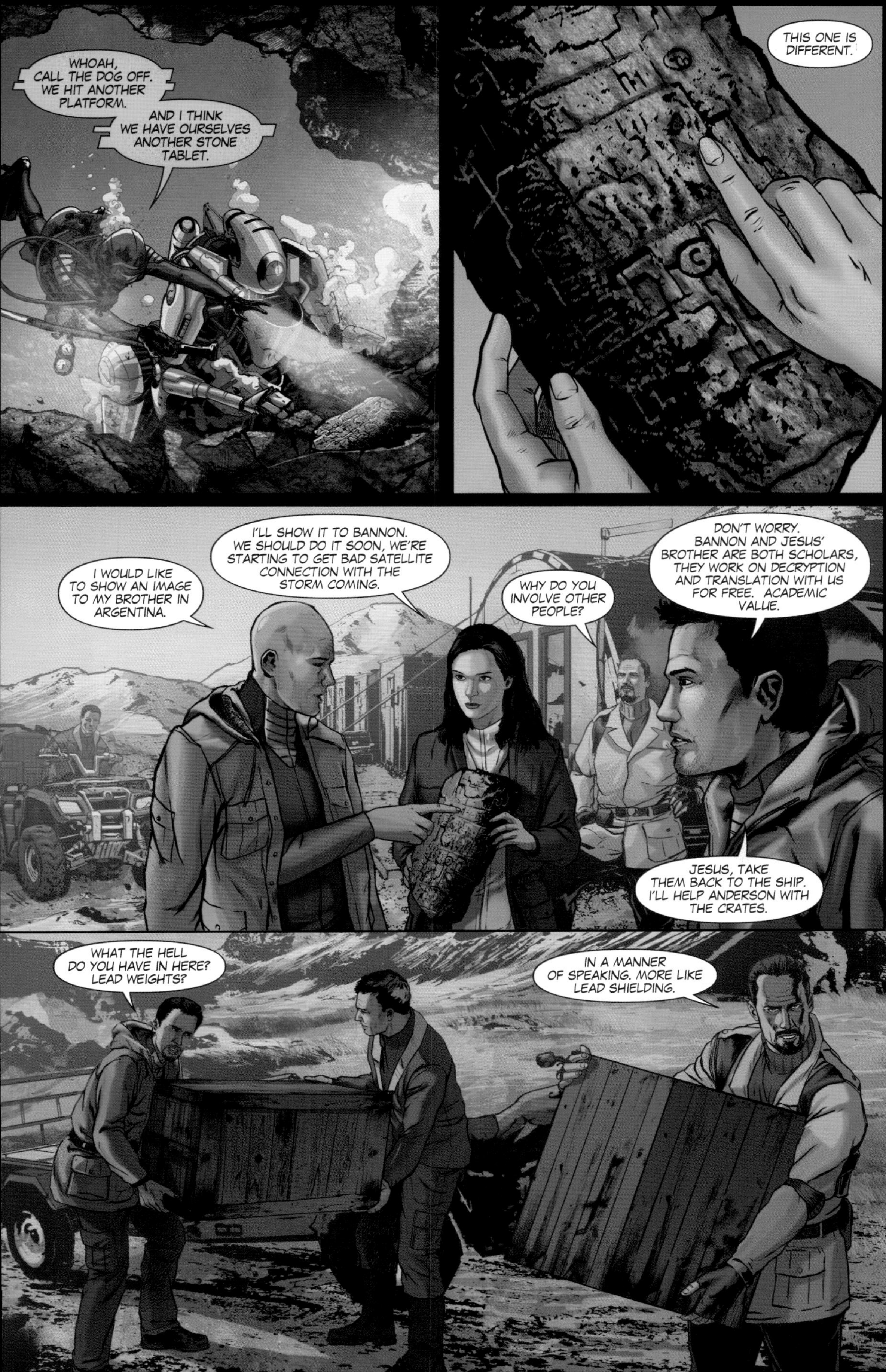

WHOAH, CALL THE DOG OFF. WE HIT ANOTHER PLATFORM.
AND I THINK WE HAVE OURSELVES ANOTHER STONE TABLET.
THIS ONE IS DIFFERENT.
I WOULD LIKE TO SHOW AN IMAGE TO MY BROTHER IN ARGENTINA.
I'LL SHOW IT TO BANNON. WE SHOULD DO IT SOON, WE'RE STARTING TO GET BAD SATELLITE CONNECTION WITH THE STORM COMING.
WHY DO YOU INVOLVE OTHER PEOPLE?
DON'T WORRY. BANNON AND JESUS' BROTHER ARE BOTH SCHOLARS, THEY WORK ON DECRYPTION AND TRANSLATION WITH US FOR FREE. ACADEMIC VALUE.
JESUS, TAKE THEM BACK TO THE SHIP. I'LL HELP ANDERSON WITH THE CRATES.
WHAT THE HELL DO YOU HAVE IN HERE? LEAD WEIGHTS?
IN A MANNER OF SPEAKING. MORE LIKE LEAD SHIELDING.

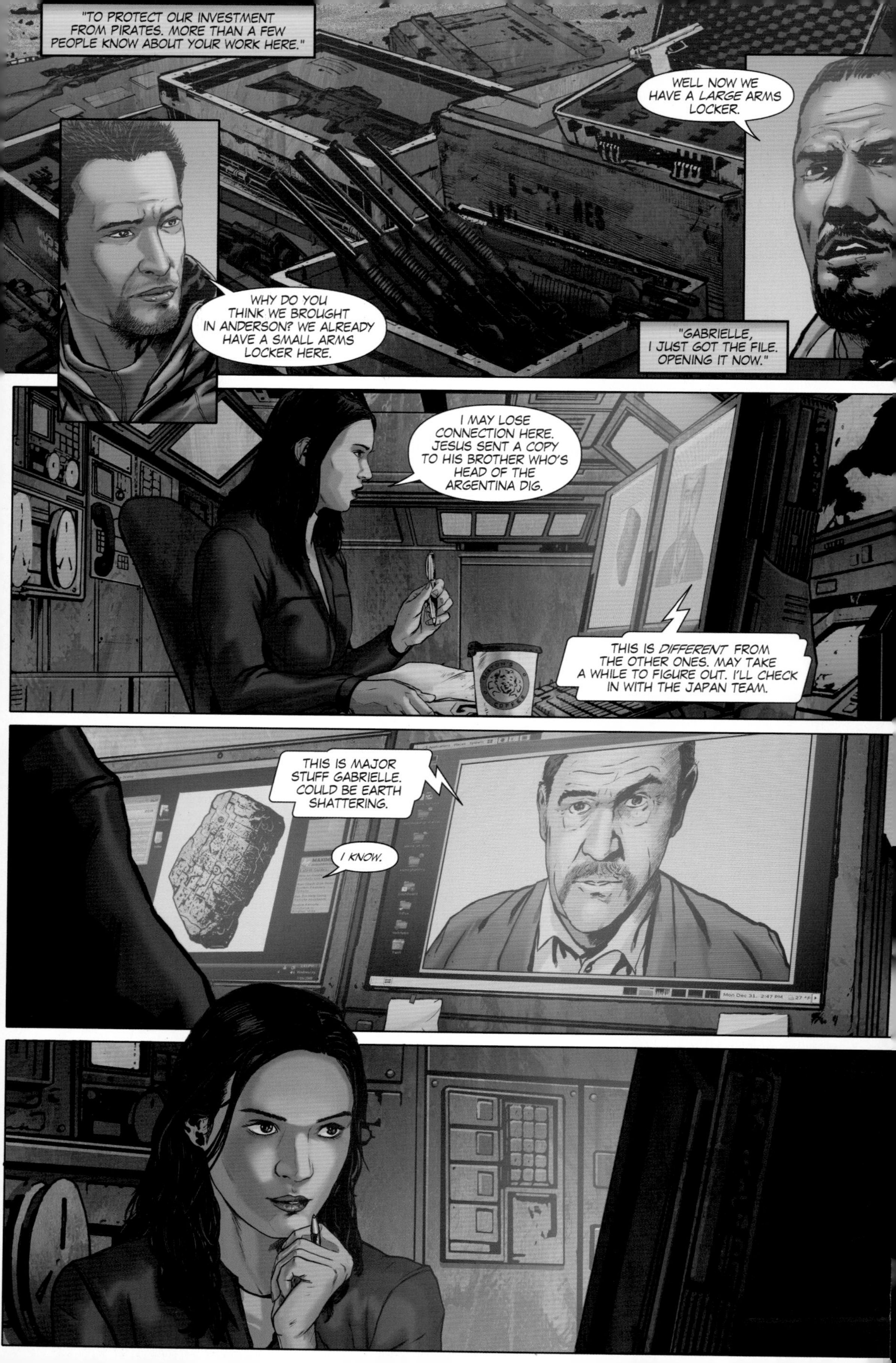
"TO PROTECT OUR INVESTMENT FROM PIRATES. MORE THAN A FEW PEOPLE KNOW ABOUT YOUR WORK HERE."
WELL NOW WE HAVE A LARGE ARMS LOCKER.
WHY DO YOU THINK WE BROUGHT IN ANDERSON? WE ALREADY HAVE A SMALL ARMS LOCKER HERE.
"GABRIELLE, I JUST GOT THE FILE. OPENING IT NOW."
I MAY LOSE CONNECTION HERE. JESUS SENT A COPY TO HIS BROTHER WHO'S HEAD OF THE ARGENTINA DIG.
THIS IS DIFFERENT FROM THE OTHER ONES. MAY TAKE A WHILE TO FIGURE OUT. I'LL CHECK IN WITH THE JAPAN TEAM.
THIS IS MAJOR STUFF GABRIELLE. COULD BE EARTH SHATTERING.
I KNOW.

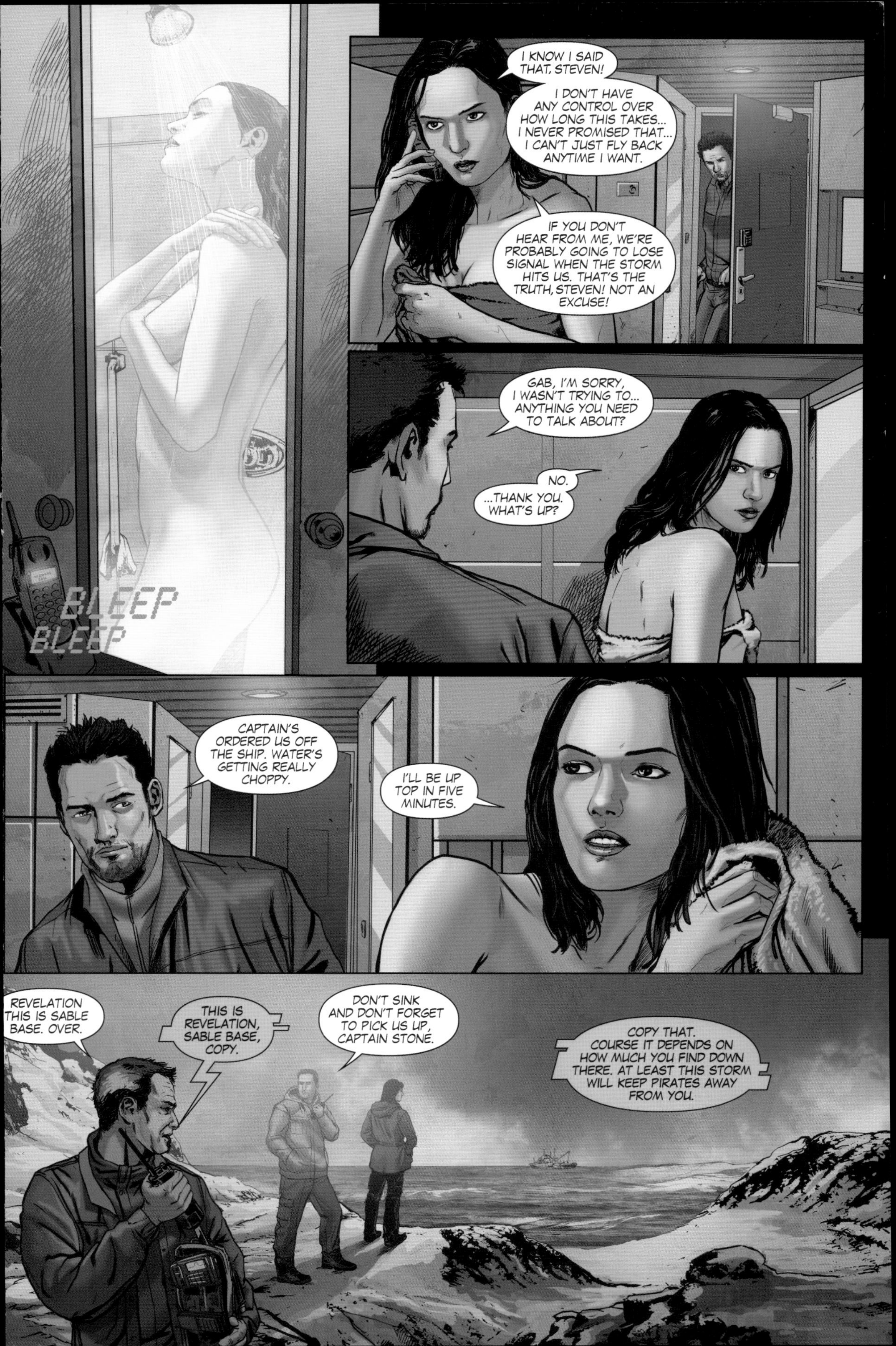
I KNOW I SAID THAT, STEVEN!
I DON'T HAVE ANY CONTROL OVER HOW LONG THIS TAKES... I NEVER PROMISED THAT... I CAN'T JUST FLY BACK ANYTIME I WANT.
IF YOU DON'T HEAR FROM ME, WE'RE PROBABLY GOING TO LOSE SIGNAL WHEN THE STORM HITS US. THAT'S THE TRUTH, STEVEN! NOT AN EXCUSE!
BLEEP
BLEEP
GAB, I'M SORRY, I WASN'T TRYING TO... ANYTHING YOU NEED TO TALK ABOUT?
NO.
...THANK YOU. WHAT'S UP?
CAPTAIN'S ORDERED US OFF THE SHIP. WATER'S GETTING REALLY CHOPPY.
I'LL BE UP TOP IN FIVE MINUTES.
REVELATION THIS IS SABLE BASE. OVER.
THIS IS REVELATION, SABLE BASE, COPY.
DON'T SINK AND DON'T FORGET TO PICK US UP, CAPTAIN STONE.
COPY THAT. COURSE IT DEPENDS ON HOW MUCH YOU FIND DOWN THERE. AT LEAST THIS STORM WILL KEEP PIRATES AWAY FROM YOU.

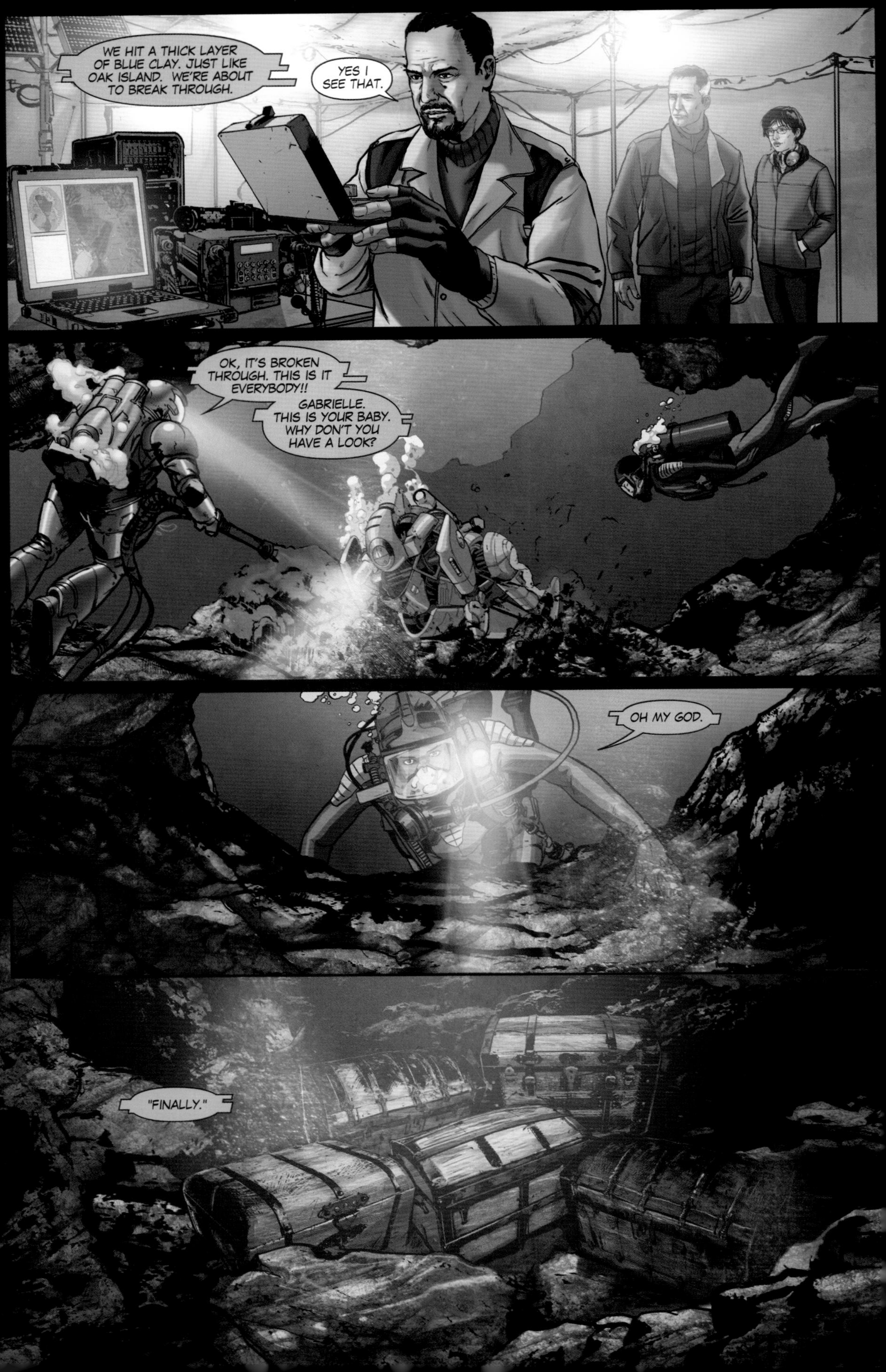
WE HIT A THICK LAYER OF BLUE CLAY. JUST LIKE OAK ISLAND. WE'RE ABOUT TO BREAK THROUGH.
YES I SEE THAT.
OK, IT'S BROKEN THROUGH. THIS IS IT EVERYBODY!!
GABRIELLE. THIS IS YOUR BABY. WHY DON'T YOU HAVE A LOOK?
OH MY GOD.
"FINALLY."

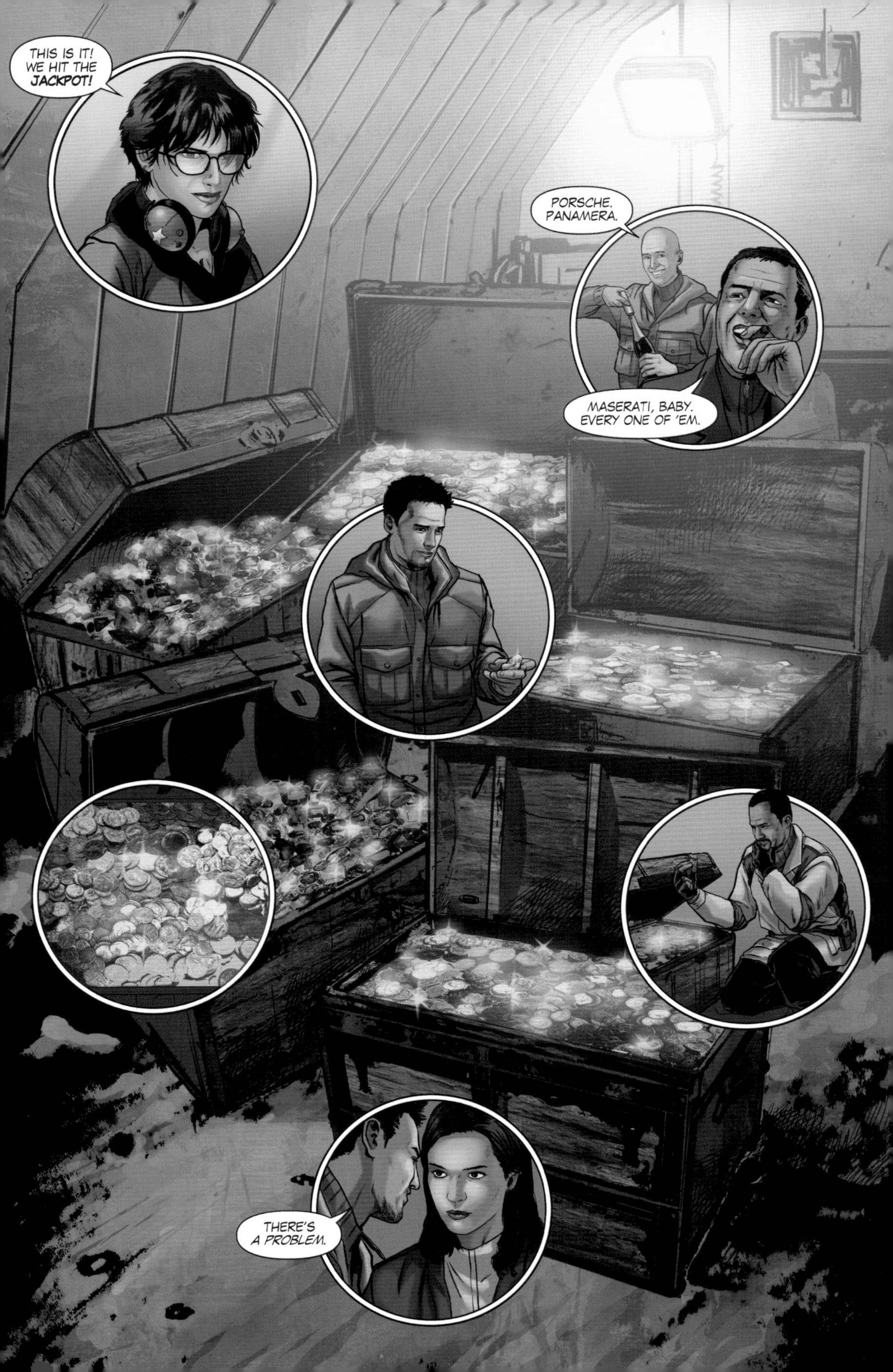
THIS IS IT! WE HIT THE **JACKPOT!**
PORSCHE. PANAMERA.
MASERATI, BABY. EVERY ONE OF 'EM.
THERE'S A PROBLEM.

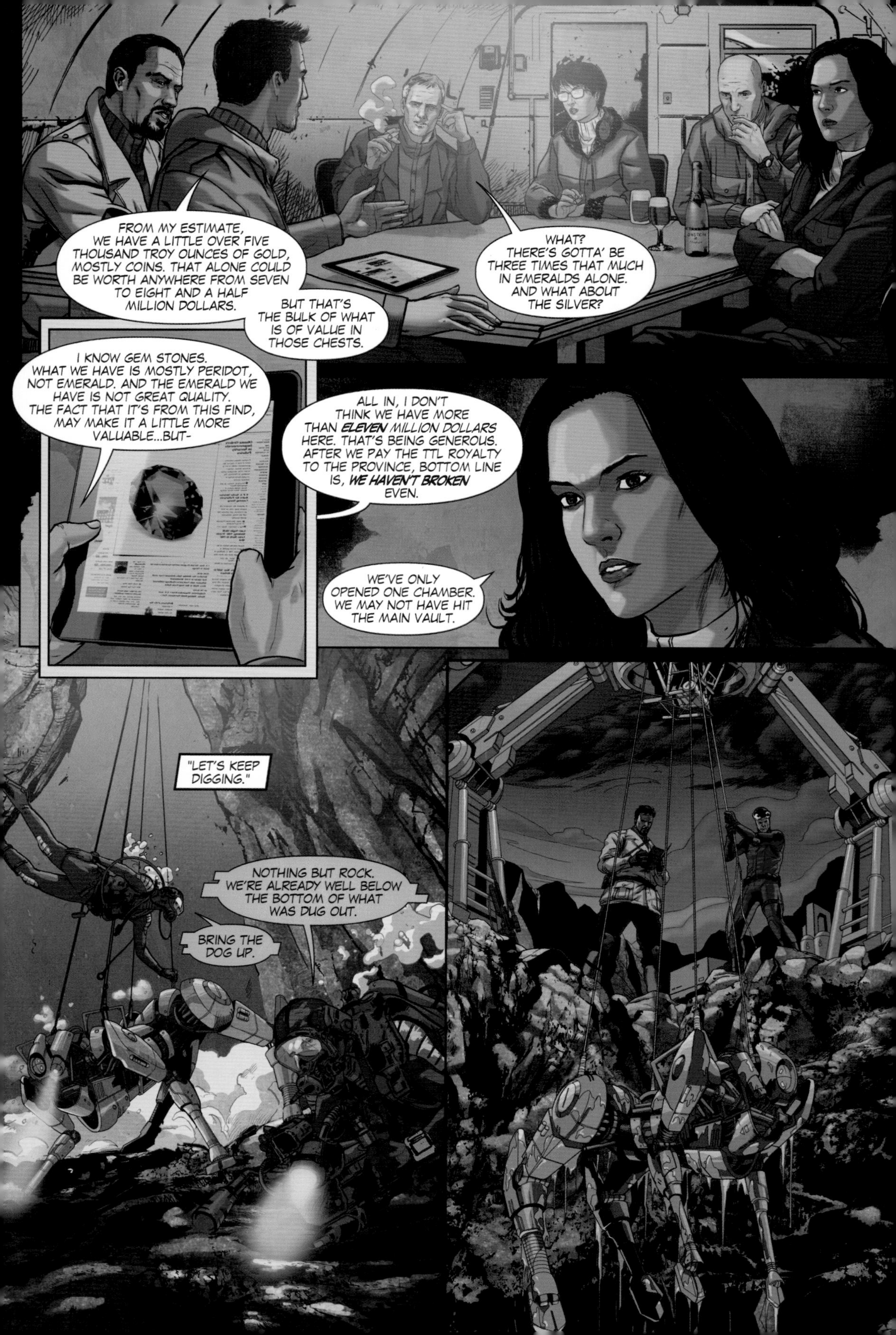
FROM MY ESTIMATE, WE HAVE A LITTLE OVER FIVE THOUSAND TROY OUNCES OF GOLD, MOSTLY COINS. THAT ALONE COULD BE WORTH ANYWHERE FROM SEVEN TO EIGHT AND A HALF MILLION DOLLARS.
BUT THAT'S THE BULK OF WHAT IS OF VALUE IN THOSE CHESTS.
WHAT? THERE'S GOTTA' BE THREE TIMES THAT MUCH IN EMERALDS ALONE. AND WHAT ABOUT THE SILVER?
I KNOW GEM STONES. WHAT WE HAVE IS MOSTLY PERIDOT, NOT EMERALD. AND THE EMERALD WE HAVE IS NOT GREAT QUALITY. THE FACT THAT IT'S FROM THIS FIND, MAY MAKE IT A LITTLE MORE VALUABLE...BUT-
ALL IN, I DON'T THINK WE HAVE MORE THAN ELEVEN MILLION DOLLARS HERE. THAT'S BEING GENEROUS. AFTER WE PAY THE TTL ROYALTY TO THE PROVINCE, BOTTOM LINE IS, WE HAVEN'T BROKEN EVEN.
WE'VE ONLY OPENED ONE CHAMBER. WE MAY NOT HAVE HIT THE MAIN VAULT.
"LET'S KEEP DIGGING."
NOTHING BUT ROCK. WE'RE ALREADY WELL BELOW THE BOTTOM OF WHAT WAS DUG OUT.
BRING THE DOG UP.

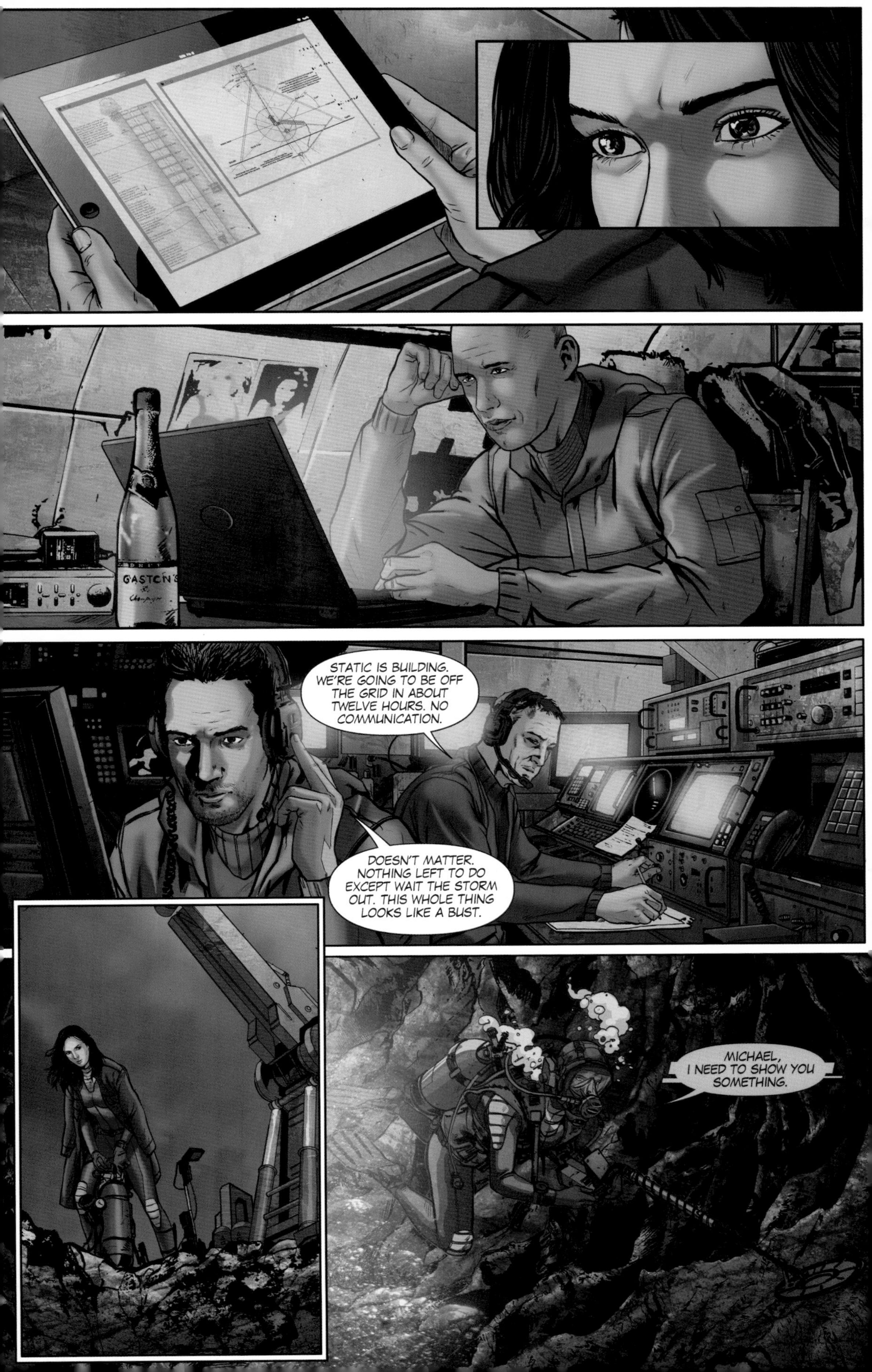
GASTON'S
STATIC IS BUILDING. WE'RE GOING TO BE OFF THE GRID IN ABOUT TWELVE HOURS. NO COMMUNICATION.
DOESN'T MATTER. NOTHING LEFT TO DO EXCEPT WAIT THE STORM OUT. THIS WHOLE THING LOOKS LIKE A BUST.
MICHAEL, I NEED TO SHOW YOU SOMETHING.

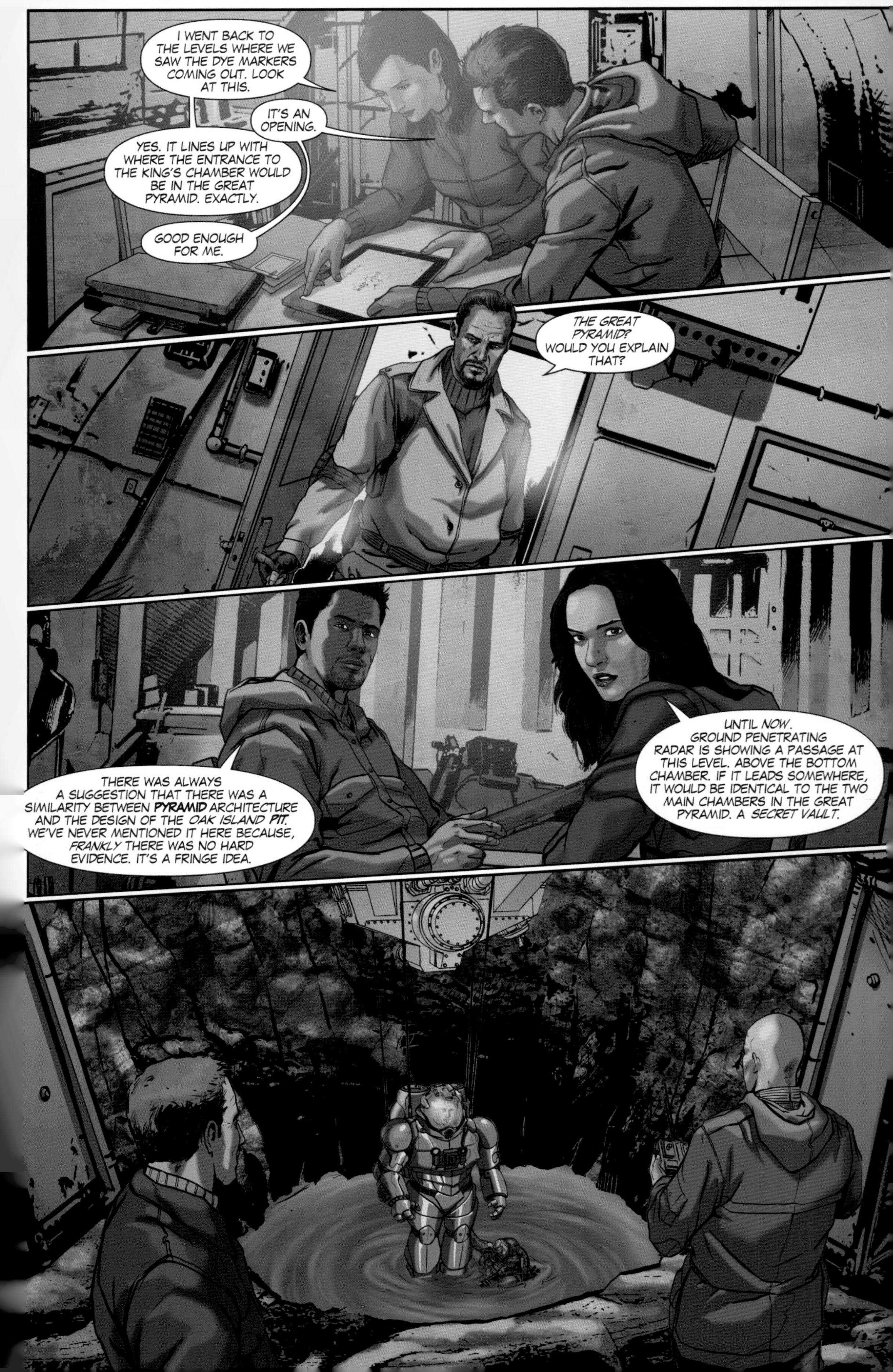
I WENT BACK TO THE LEVELS WHERE WE SAW THE DYE MARKERS COMING OUT. LOOK AT THIS.
IT'S AN OPENING.
YES. IT LINES UP WITH WHERE THE ENTRANCE TO THE KING'S CHAMBER WOULD BE IN THE GREAT PYRAMID. EXACTLY.
GOOD ENOUGH FOR ME.
THE GREAT PYRAMID? WOULD YOU EXPLAIN THAT?
THERE WAS ALWAYS A SUGGESTION THAT THERE WAS A SIMILARITY BETWEEN PYRAMID ARCHITECTURE AND THE DESIGN OF THE OAK ISLAND PIT. WE'VE NEVER MENTIONED IT HERE BECAUSE, FRANKLY THERE WAS NO HARD EVIDENCE. IT'S A FRINGE IDEA.
UNTIL NOW. GROUND PENETRATING RADAR IS SHOWING A PASSAGE AT THIS LEVEL. ABOVE THE BOTTOM CHAMBER. IF IT LEADS SOMEWHERE, IT WOULD BE IDENTICAL TO THE TWO MAIN CHAMBERS IN THE GREAT PYRAMID. A SECRET VAULT.

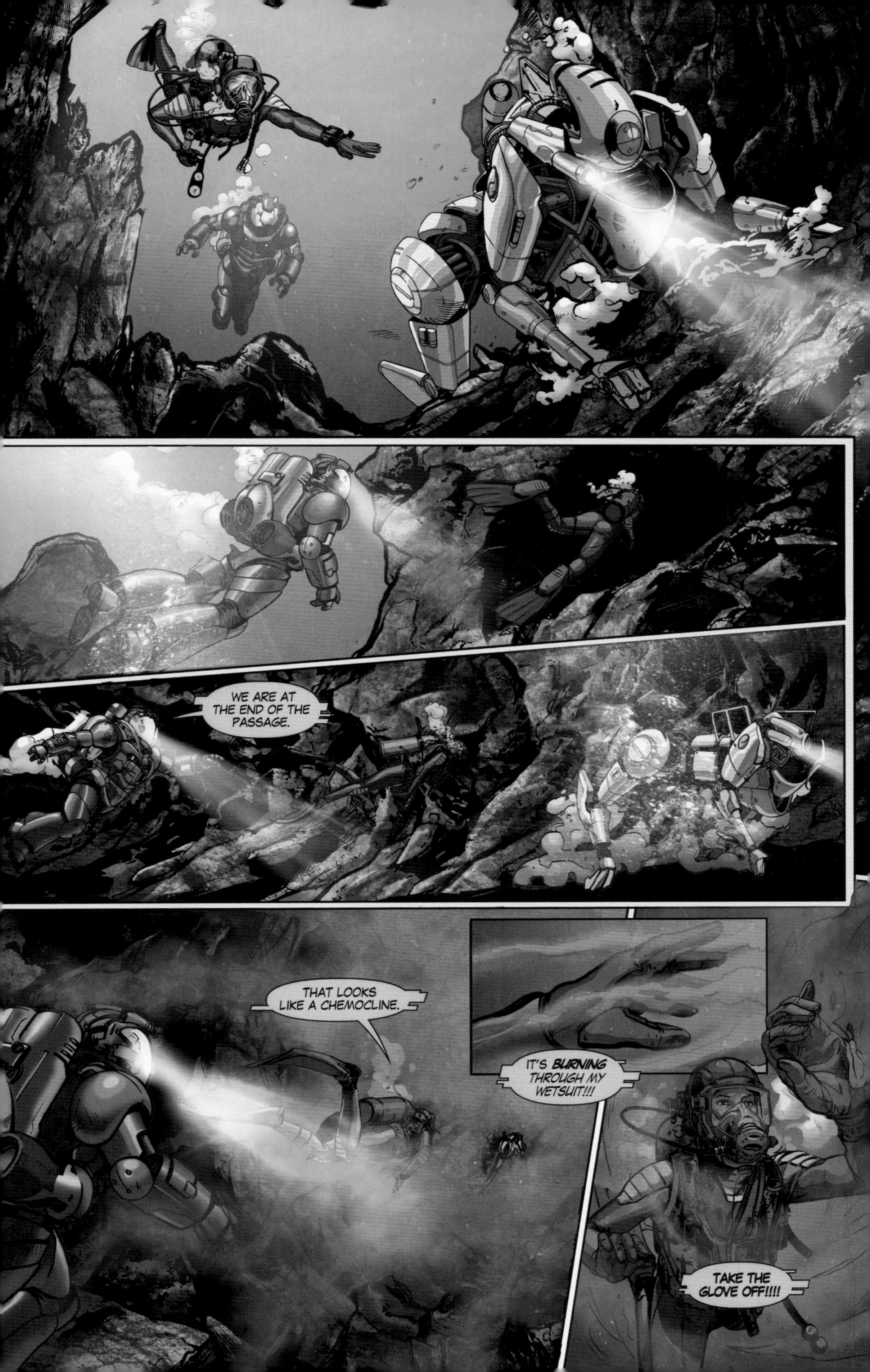
WE ARE AT THE END OF THE PASSAGE.
THAT LOOKS LIKE A CHEMOCLINE.
IT'S BURNING THROUGH MY WETSUIT!!!
TAKE THE GLOVE OFF!!!!

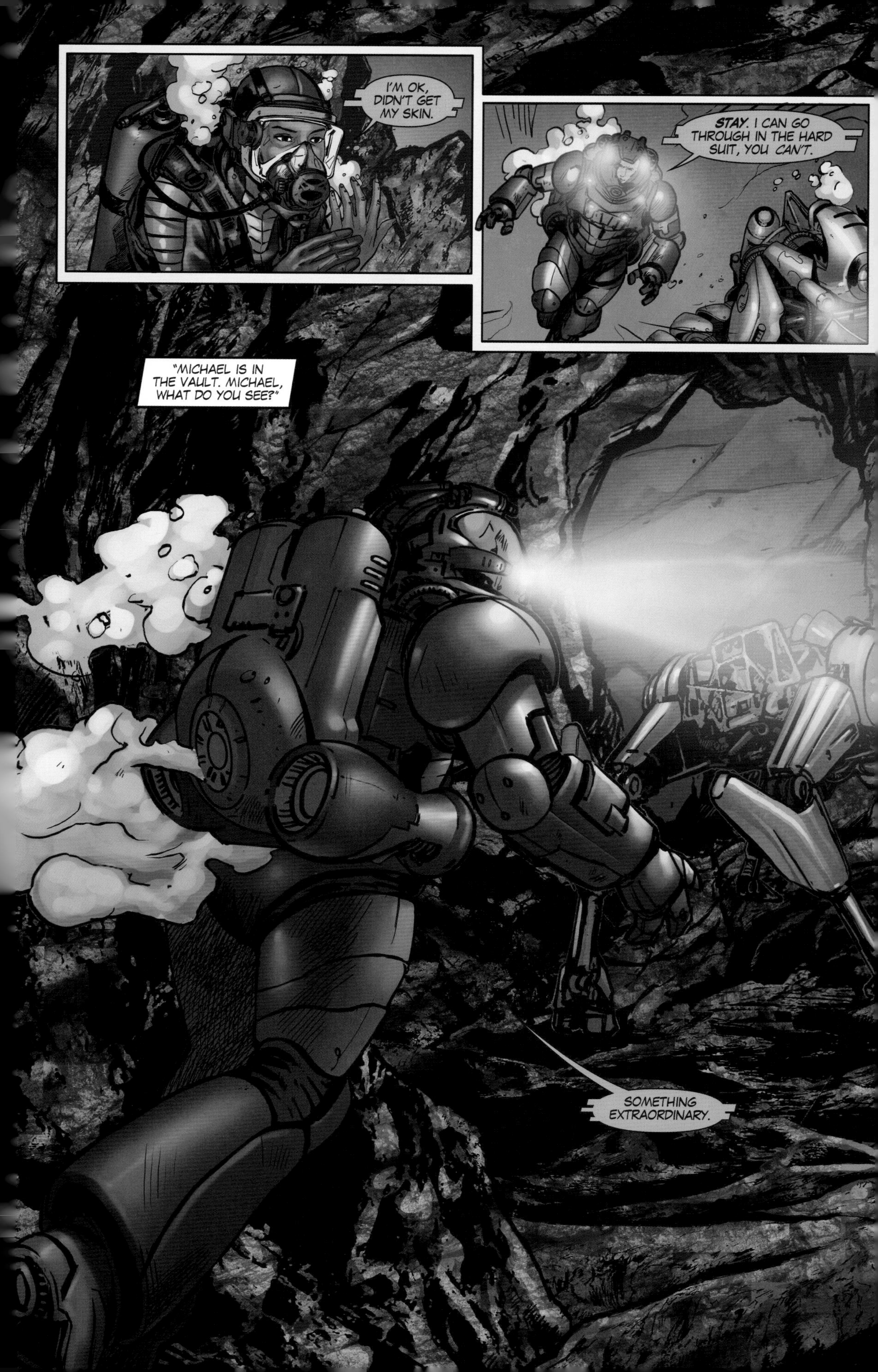
I'M OK, DIDN'T GET MY SKIN.
STAY. I CAN GO THROUGH IN THE HARD SUIT, YOU CAN'T.
"MICHAEL IS IN THE VAULT. MICHAEL, WHAT DO YOU SEE?"
SOMETHING EXTRAORDINARY.

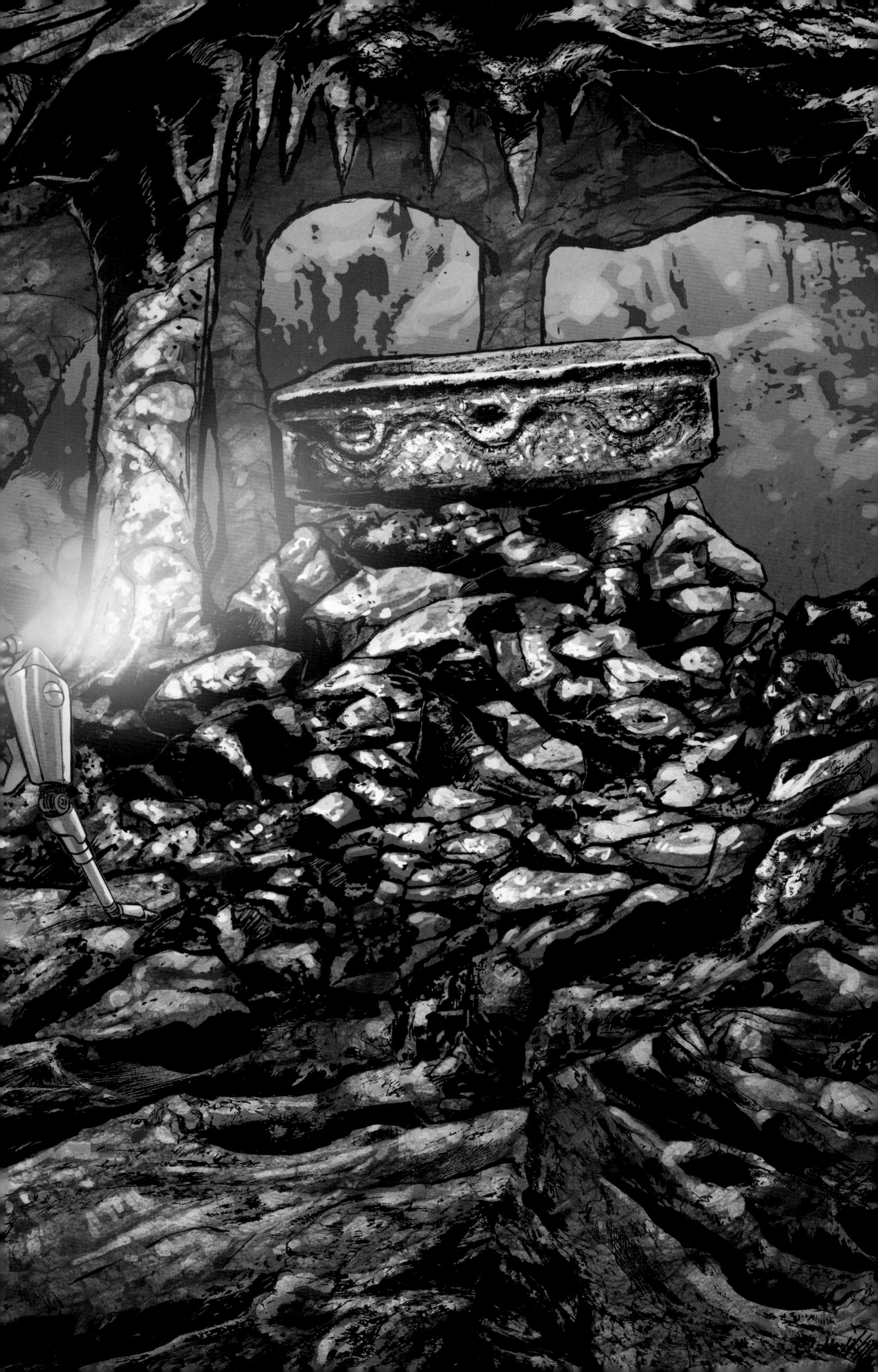

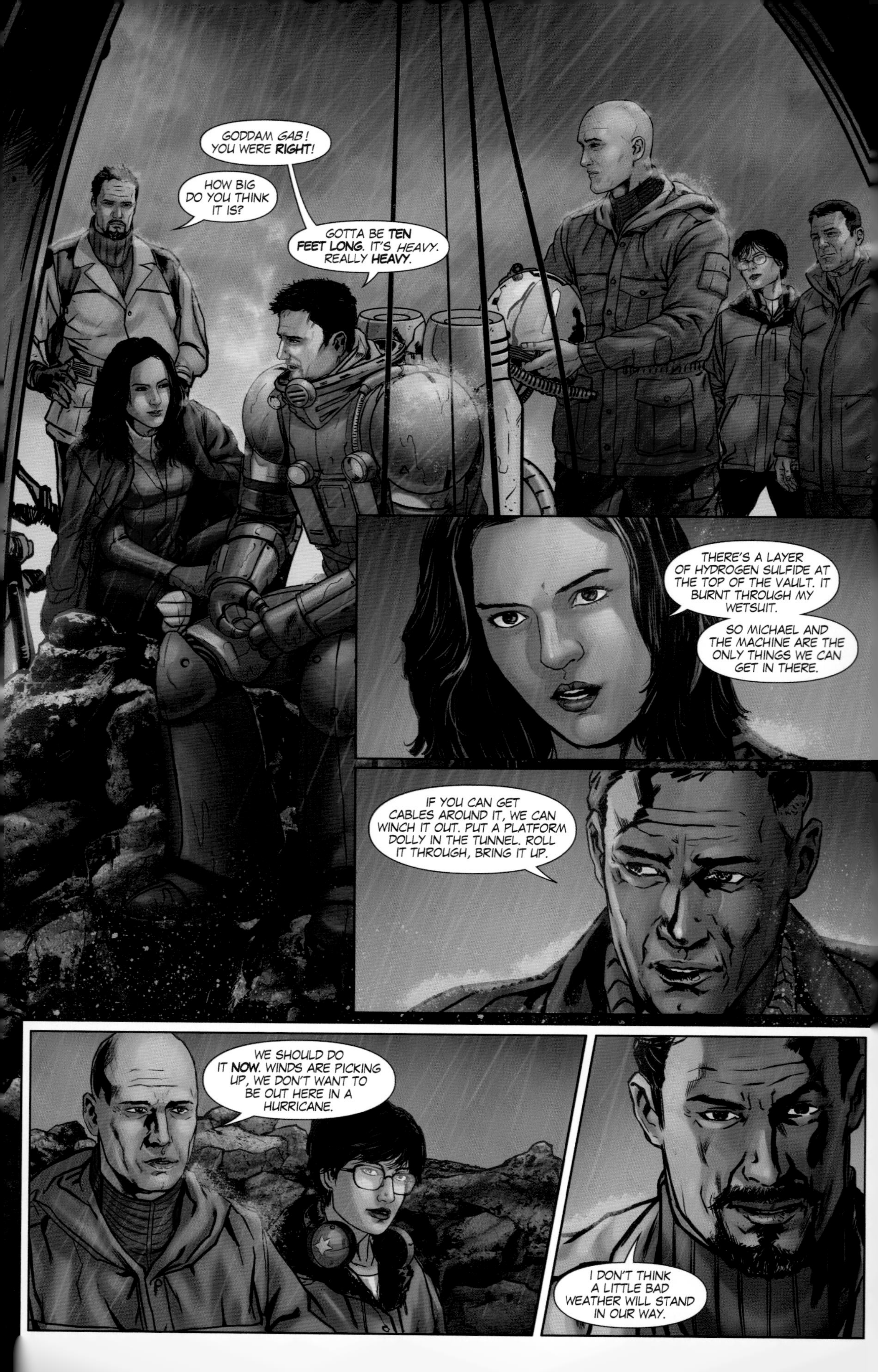
GODDAM GAB! YOU WERE RIGHT!
HOW BIG DO YOU THINK IT IS?
GOTTA BE TEN FEET LONG. IT'S HEAVY. REALLY HEAVY.
THERE'S A LAYER OF HYDROGEN SULFIDE AT THE TOP OF THE VAULT. IT BURNT THROUGH MY WETSUIT.
SO MICHAEL AND THE MACHINE ARE THE ONLY THINGS WE CAN GET IN THERE.
IF YOU CAN GET CABLES AROUND IT, WE CAN WINCH IT OUT. PUT A PLATFORM DOLLY IN THE TUNNEL. ROLL IT THROUGH, BRING IT UP.
WE SHOULD DO IT NOW. WINDS ARE PICKING UP, WE DON'T WANT TO BE OUT HERE IN A HURRICANE.
I DON'T THINK A LITTLE BAD WEATHER WILL STAND IN OUR WAY.

OK. EVERYONE STEP BACK FOR A SECOND WHILE I IMAGE IT.

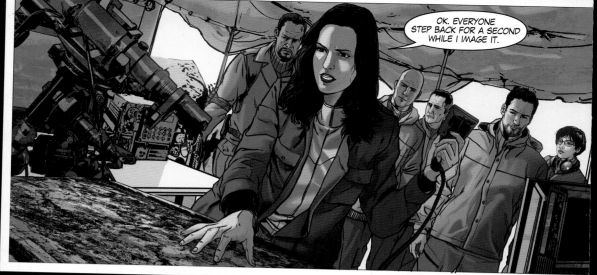

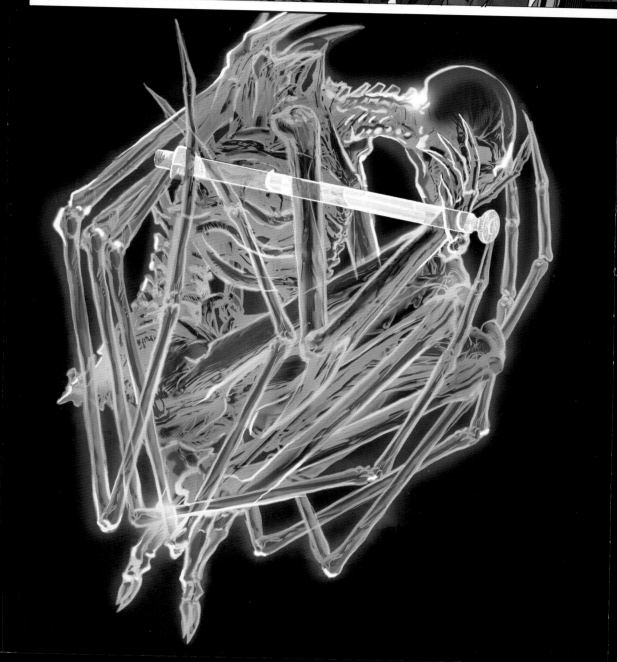

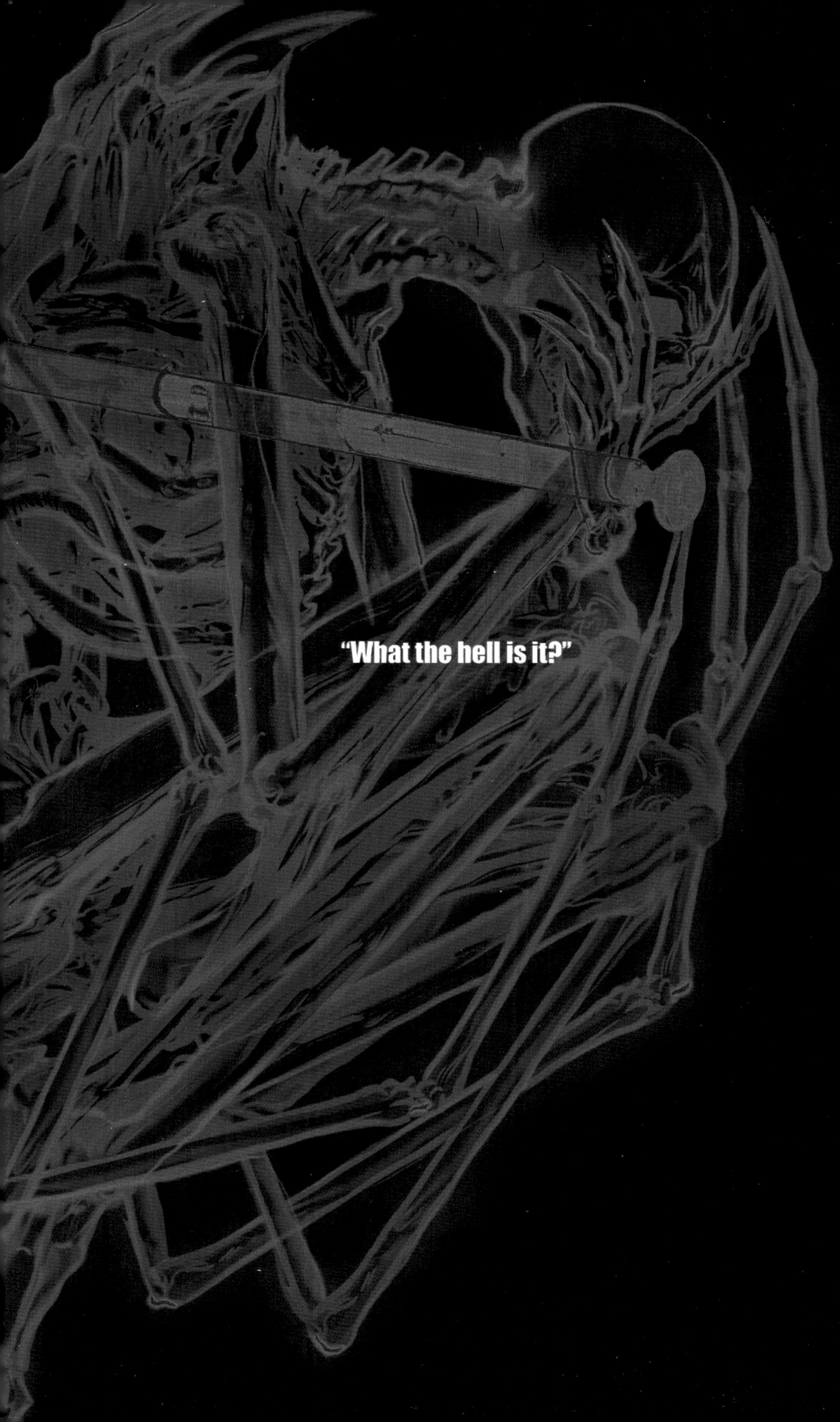
"What the hell is it?"

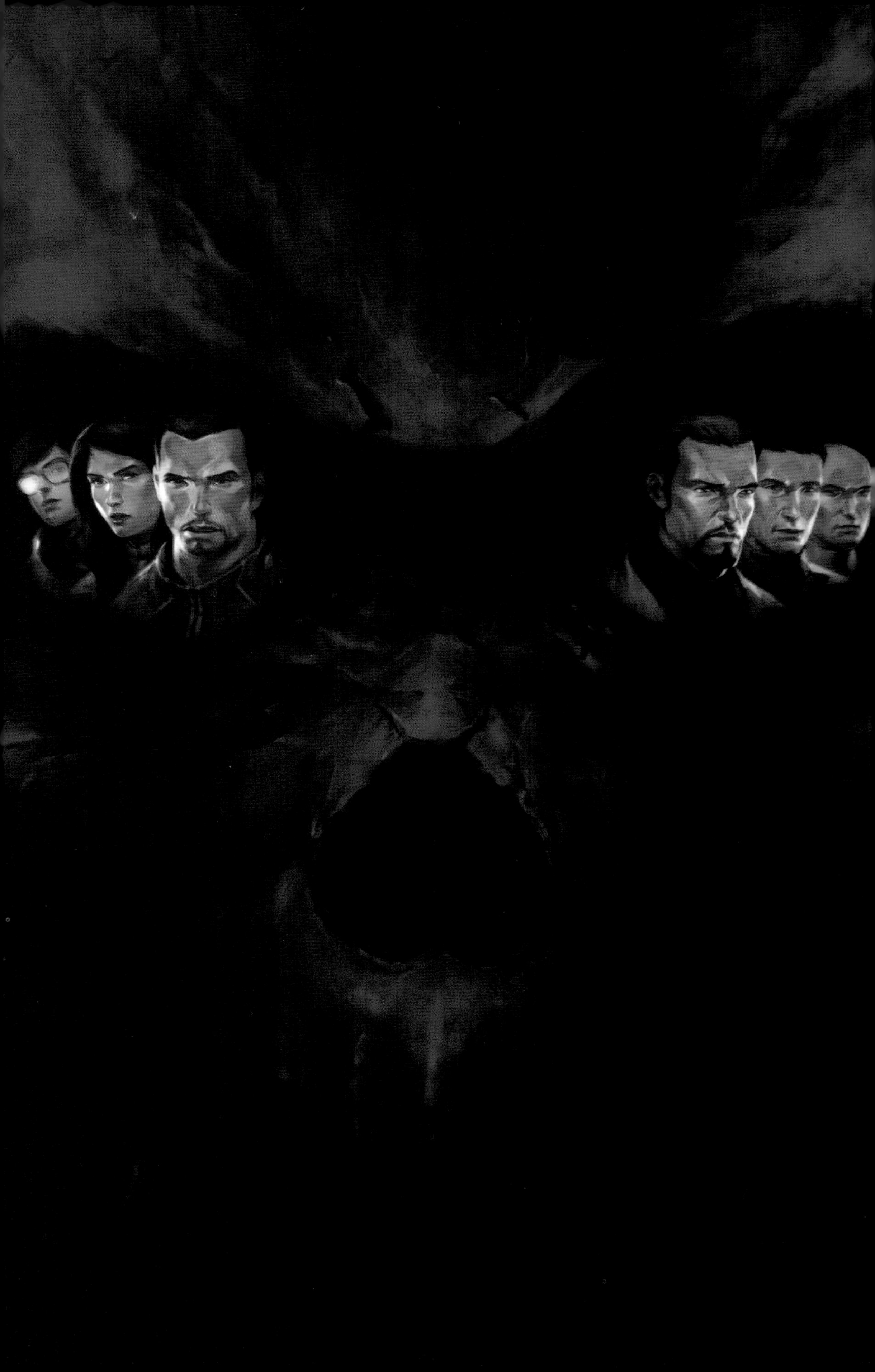

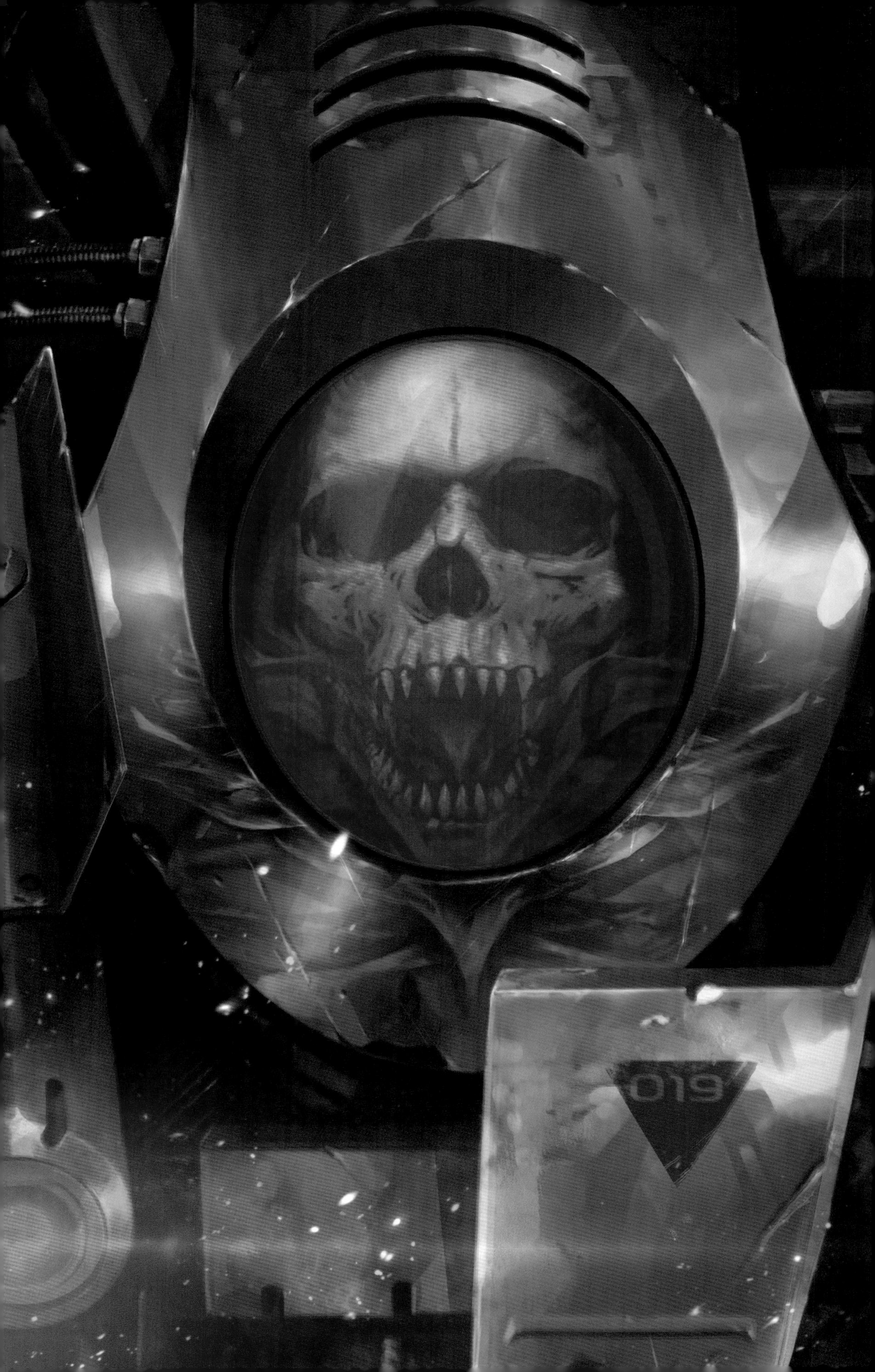
019

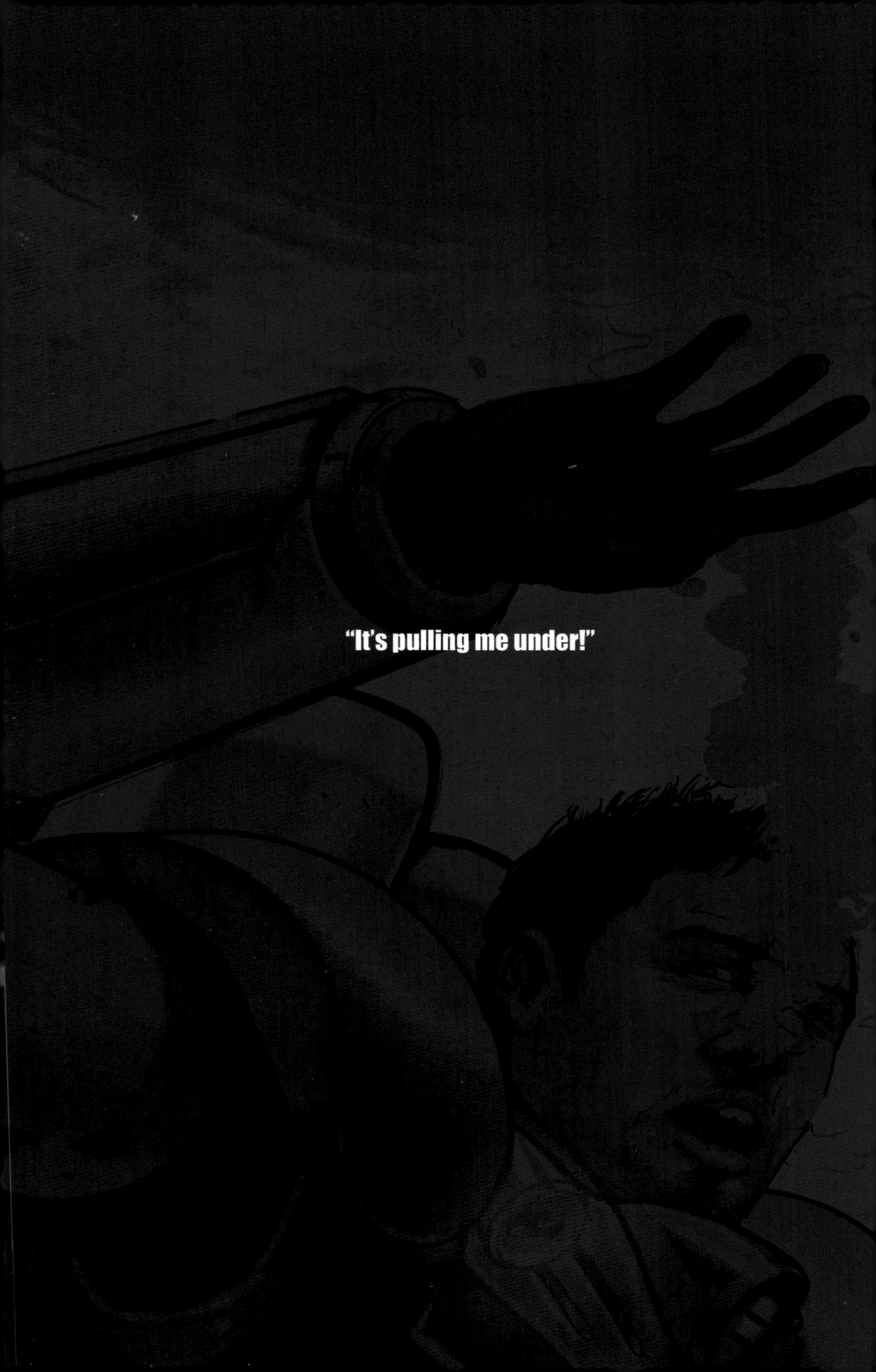
“It’s pulling me under!”

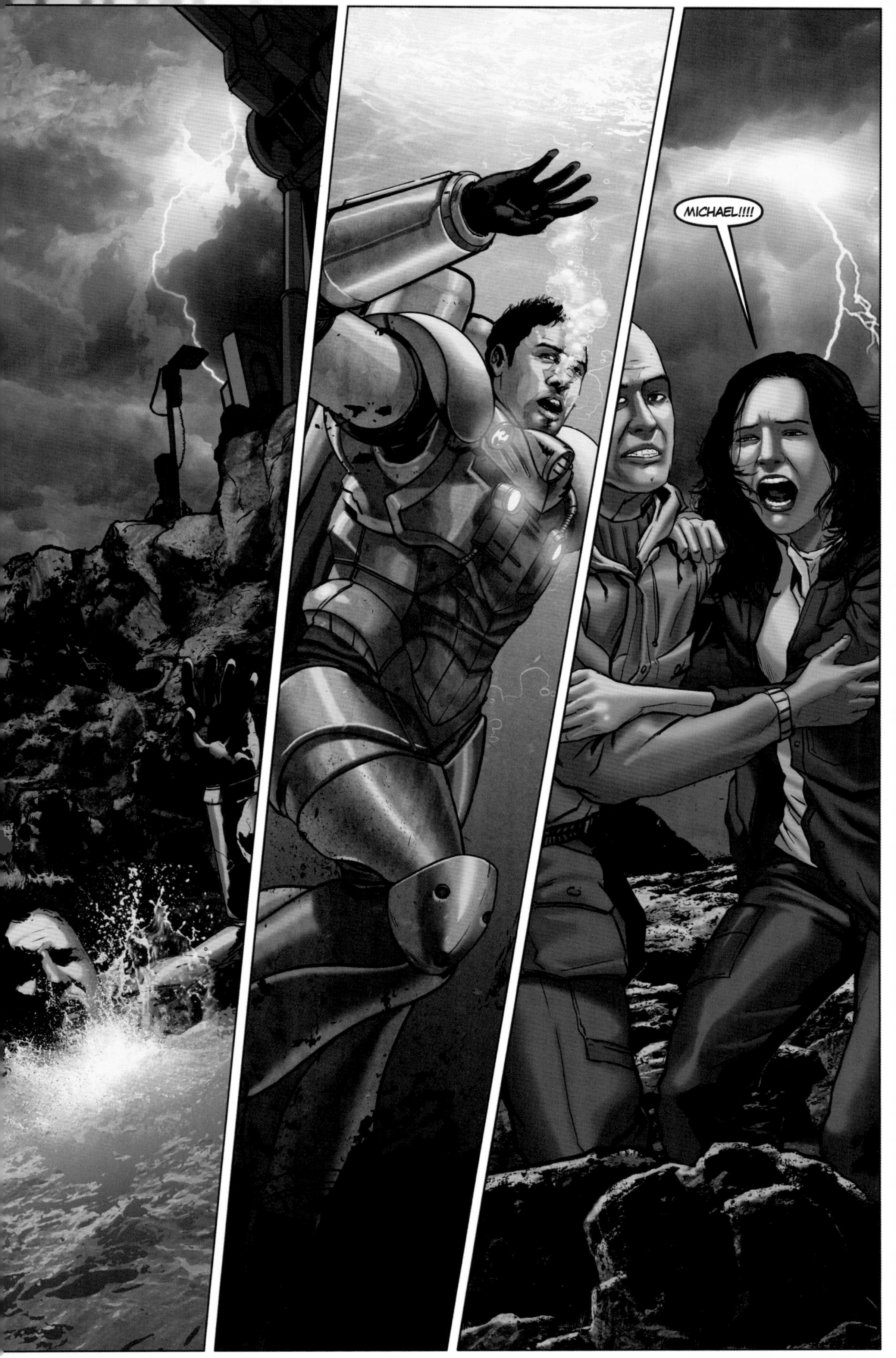
MICHAEL!!!!

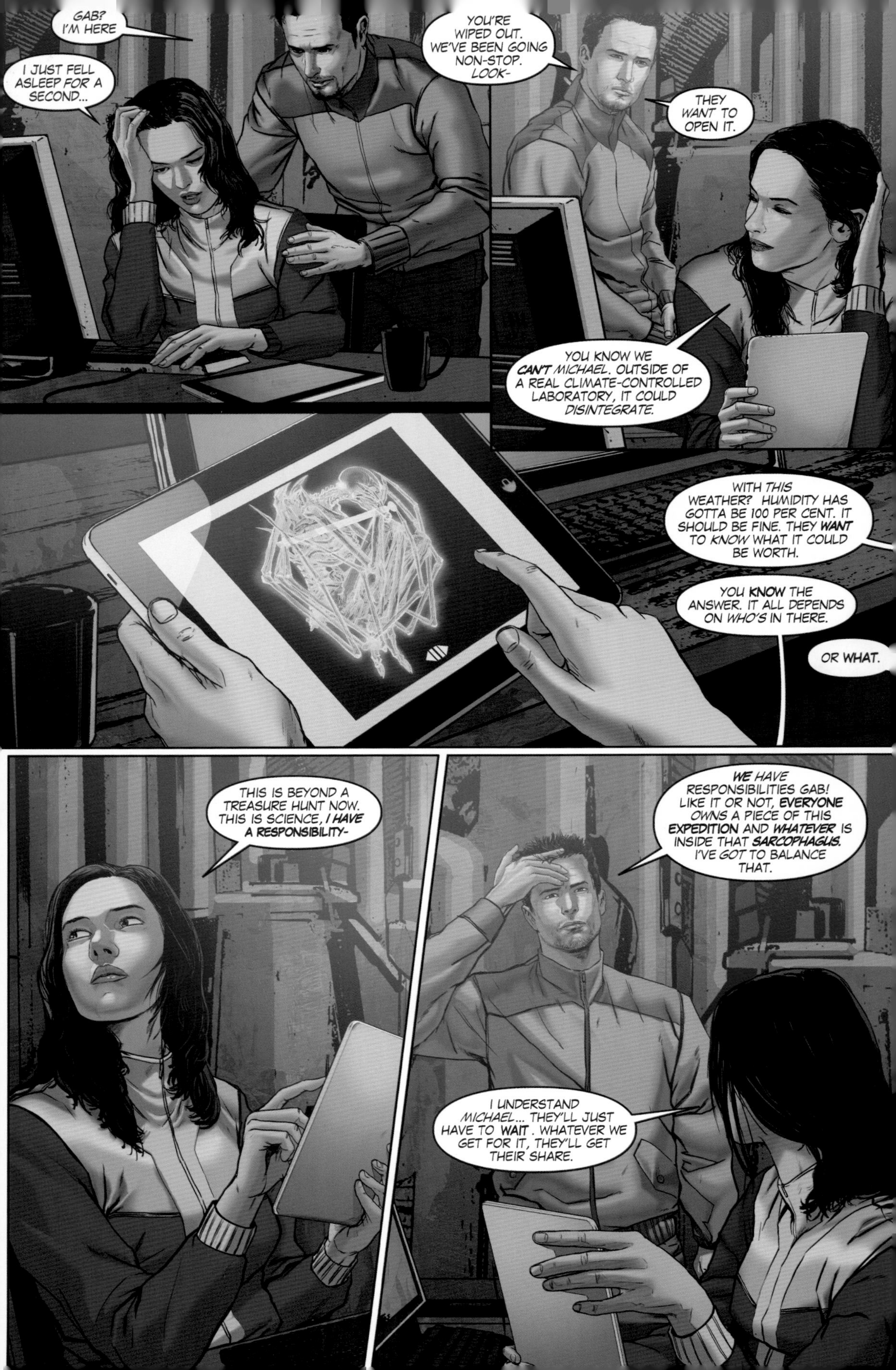
GAB? I'M HERE
I JUST FELL ASLEEP FOR A SECOND...
YOU'RE WIPED OUT. WE'VE BEEN GOING NON-STOP. LOOK-
THEY WANT TO OPEN IT.
YOU KNOW WE CAN'T MICHAEL. OUTSIDE OF A REAL CLIMATE-CONTROLLED LABORATORY, IT COULD DISINTEGRATE.
WITH THIS WEATHER? HUMIDITY HAS GOTTA BE 100 PER CENT. IT SHOULD BE FINE. THEY WANT TO KNOW WHAT IT COULD BE WORTH.
YOU KNOW THE ANSWER. IT ALL DEPENDS ON WHO'S IN THERE.
OR WHAT.
THIS IS BEYOND A TREASURE HUNT NOW. THIS IS SCIENCE, I HAVE A RESPONSIBILITY-
WE HAVE RESPONSIBILITIES GAB! LIKE IT OR NOT, EVERYONE OWNS A PIECE OF THIS EXPEDITION AND WHATEVER IS INSIDE THAT SARCOPHAGUS. I'VE GOT TO BALANCE THAT.
I UNDERSTAND MICHAEL... THEY'LL JUST HAVE TO WAIT. WHATEVER WE GET FOR IT, THEY'LL GET THEIR SHARE.

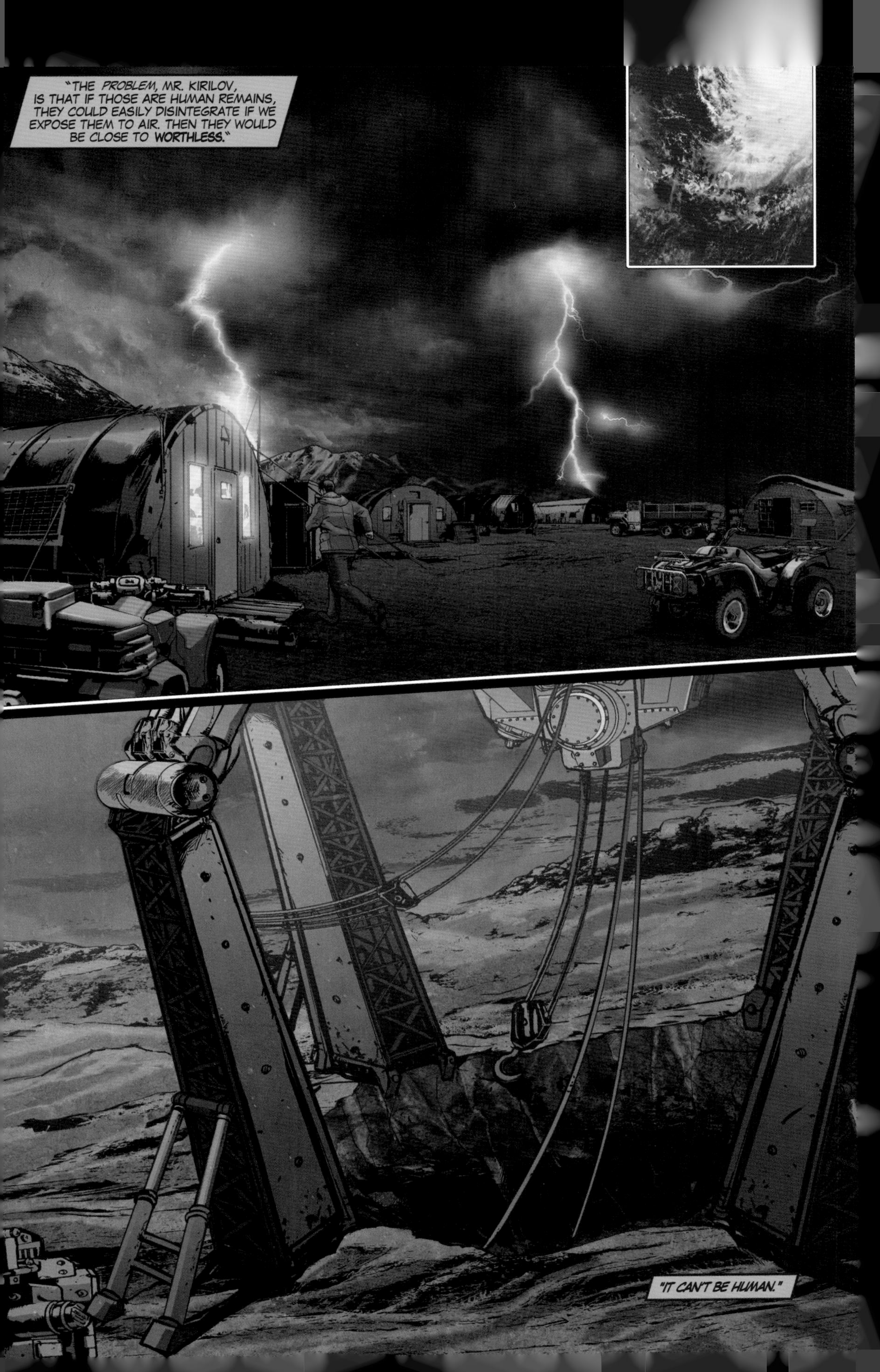
"THE PROBLEM, MR. KIRILOV, IS THAT IF THOSE ARE HUMAN REMAINS, THEY COULD EASILY DISINTEGRATE IF WE EXPOSE THEM TO AIR. THEN THEY WOULD BE CLOSE TO WORTHLESS."
"IT CAN'T BE HUMAN."

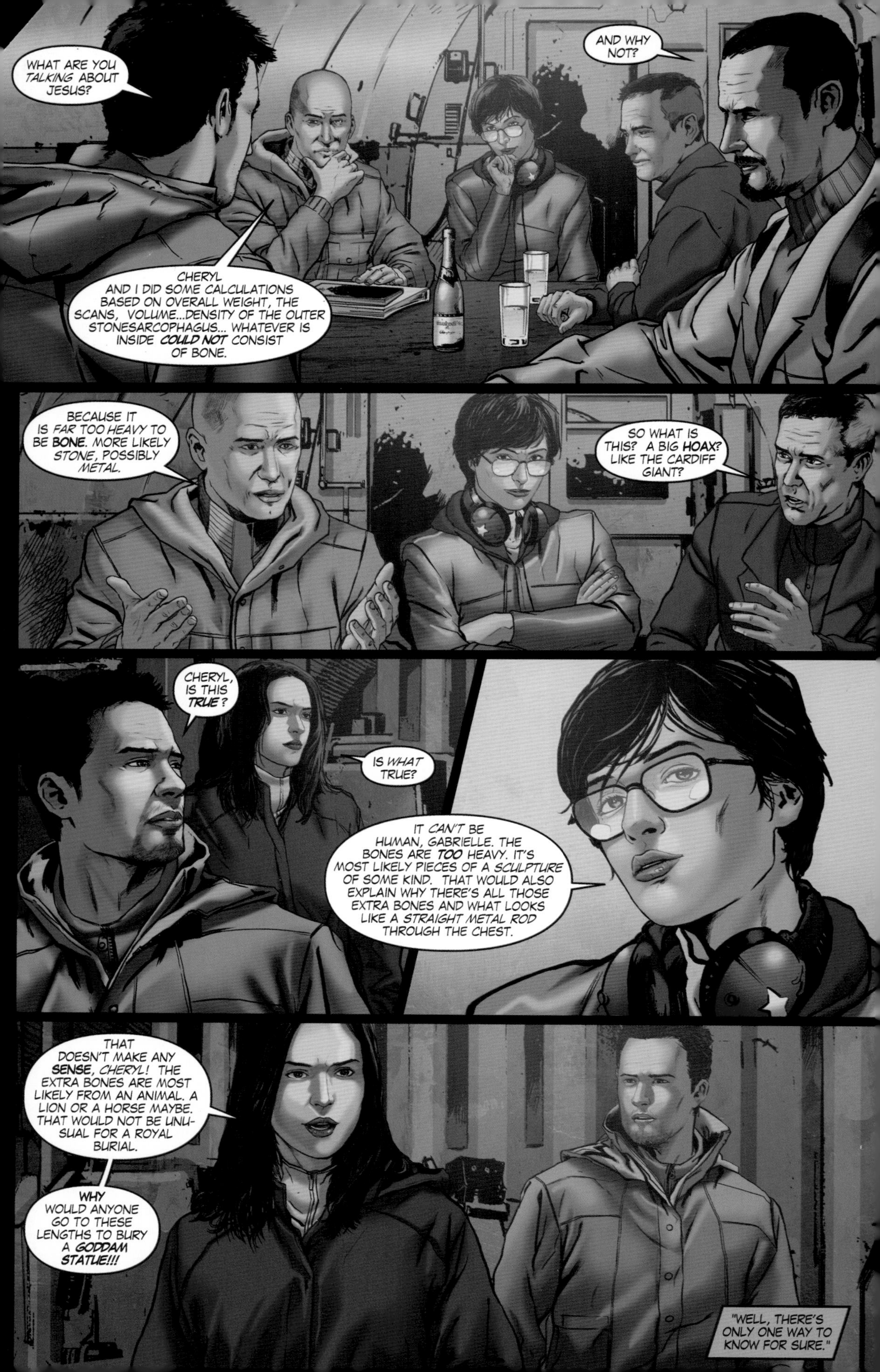
WHAT ARE YOU TALKING ABOUT JESUS?
AND WHY NOT?
CHERYL AND I DID SOME CALCULATIONS BASED ON OVERALL WEIGHT, THE SCANS, VOLUME...DENSITY OF THE OUTER STONESARCOPHAGUS... WHATEVER IS INSIDE COULD NOT CONSIST OF BONE.
BECAUSE IT IS FAR TOO HEAVY TO BE BONE. MORE LIKELY STONE, POSSIBLY METAL.
SO WHAT IS THIS? A BIG HOAX? LIKE THE CARDIFF GIANT?
CHERYL, IS THIS TRUE?
IS WHAT TRUE?
IT CAN'T BE HUMAN, GABRIELLE. THE BONES ARE TOO HEAVY. IT'S MOST LIKELY PIECES OF A SCULPTURE OF SOME KIND. THAT WOULD ALSO EXPLAIN WHY THERE'S ALL THOSE EXTRA BONES AND WHAT LOOKS LIKE A STRAIGHT METAL ROD THROUGH THE CHEST.
THAT DOESN'T MAKE ANY SENSE, CHERYL! THE EXTRA BONES ARE MOST LIKELY FROM AN ANIMAL. A LION OR A HORSE MAYBE. THAT WOULD NOT BE UNUSUAL FOR A ROYAL BURIAL.
WHY WOULD ANYONE GO TO THESE LENGTHS TO BURY A GODDAM STATUE!!!
"WELL, THERE'S ONLY ONE WAY TO KNOW FOR SURE."

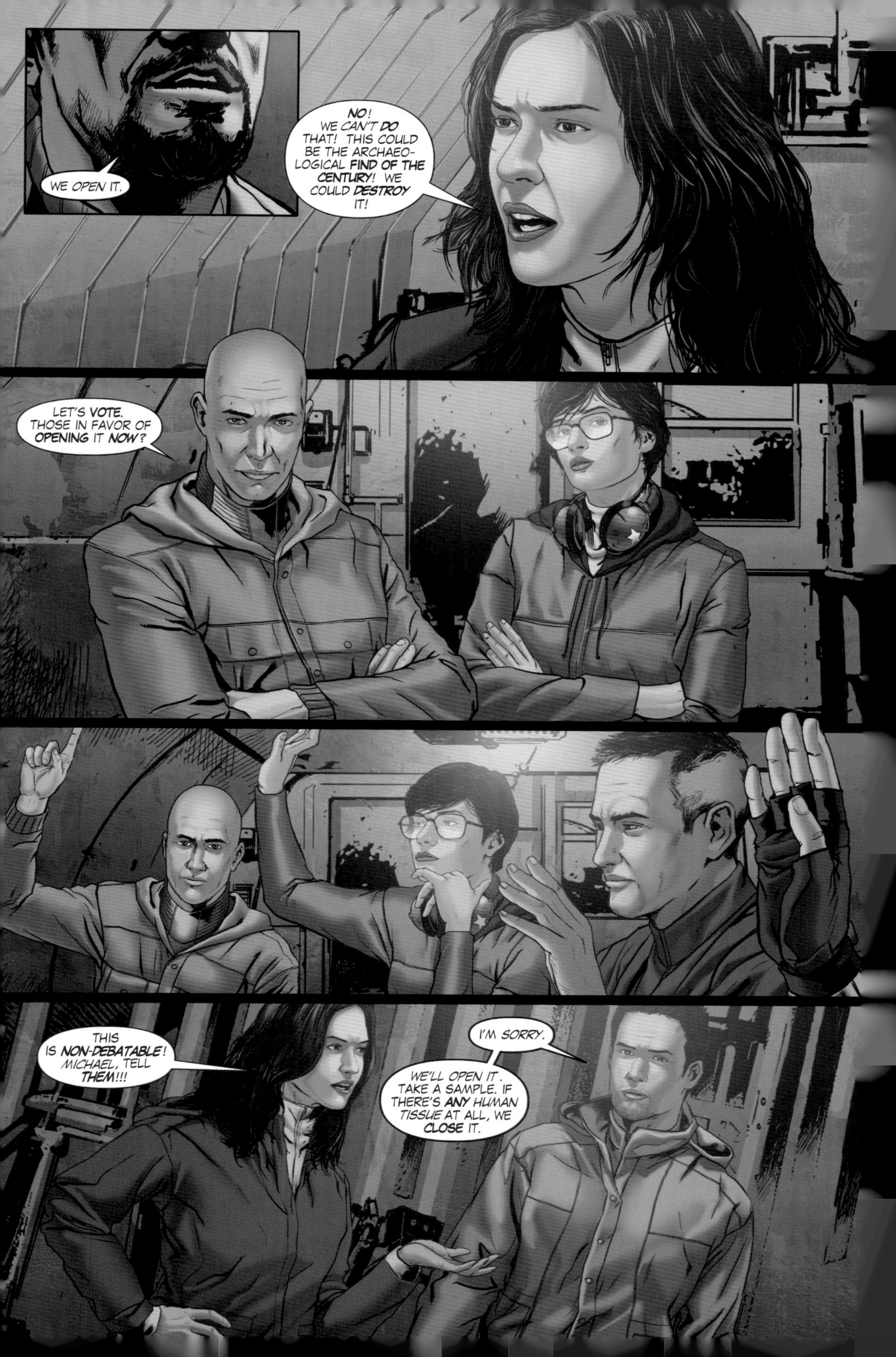
WE OPEN IT.
NO! WE CAN'T DO THAT! THIS COULD BE THE ARCHAEO-LOGICAL FIND OF THE CENTURY! WE COULD DESTROY IT!
LET'S VOTE. THOSE IN FAVOR OF OPENING IT NOW?
THIS IS NON-DEBATABLE! MICHAEL, TELL THEM!!!
I'M SORRY.
WE'LL OPEN IT. TAKE A SAMPLE. IF THERE'S ANY HUMAN TISSUE AT ALL, WE CLOSE IT.

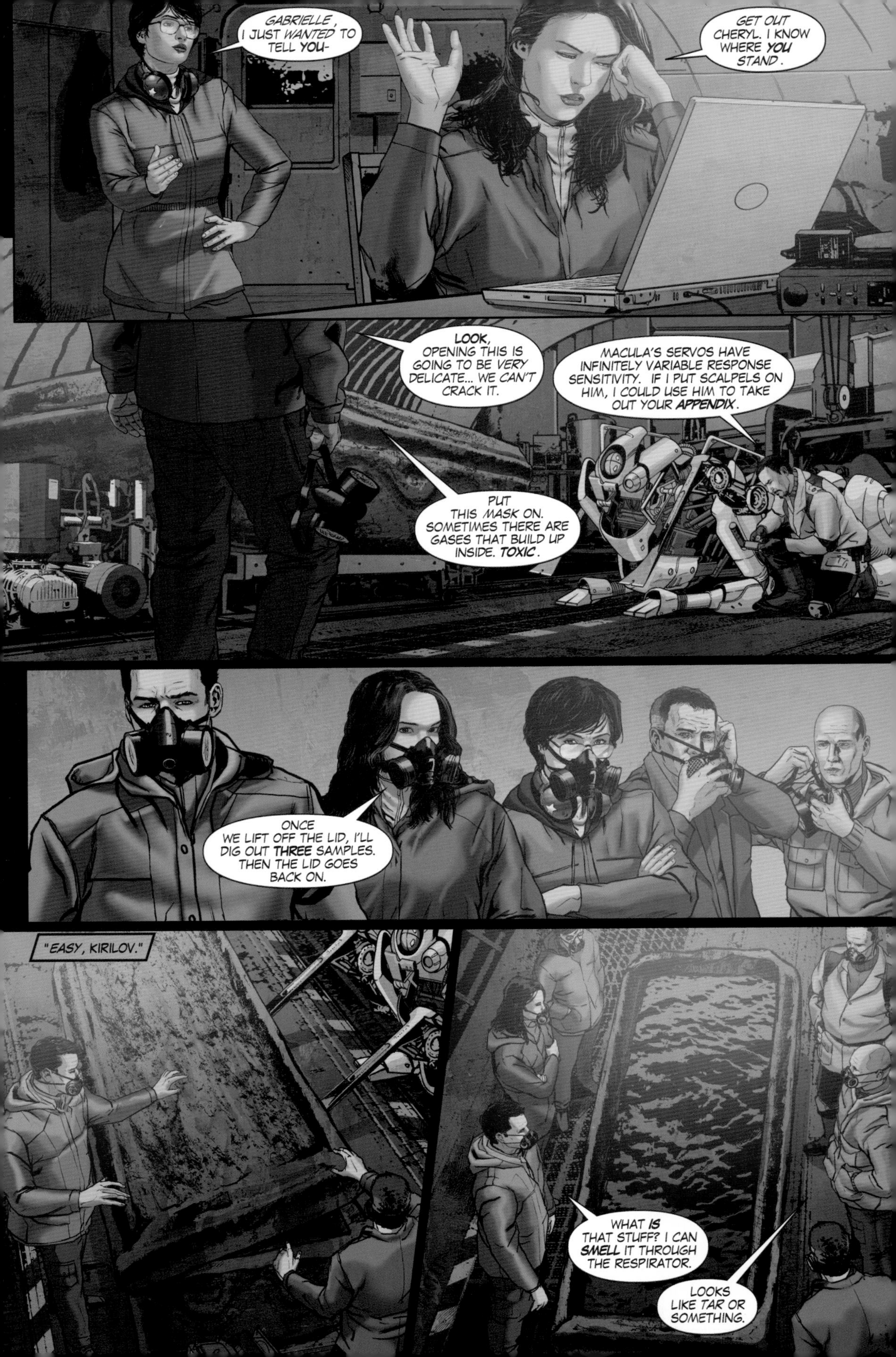
GABRIELLE, I JUST WANTED TO TELL YOU-
GET OUT CHERYL. I KNOW WHERE YOU STAND.
LOOK, OPENING THIS IS GOING TO BE VERY DELICATE... WE CAN'T CRACK IT.
MACULA'S SERVOS HAVE INFINITELY VARIABLE RESPONSE SENSITIVITY. IF I PUT SCALPELS ON HIM, I COULD USE HIM TO TAKE OUT YOUR APPENDIX.
PUT THIS MASK ON. SOMETIMES THERE ARE GASES THAT BUILD UP INSIDE. TOXIC.
ONCE WE LIFT OFF THE LID, I'LL DIG OUT THREE SAMPLES. THEN THE LID GOES BACK ON.
"EASY, KIRILOV."
WHAT IS THAT STUFF? I CAN SMELL IT THROUGH THE RESPIRATOR.
LOOKS LIKE TAR OR SOMETHING.

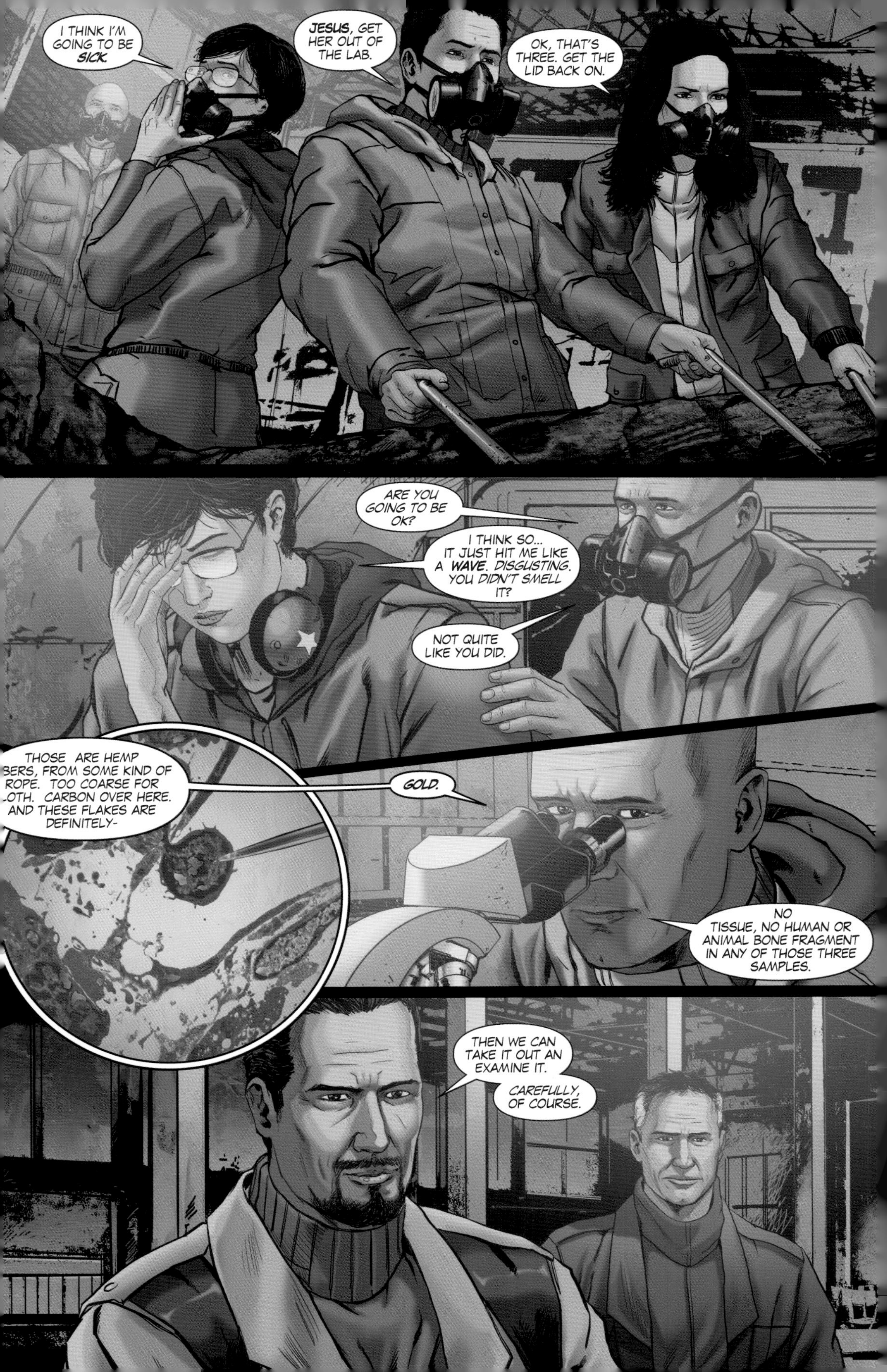
I THINK I'M GOING TO BE SICK.
JESUS, GET HER OUT OF THE LAB.
OK, THAT'S THREE. GET THE LID BACK ON.
ARE YOU GOING TO BE OK?
I THINK SO... IT JUST HIT ME LIKE A WAVE. DISGUSTING. YOU DIDN'T SMELL IT?
NOT QUITE LIKE YOU DID.
THOSE ARE HEMP BERS, FROM SOME KIND OF ROPE. TOO COARSE FOR LOTH. CARBON OVER HERE. AND THESE FLAKES ARE DEFINITELY-
GOLD.
NO TISSUE, NO HUMAN OR ANIMAL BONE FRAGMENT IN ANY OF THOSE THREE SAMPLES.
THEN WE CAN TAKE IT OUT AN EXAMINE IT.
CAREFULLY, OF COURSE.

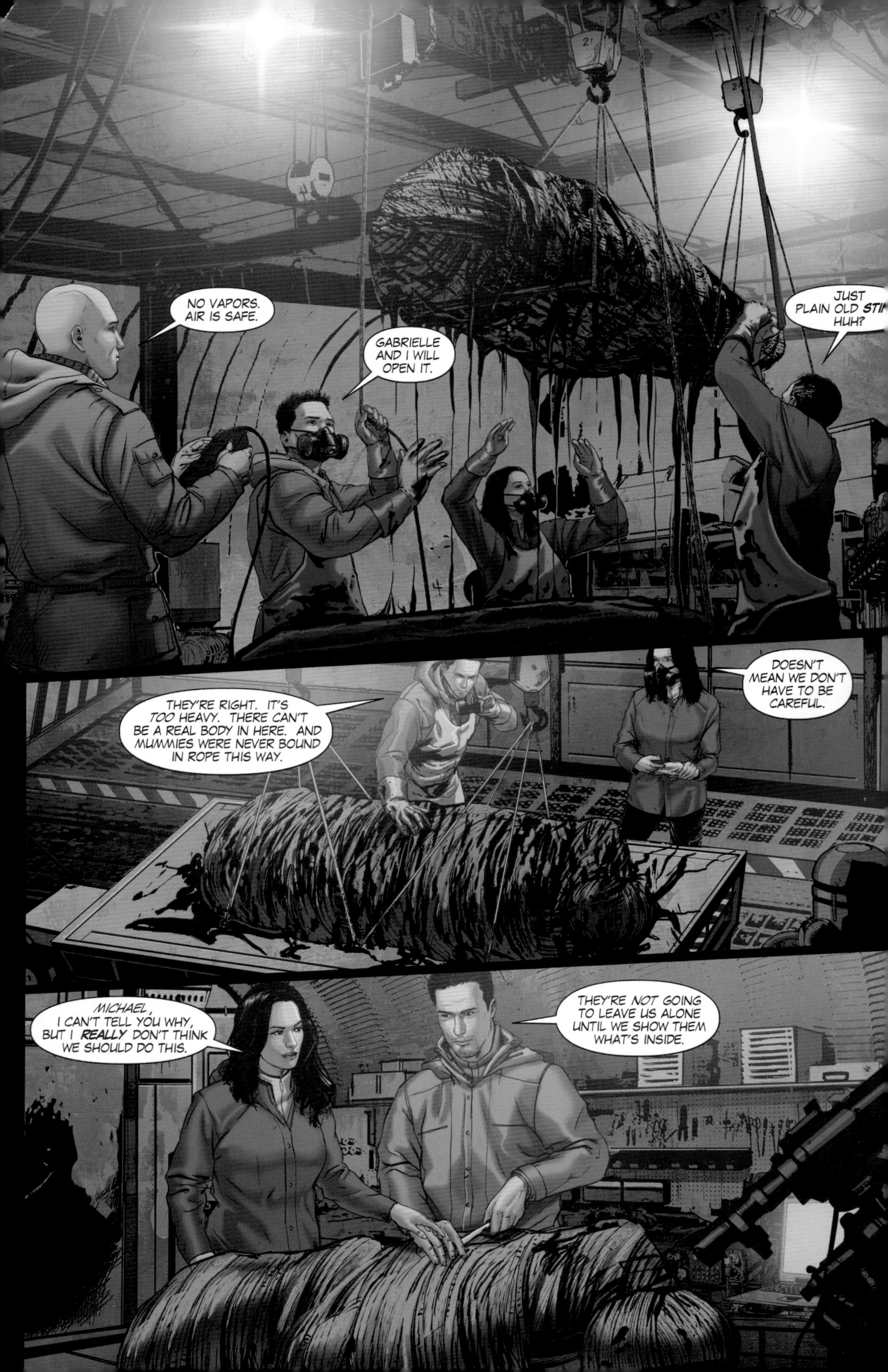
NO VAPORS. AIR IS SAFE.
GABRIELLE AND I WILL OPEN IT.
JUST PLAIN OLD STI... HUH?
THEY'RE RIGHT. IT'S TOO HEAVY. THERE CAN'T BE A REAL BODY IN HERE. AND MUMMIES WERE NEVER BOUND IN ROPE THIS WAY.
DOESN'T MEAN WE DON'T HAVE TO BE CAREFUL.
MICHAEL, I CAN'T TELL YOU WHY, BUT I REALLY DON'T THINK WE SHOULD DO THIS.
THEY'RE NOT GOING TO LEAVE US ALONE UNTIL WE SHOW THEM WHAT'S INSIDE.

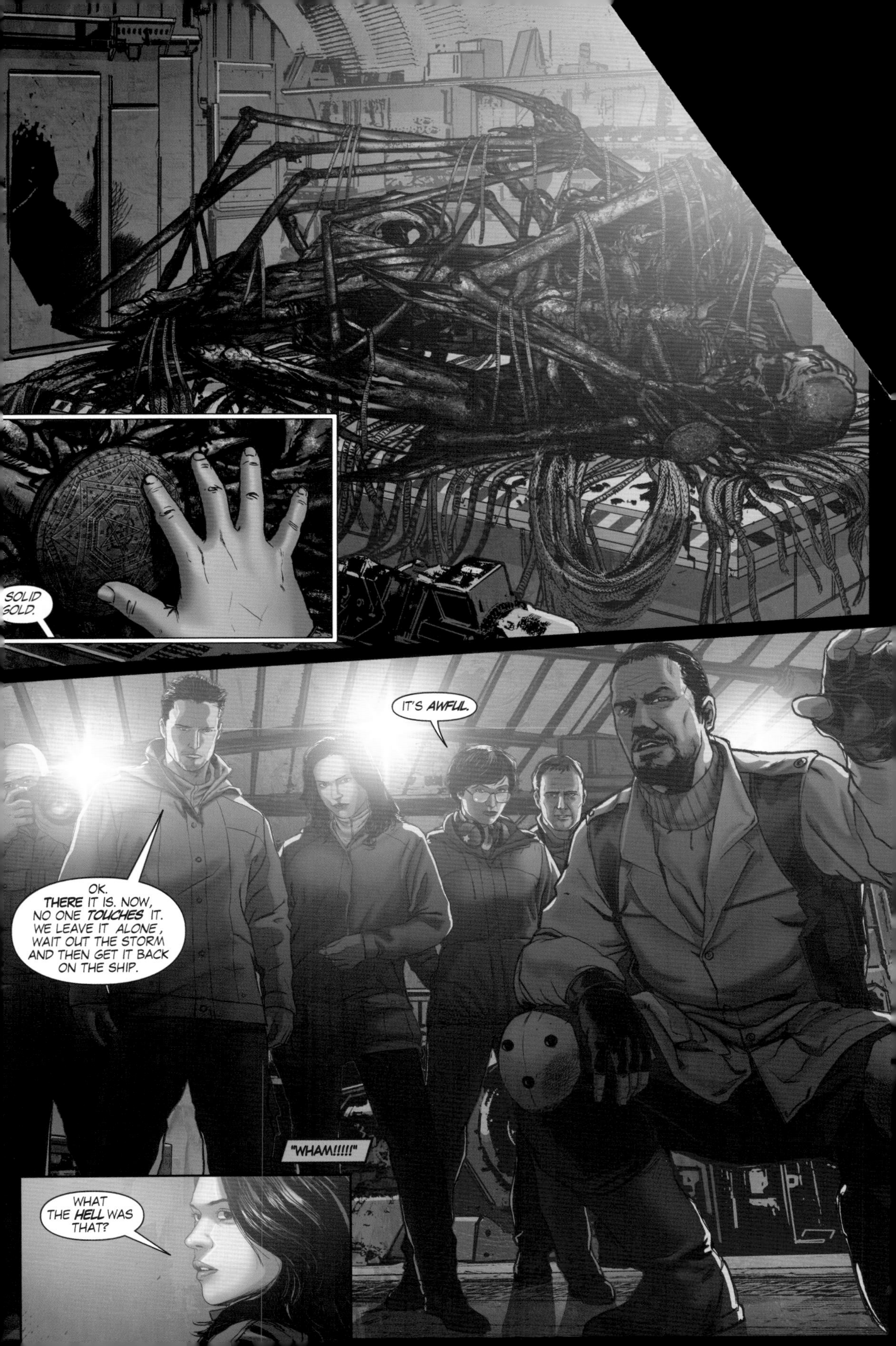
SOLID GOLD.
IT'S AWFUL.
OK. THERE IT IS. NOW, NO ONE TOUCHES IT. WE LEAVE IT ALONE, WAIT OUT THE STORM AND THEN GET IT BACK ON THE SHIP.
"WHAM!!!!!"
WHAT THE HELL WAS THAT?

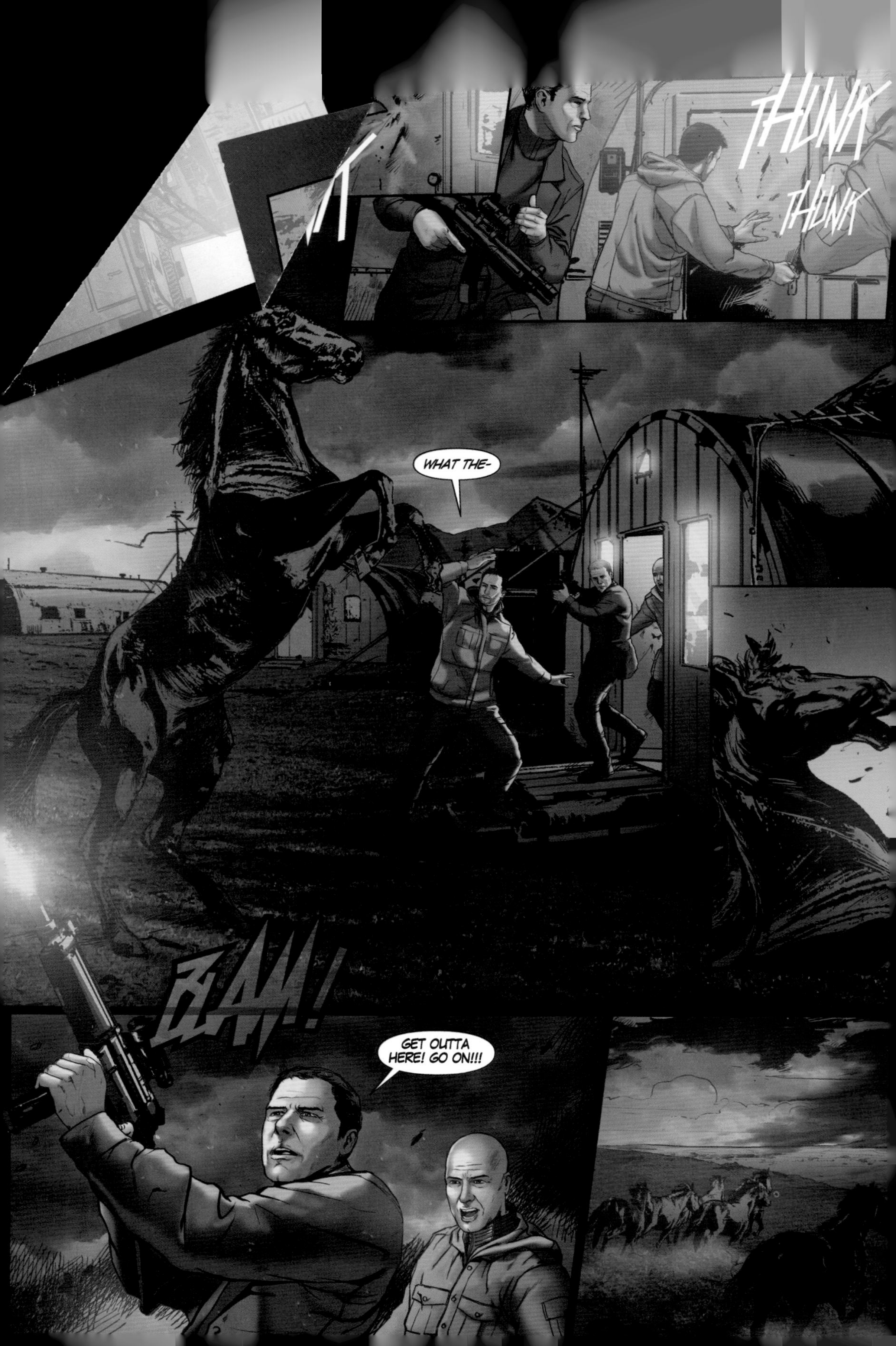
THUNK
THUNK
WHAT THE-
BLAM!
GET OUTTA HERE! GO ON!!!

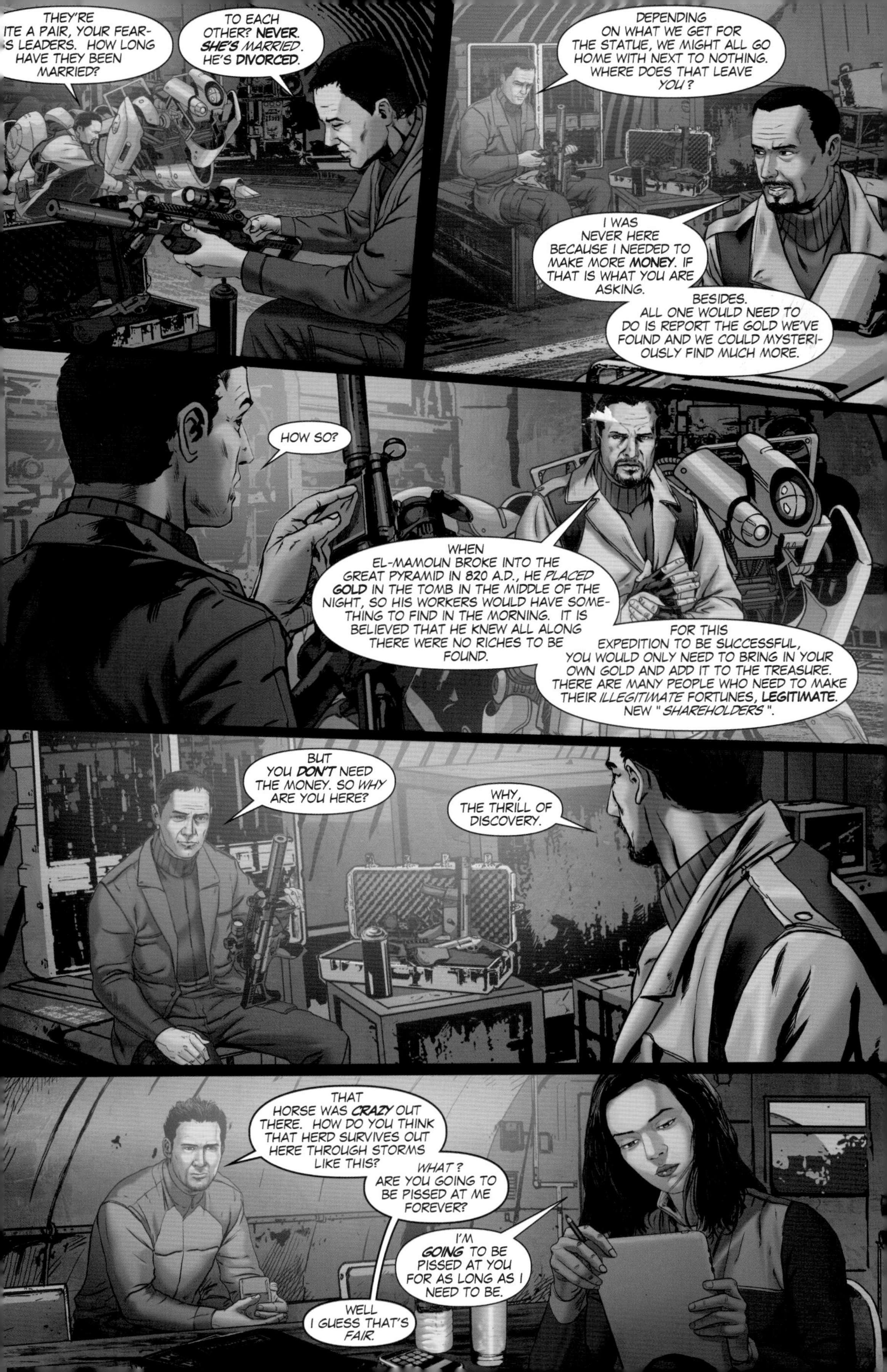
THEY'RE
ITE A PAIR, YOUR FEAR-
S LEADERS. HOW LONG HAVE THEY BEEN MARRIED?
TO EACH OTHER? NEVER. SHE'S MARRIED. HE'S DIVORCED.
DEPENDING ON WHAT WE GET FOR THE STATUE, WE MIGHT ALL GO HOME WITH NEXT TO NOTHING. WHERE DOES THAT LEAVE YOU?
I WAS NEVER HERE BECAUSE I NEEDED TO MAKE MORE MONEY. IF THAT IS WHAT YOU ARE ASKING.
BESIDES. ALL ONE WOULD NEED TO DO IS REPORT THE GOLD WE'VE FOUND AND WE COULD MYSTERIOUSLY FIND MUCH MORE.
HOW SO?
WHEN EL-MAMOUN BROKE INTO THE GREAT PYRAMID IN 820 A.D., HE PLACED GOLD IN THE TOMB IN THE MIDDLE OF THE NIGHT, SO HIS WORKERS WOULD HAVE SOMETHING TO FIND IN THE MORNING. IT IS BELIEVED THAT HE KNEW ALL ALONG THERE WERE NO RICHES TO BE FOUND.
FOR THIS EXPEDITION TO BE SUCCESSFUL, YOU WOULD ONLY NEED TO BRING IN YOUR OWN GOLD AND ADD IT TO THE TREASURE. THERE ARE MANY PEOPLE WHO NEED TO MAKE THEIR ILLEGITIMATE FORTUNES, LEGITIMATE. NEW "SHAREHOLDERS".
BUT YOU DON'T NEED THE MONEY. SO WHY ARE YOU HERE?
WHY, THE THRILL OF DISCOVERY.
THAT HORSE WAS CRAZY OUT THERE. HOW DO YOU THINK THAT HERD SURVIVES OUT HERE THROUGH STORMS LIKE THIS?
WHAT? ARE YOU GOING TO BE PISSED AT ME FOREVER?
I'M GOING TO BE PISSED AT YOU FOR AS LONG AS I NEED TO BE.
WELL I GUESS THAT'S FAIR.

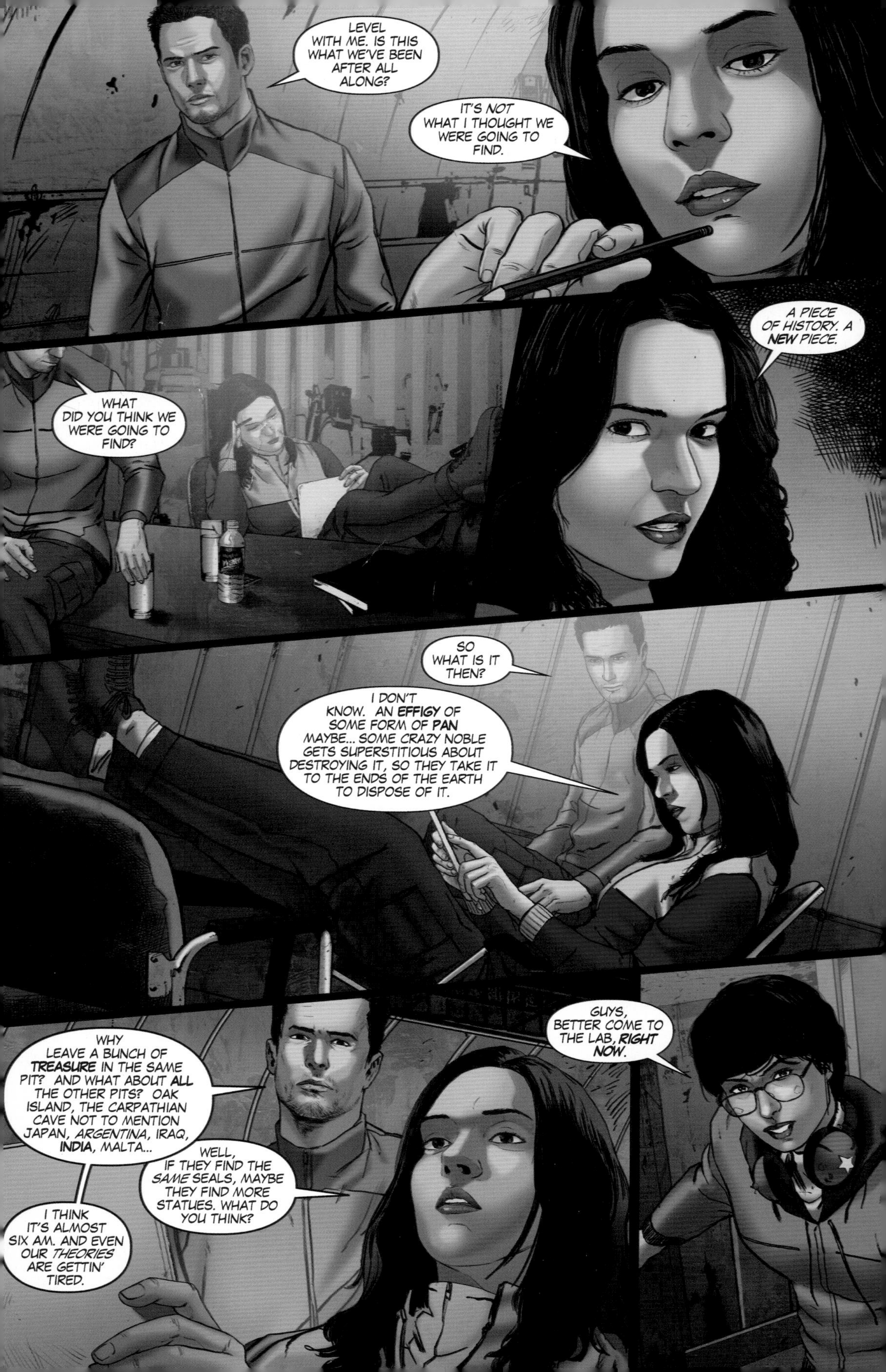
LEVEL WITH ME. IS THIS WHAT WE'VE BEEN AFTER ALL ALONG?
IT'S *NOT* WHAT I THOUGHT WE WERE GOING TO FIND.
WHAT DID YOU THINK WE WERE GOING TO FIND?
A PIECE OF HISTORY. A **NEW** PIECE.
SO WHAT IS IT THEN?
I DON'T KNOW. AN **EFFIGY** OF SOME FORM OF **PAN** MAYBE... SOME CRAZY NOBLE GETS SUPERSTITIOUS ABOUT DESTROYING IT, SO THEY TAKE IT TO THE ENDS OF THE EARTH TO DISPOSE OF IT.
WHY LEAVE A BUNCH OF **TREASURE** IN THE SAME PIT? AND WHAT ABOUT **ALL** THE OTHER PITS? OAK ISLAND, THE CARPATHIAN CAVE NOT TO MENTION JAPAN, *ARGENTINA*, IRAQ, **INDIA**, MALTA...
WELL, IF THEY FIND THE *SAME* SEALS, MAYBE THEY FIND MORE STATUES. WHAT DO YOU THINK?
I THINK IT'S ALMOST SIX AM. AND EVEN OUR *THEORIES* ARE GETTIN' TIRED.
GUYS, BETTER COME TO THE LAB, **RIGHT NOW**.

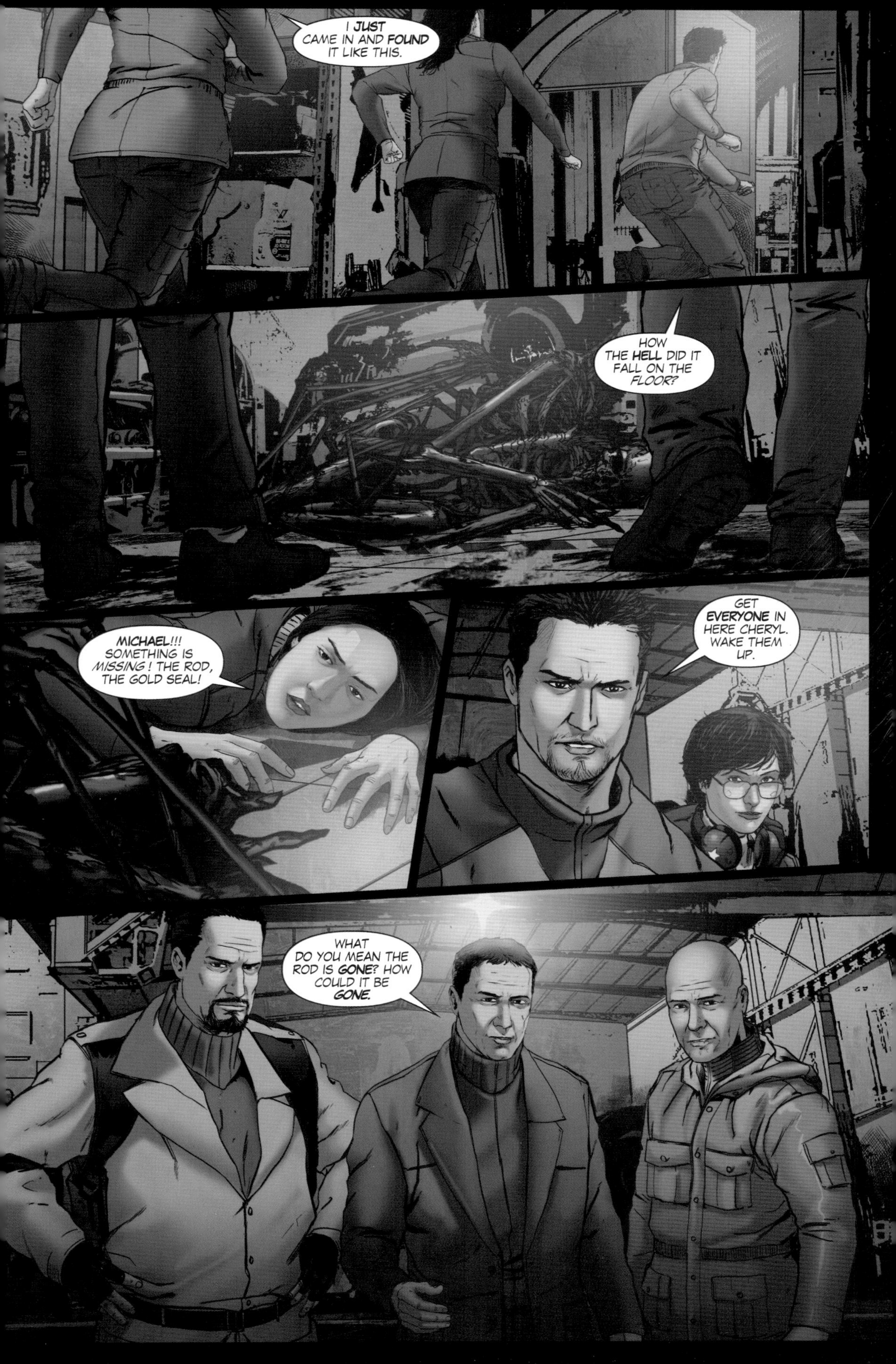
I **JUST** CAME IN AND **FOUND** IT LIKE THIS.
HOW THE **HELL** DID IT FALL ON THE *FLOOR?*
MICHAEL!!! SOMETHING IS *MISSING* ! THE ROD, THE GOLD SEAL!
GET **EVERYONE** IN HERE CHERYL. WAKE THEM UP.
WHAT DO YOU MEAN THE ROD IS **GONE**? HOW COULD IT BE ***GONE.***

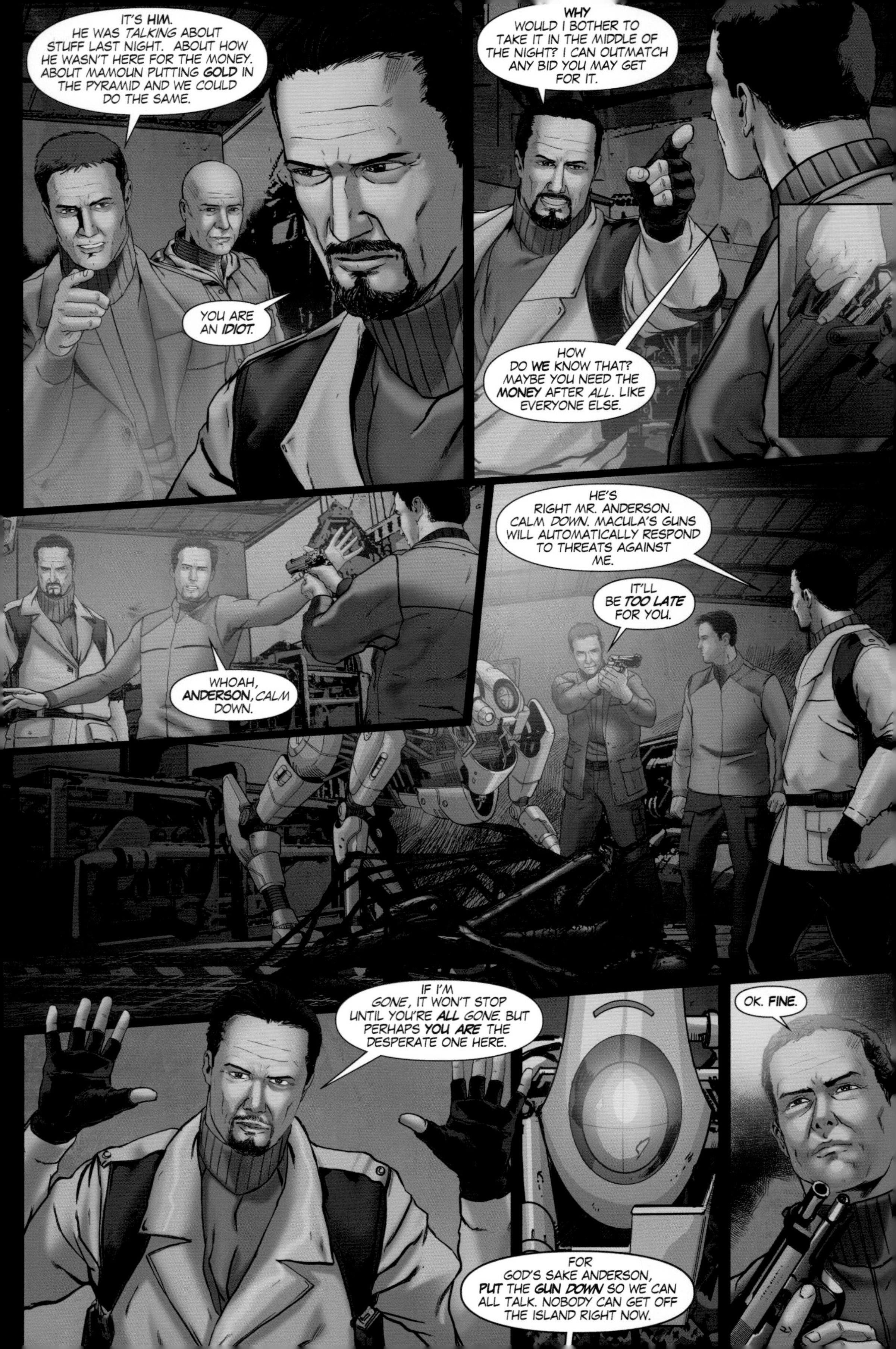

IT'S **HIM**. HE WAS *TALKING* ABOUT STUFF LAST NIGHT. ABOUT HOW HE WASN'T HERE FOR THE MONEY. ABOUT MAMOUN PUTTING **GOLD** IN THE PYRAMID AND WE COULD DO THE SAME.
YOU ARE AN ***IDIOT***.
WHY WOULD I BOTHER TO TAKE IT IN THE MIDDLE OF THE NIGHT? I CAN OUTMATCH ANY BID YOU MAY GET FOR IT.
HOW DO **WE** KNOW THAT? MAYBE YOU NEED THE **MONEY** AFTER *ALL*. LIKE EVERYONE ELSE.
WHOAH, **ANDERSON**, CALM DOWN.
HE'S RIGHT MR. ANDERSON. CALM *DOWN*. MACULA'S GUNS WILL AUTOMATICALLY RESPOND TO THREATS AGAINST ME.
IT'LL BE ***TOO LATE*** FOR YOU.
IF I'M *GONE*, IT WON'T STOP UNTIL YOU'RE ***ALL*** GONE. BUT PERHAPS **YOU *ARE*** THE DESPERATE ONE HERE.
OK. **FINE**.
FOR GOD'S SAKE ANDERSON, **PUT** THE **GUN *DOWN*** SO WE CAN ALL TALK. NOBODY CAN GET OFF THE ISLAND RIGHT NOW.

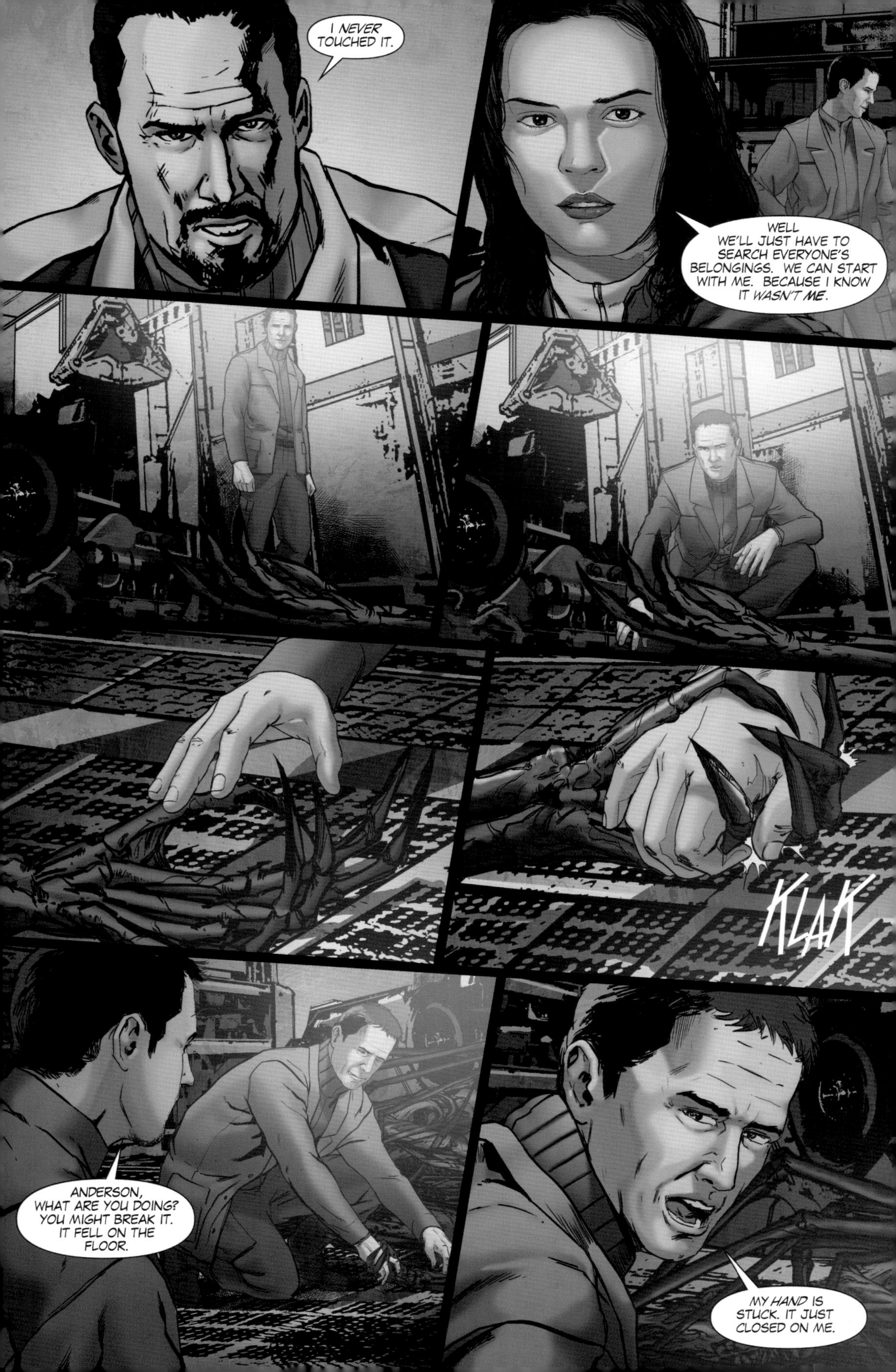
I NEVER TOUCHED IT.
WELL WE'LL JUST HAVE TO SEARCH EVERYONE'S BELONGINGS. WE CAN START WITH ME. BECAUSE I KNOW IT WASN'T ME.
KLAK
ANDERSON, WHAT ARE YOU DOING? YOU MIGHT BREAK IT. IT FELL ON THE FLOOR.
MY HAND IS STUCK. IT JUST CLOSED ON ME.

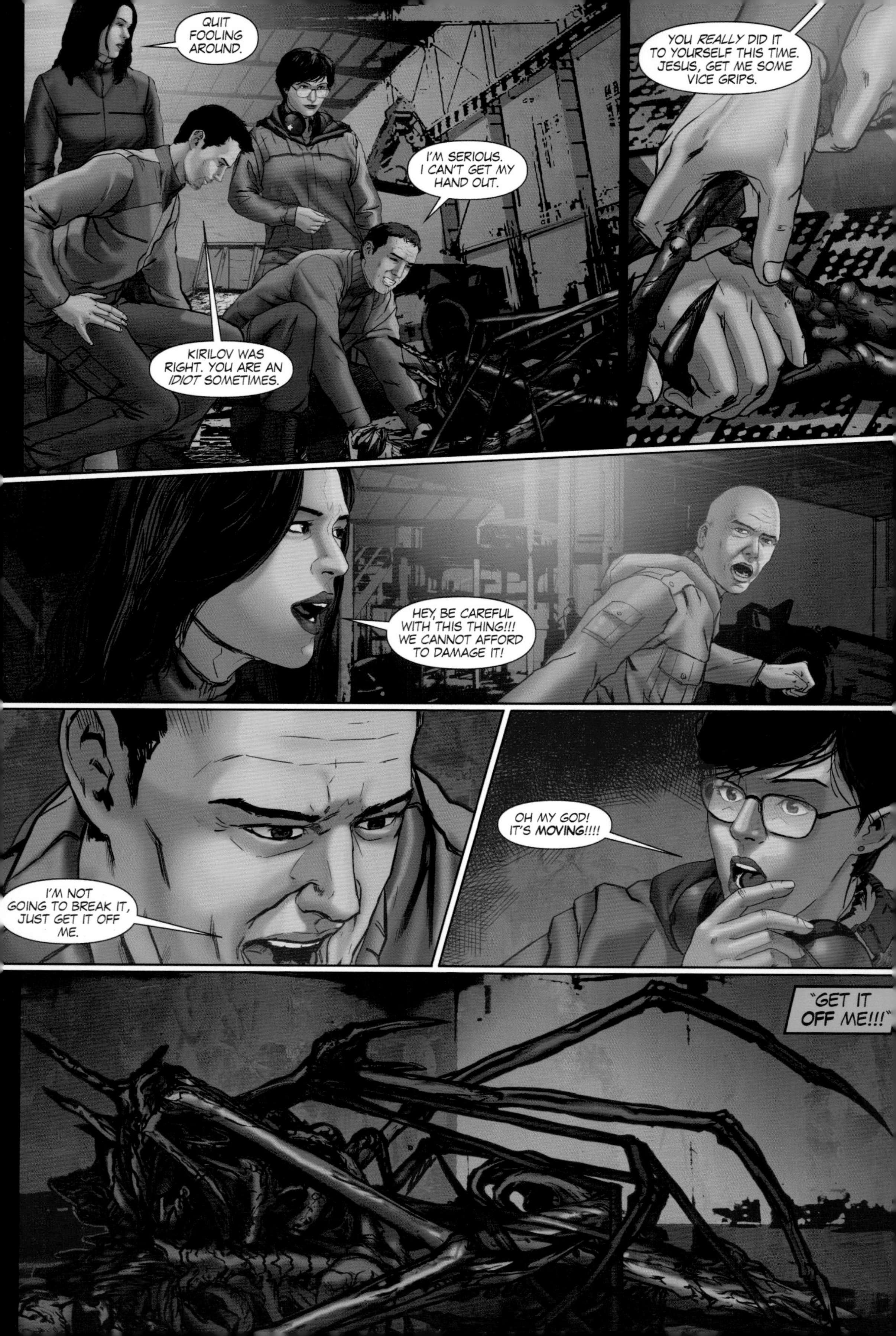
QUIT FOOLING AROUND.
I'M SERIOUS. I CAN'T GET MY HAND OUT.
KIRILOV WAS RIGHT. YOU ARE AN *IDIOT* SOMETIMES.
YOU *REALLY* DID IT TO YOURSELF THIS TIME. JESUS, GET ME SOME VICE GRIPS.
HEY, BE CAREFUL WITH THIS THING!!! WE CANNOT AFFORD TO DAMAGE IT!
I'M NOT GOING TO BREAK IT, JUST GET IT OFF ME.
OH MY GOD! IT'S **MOVING**!!!!
"GET IT **OFF ME**!!!"

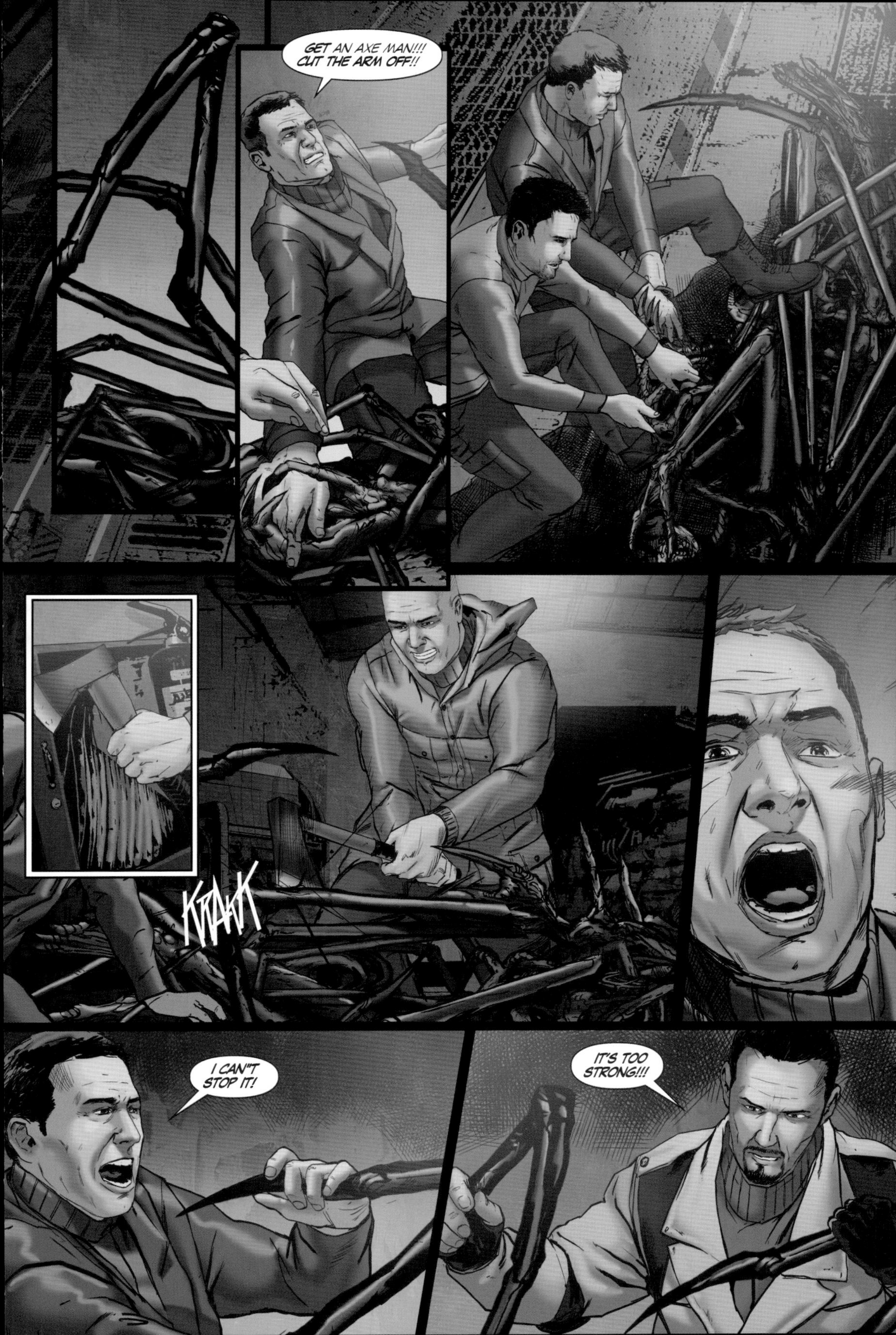
GET AN AXE MAN!!!
CUT THE ARM OFF!!
KRAKK
I CAN"T
STOP IT!
IT'S TOO
STRONG!!!

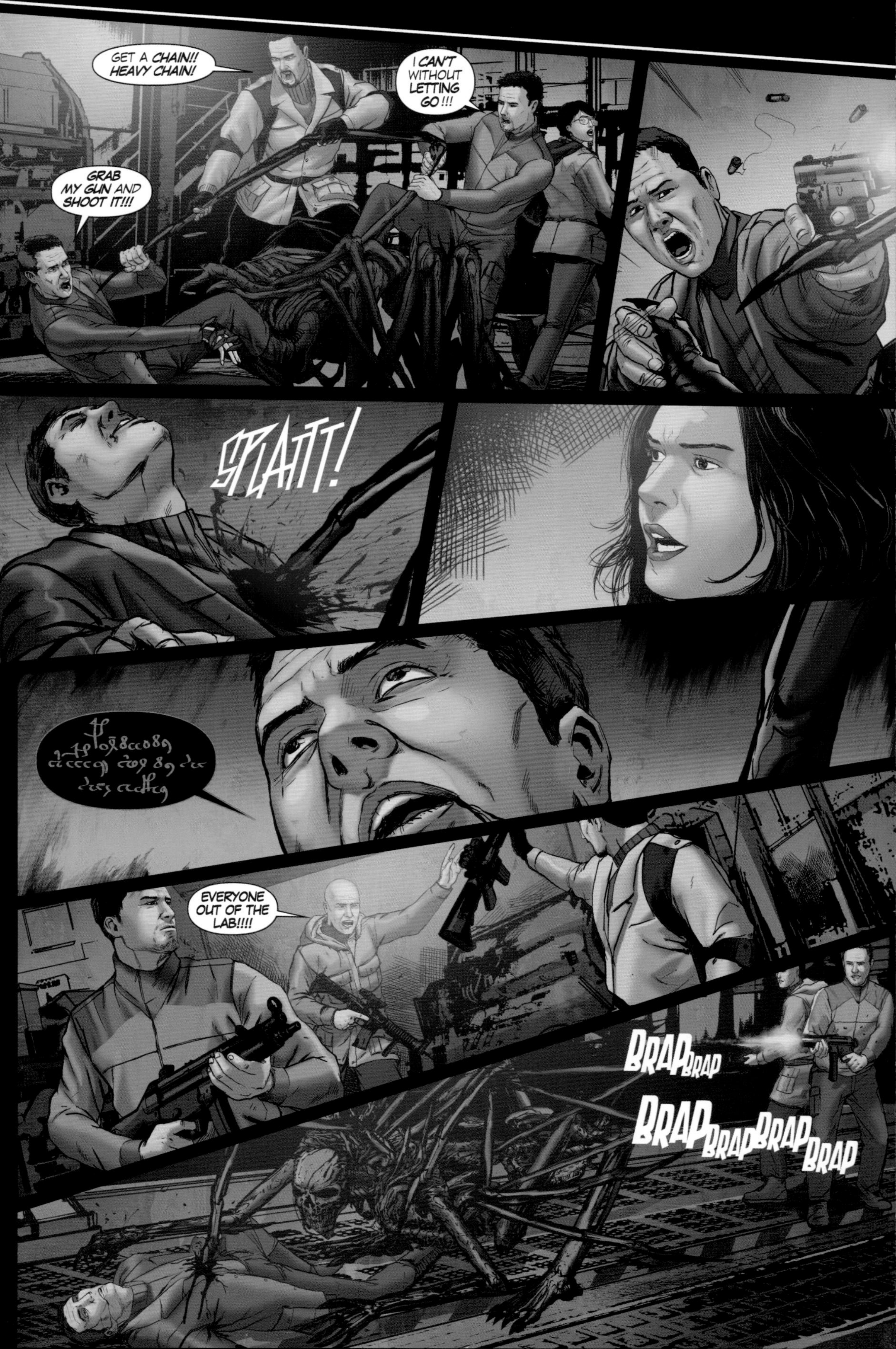
GET A CHAIN!! HEAVY CHAIN!
I CAN'T WITHOUT LETTING GO!!!
GRAB MY GUN AND SHOOT IT!!!
SPLATT!
EVERYONE OUT OF THE LAB!!!!
BRAPBRAP
BRAPBRAPBRAPBRAP

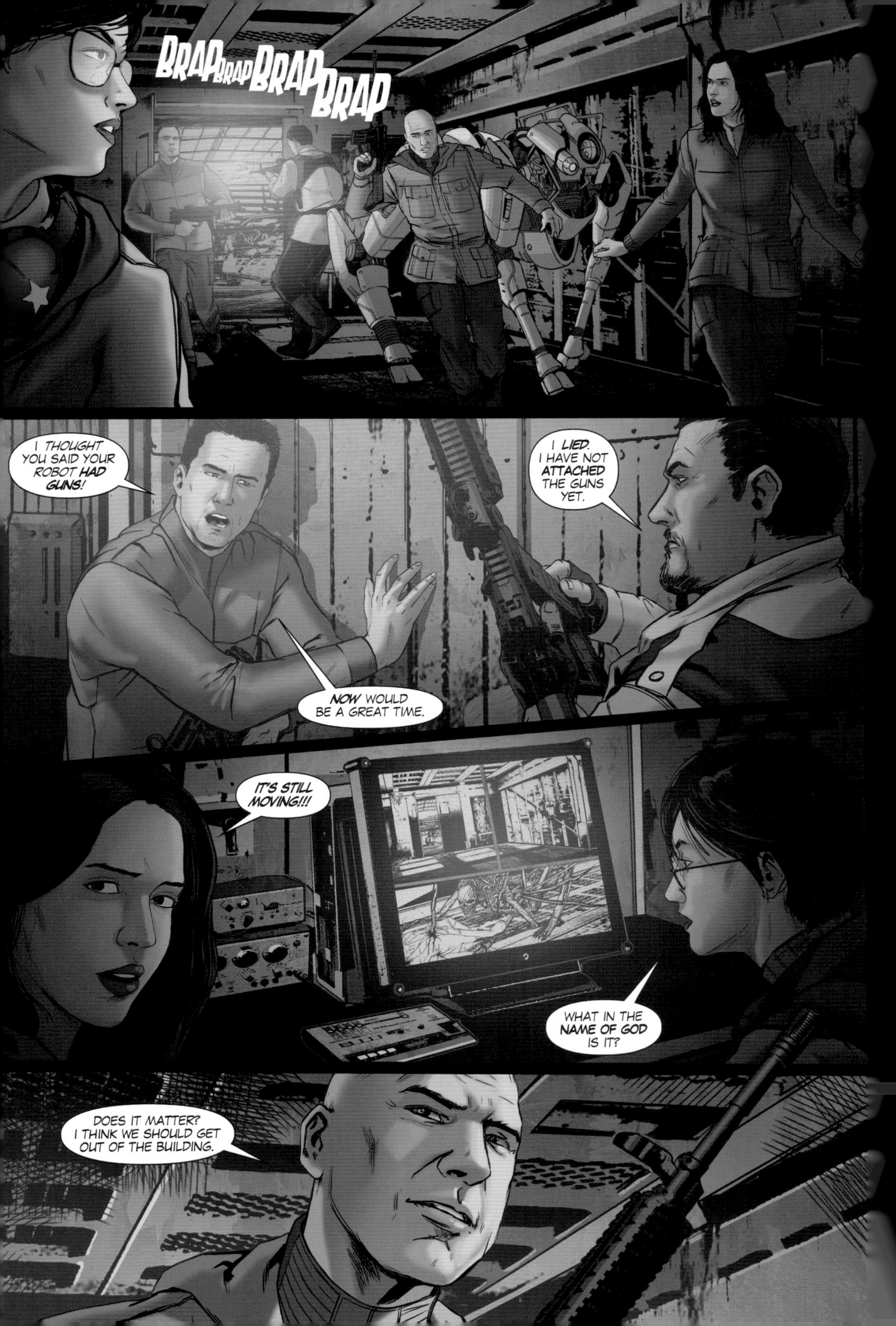
BRAP brap BRAP BRAP
I THOUGHT YOU SAID YOUR ROBOT HAD GUNS!
I LIED. I HAVE NOT ATTACHED THE GUNS YET.
NOW WOULD BE A GREAT TIME.
IT'S STILL MOVING!!!
WHAT IN THE NAME OF GOD IS IT?
DOES IT MATTER? I THINK WE SHOULD GET OUT OF THE BUILDING.

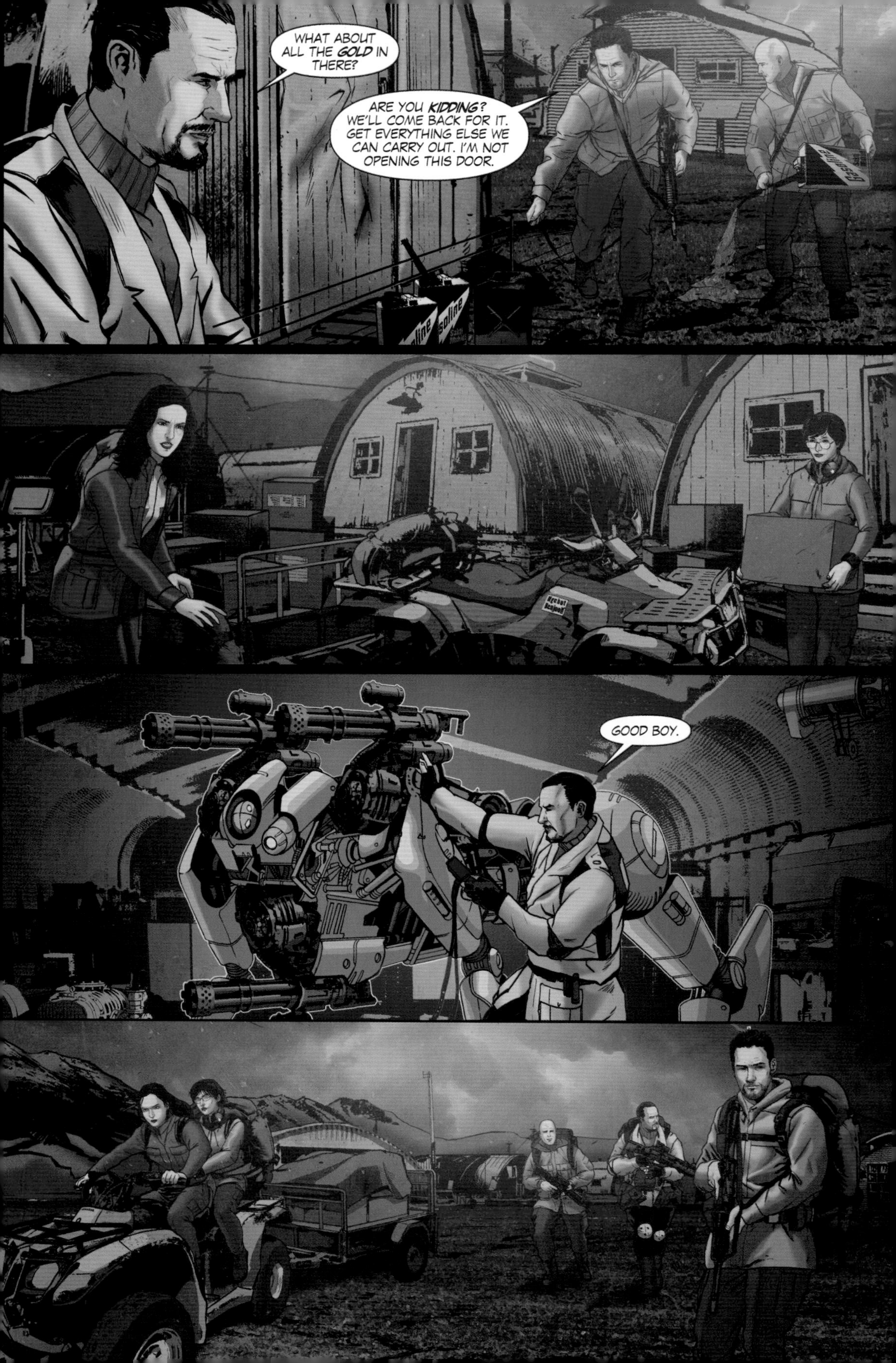
WHAT ABOUT ALL THE **GOLD** IN THERE?
ARE YOU **KIDDING**? WE'LL COME BACK FOR IT. GET EVERYTHING ELSE WE CAN CARRY OUT. I'M NOT OPENING THIS DOOR.
GOOD BOY.

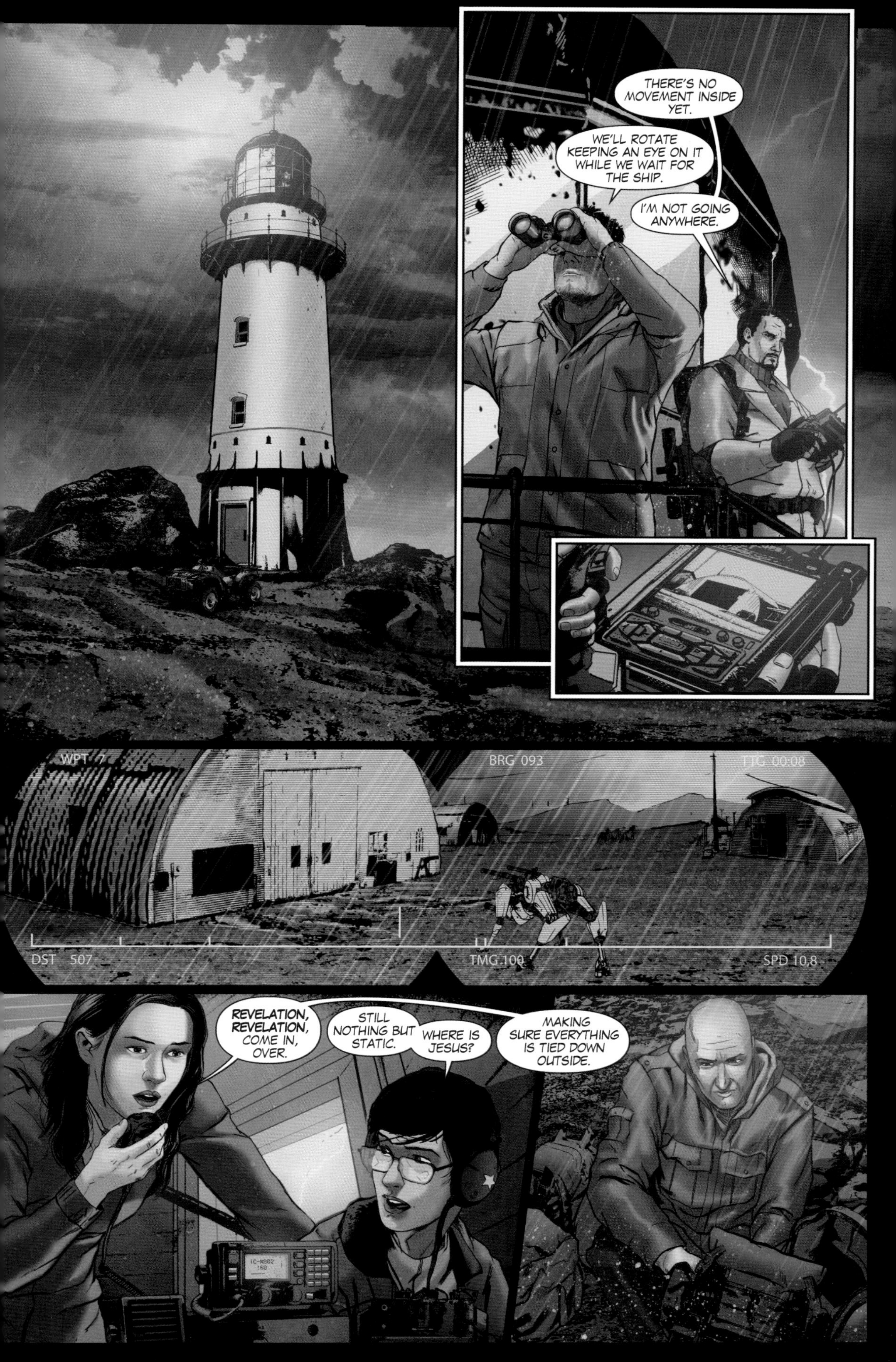

THERE'S NO MOVEMENT INSIDE YET.
WE'LL ROTATE KEEPING AN EYE ON IT WHILE WE WAIT FOR THE SHIP.
I'M NOT GOING ANYWHERE.
WPT 7
BRG 093
TTG 00:08
DST 507
TMG 100
SPD 10,8
REVELATION, REVELATION, COME IN, OVER.
STILL NOTHING BUT STATIC.
WHERE IS JESUS?
MAKING SURE EVERYTHING IS TIED DOWN OUTSIDE.

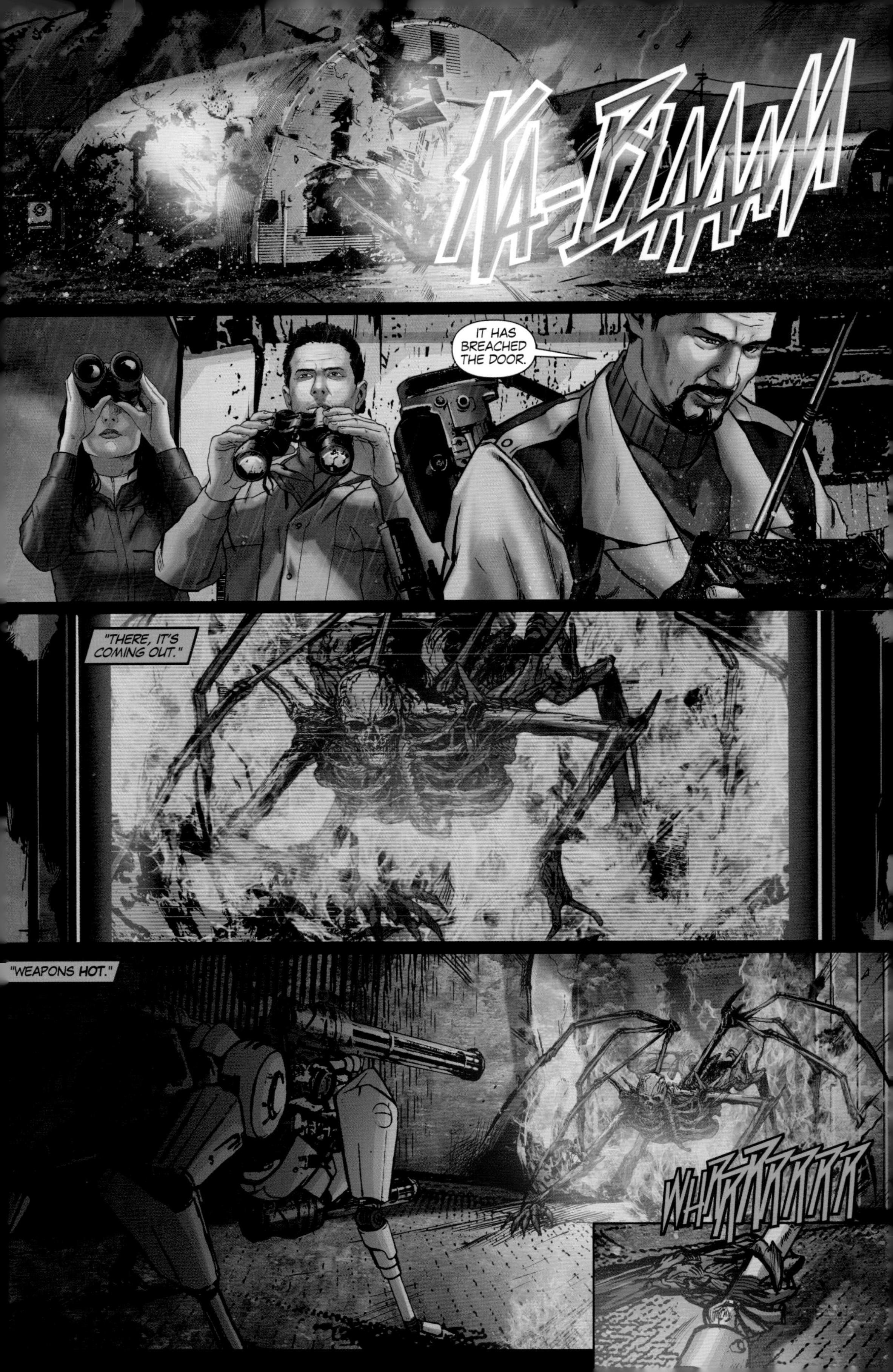
KA-BLAMM
IT HAS BREACHED THE DOOR.
"THERE, IT'S COMING OUT."
"WEAPONS HOT."
WHRRRRRRR

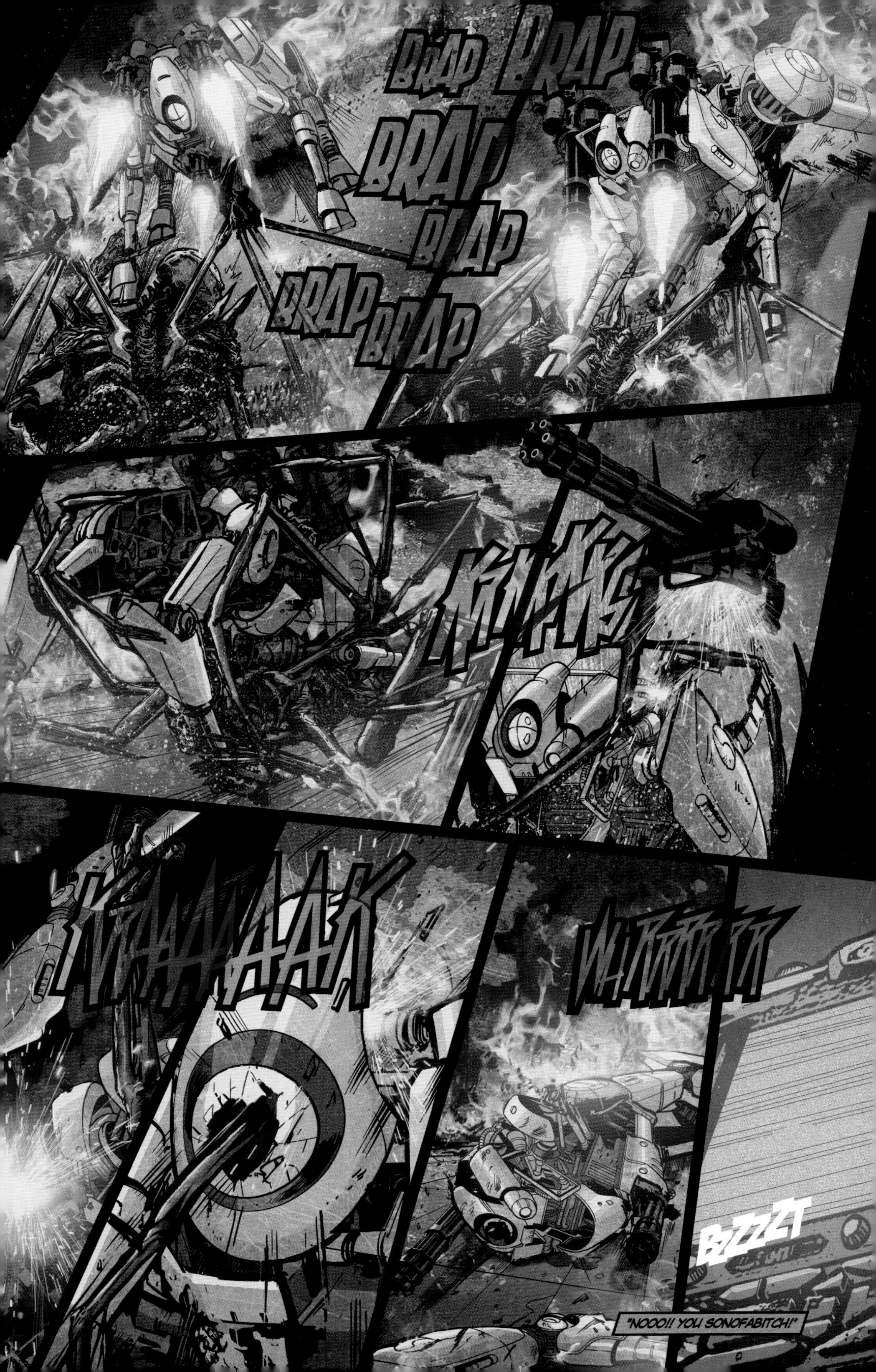
BRAP BRAP
BRAP
BRAP
BRAP BRAP
KRAAAK
WHRRRRRR
BZZZZT
"NOOO!! YOU SONOFABITCH!"

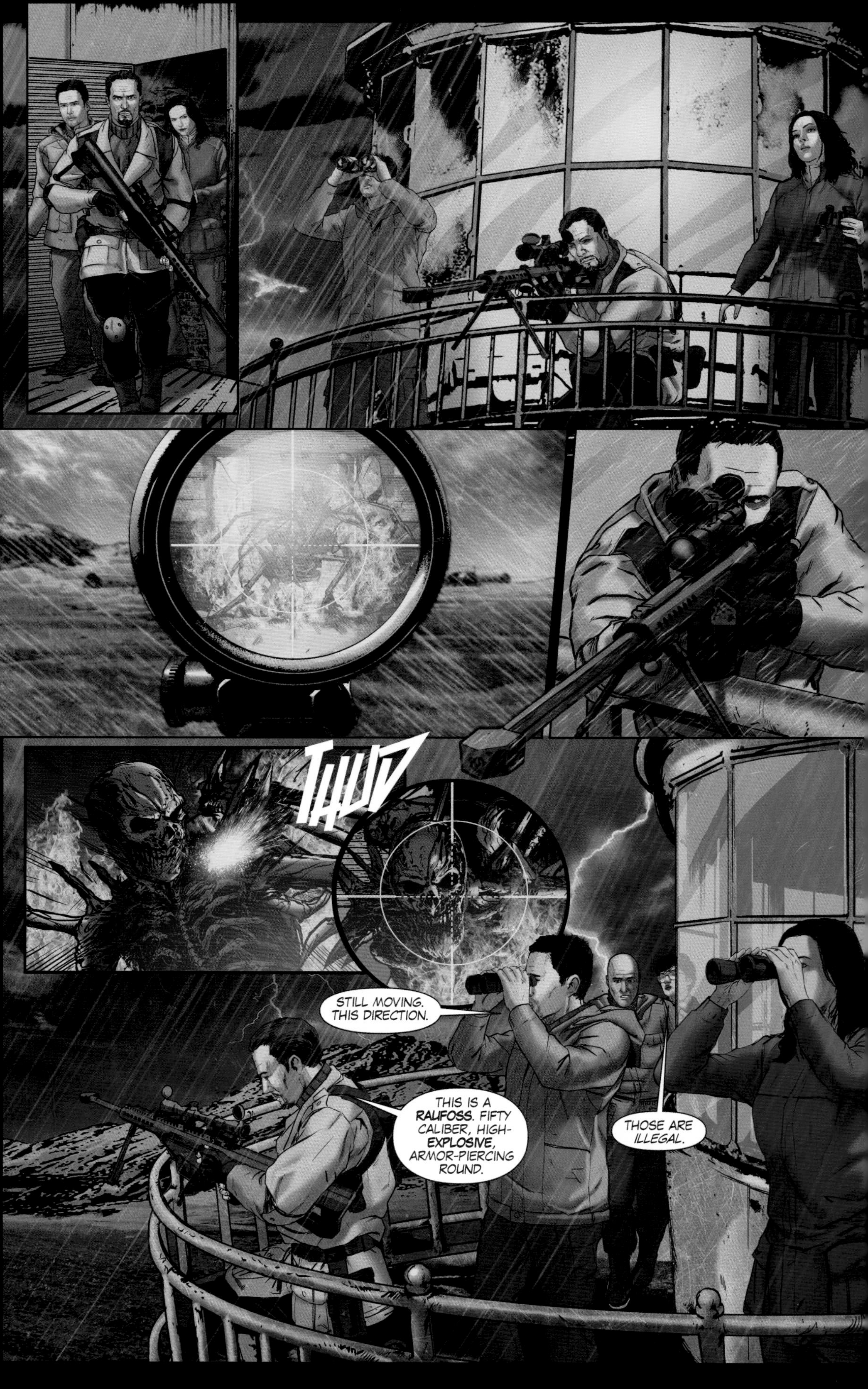
THUD
STILL MOVING. THIS DIRECTION.
THIS IS A **RAUFOSS.** FIFTY CALIBER, HIGH-**EXPLOSIVE,** ARMOR-PIERCING ROUND.
THOSE ARE ILLEGAL.

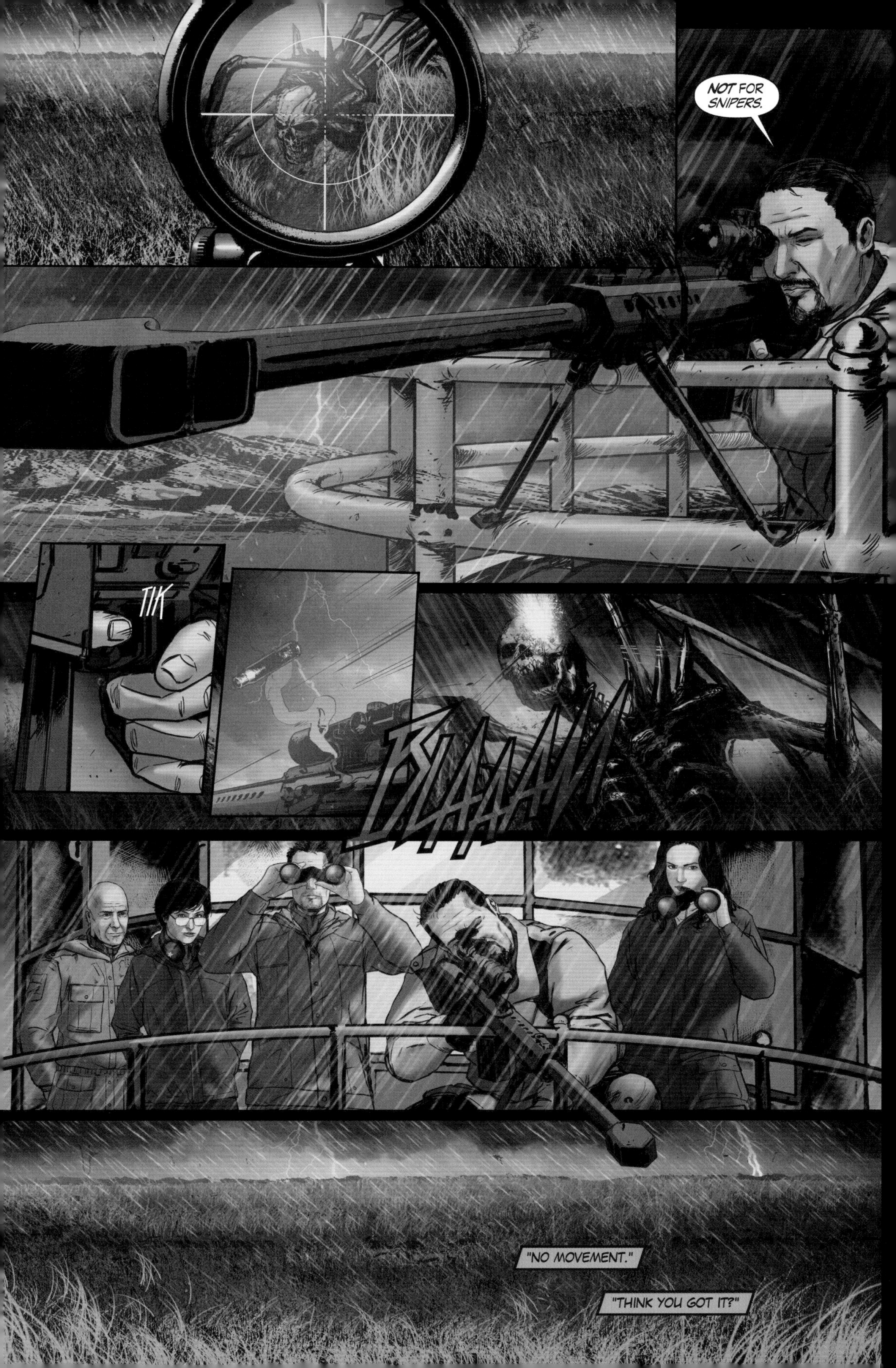

NOT FOR SNIPERS.
TIK
BLAAM
"NO MOVEMENT."
"THINK YOU GOT IT?"

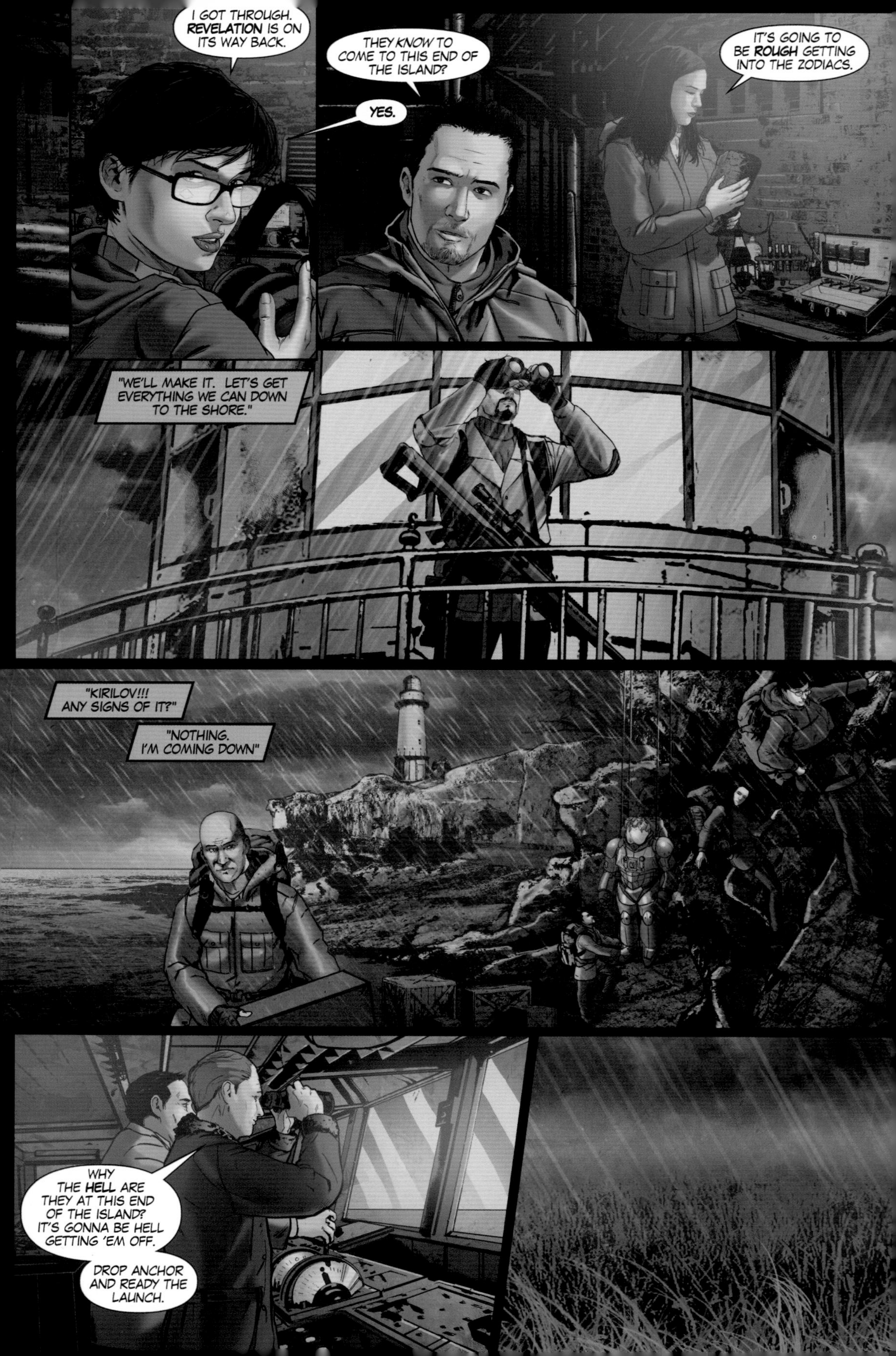
I GOT THROUGH. REVELATION IS ON ITS WAY BACK.
THEY KNOW TO COME TO THIS END OF THE ISLAND?
YES.
IT'S GOING TO BE ROUGH GETTING INTO THE ZODIACS.
"WE'LL MAKE IT. LET'S GET EVERYTHING WE CAN DOWN TO THE SHORE."
"KIRILOV!!! ANY SIGNS OF IT?"
"NOTHING. I'M COMING DOWN"
WHY THE HELL ARE THEY AT THIS END OF THE ISLAND? IT'S GONNA BE HELL GETTING 'EM OFF.
DROP ANCHOR AND READY THE LAUNCH.

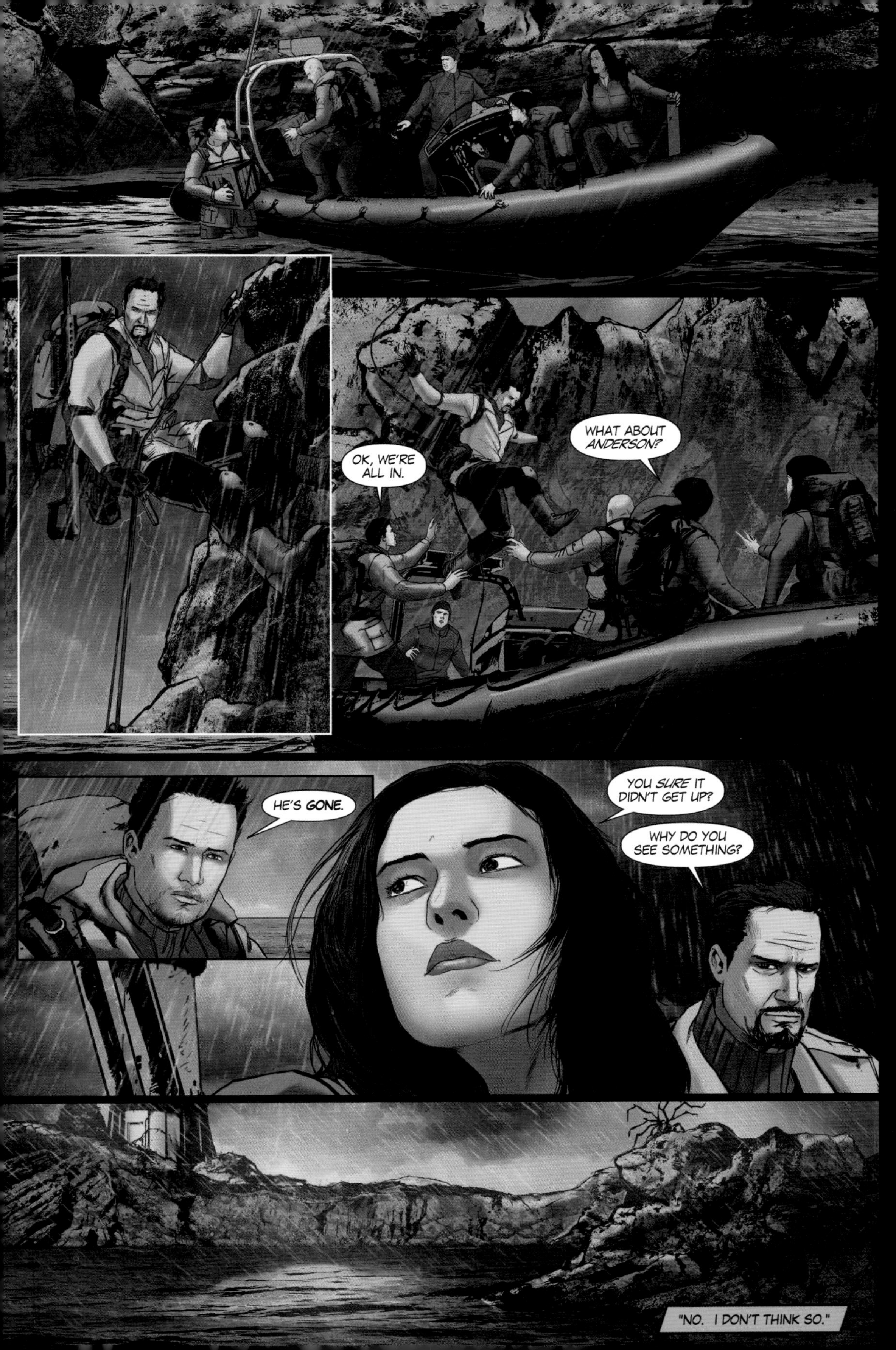
OK, WE'RE ALL IN.
WHAT ABOUT ANDERSON?
HE'S GONE.
YOU SURE IT DIDN'T GET UP?
WHY DO YOU SEE SOMETHING?
"NO. I DON'T THINK SO."

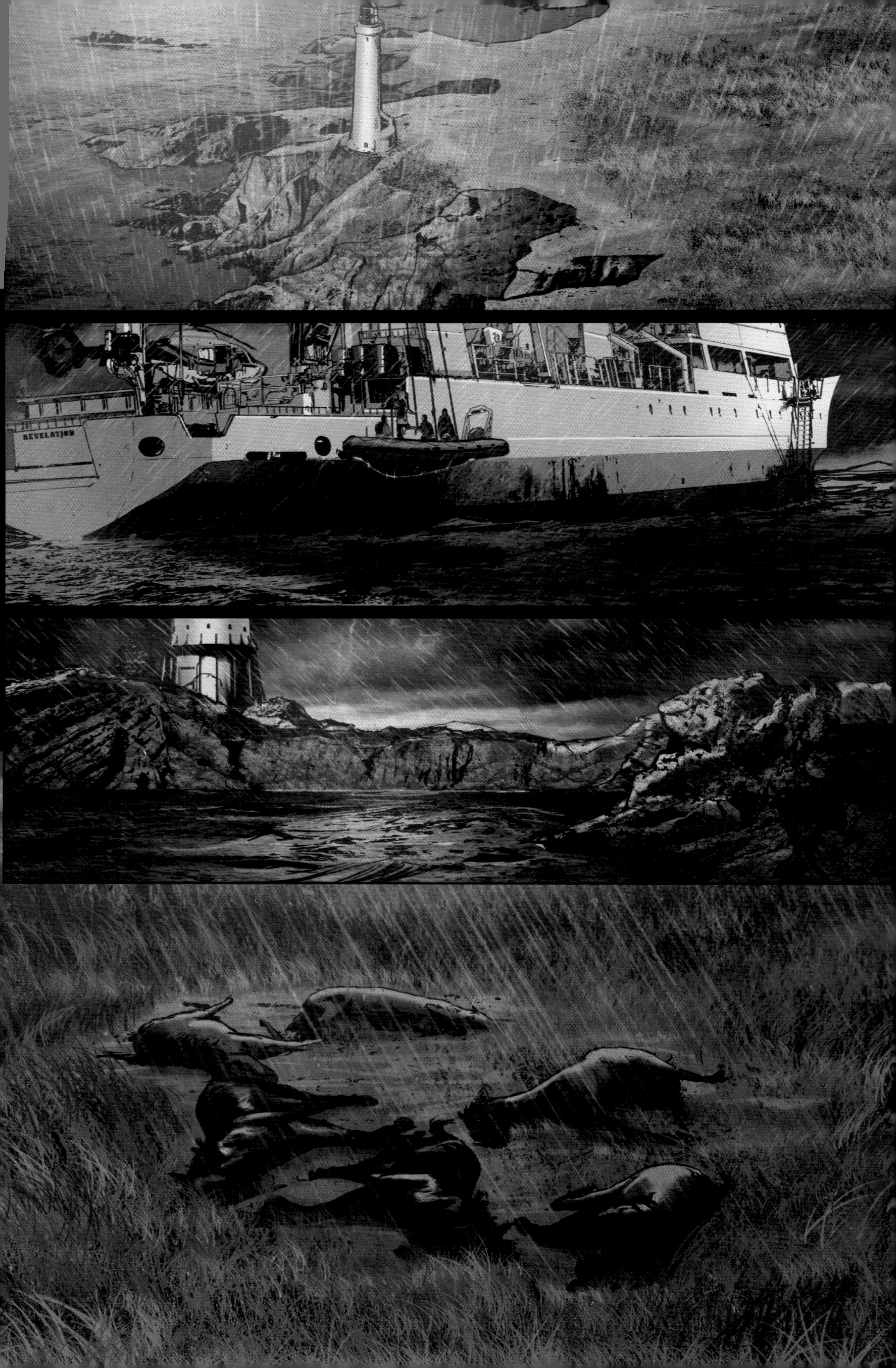
REVELATION

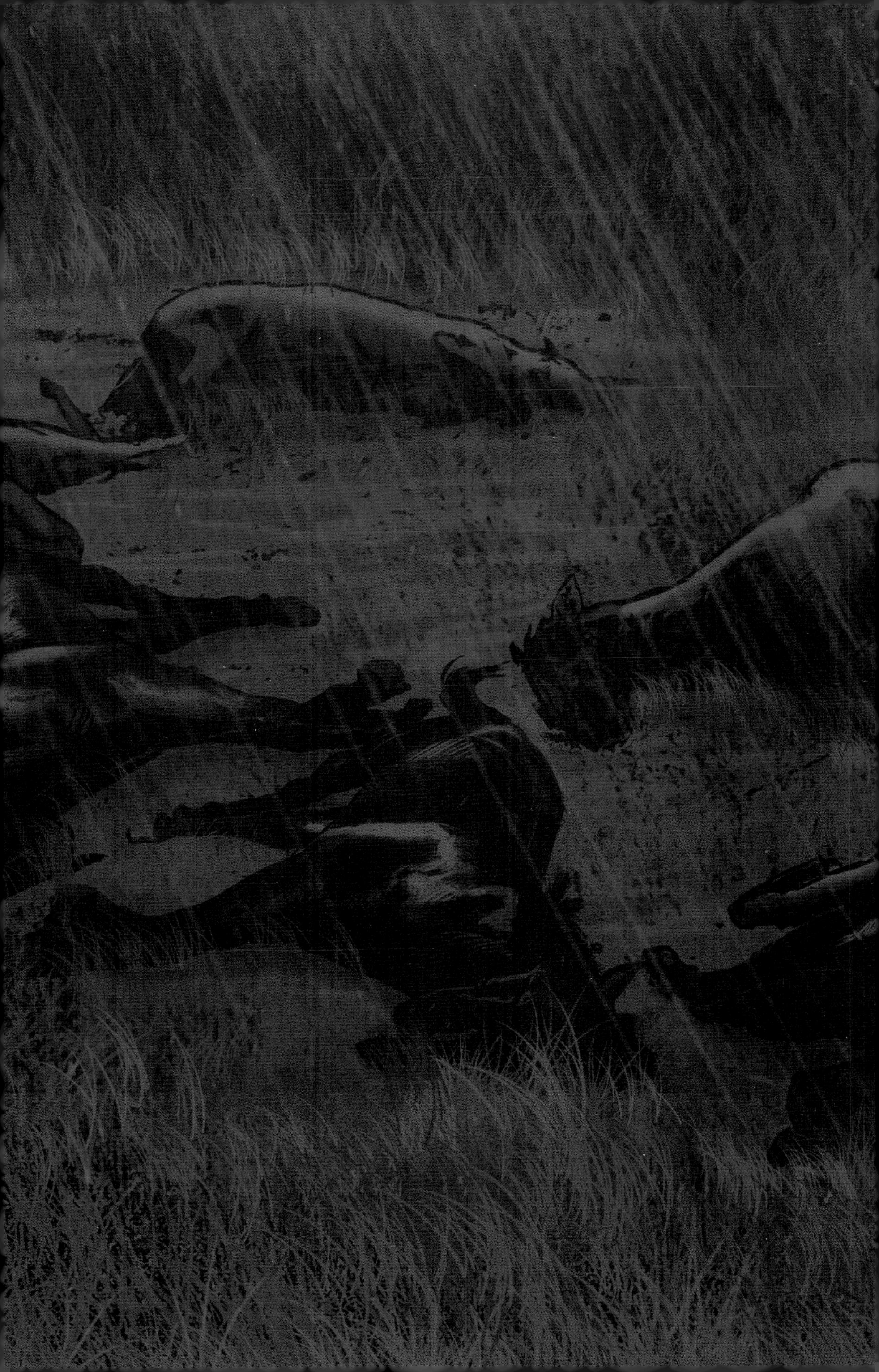

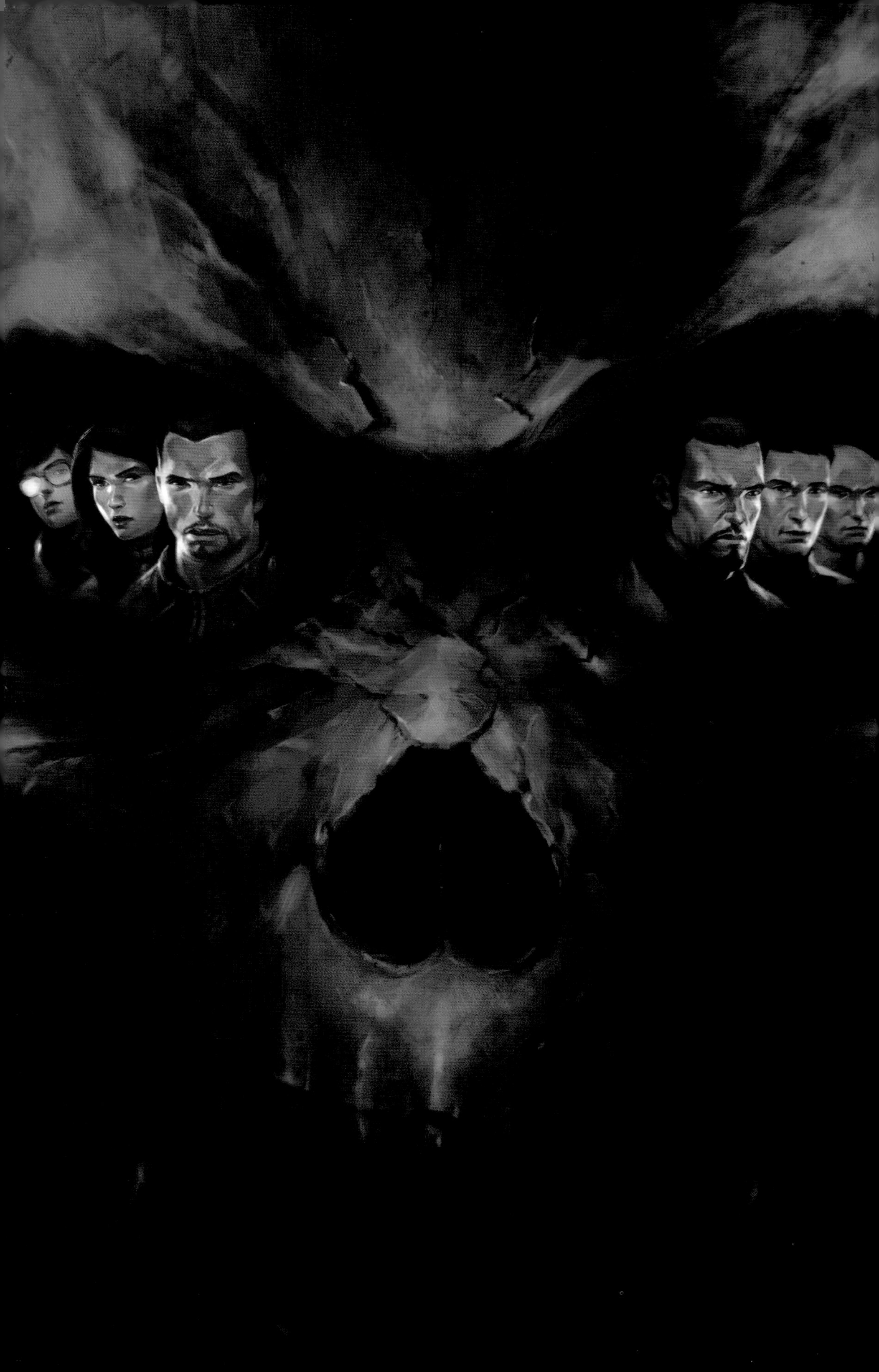

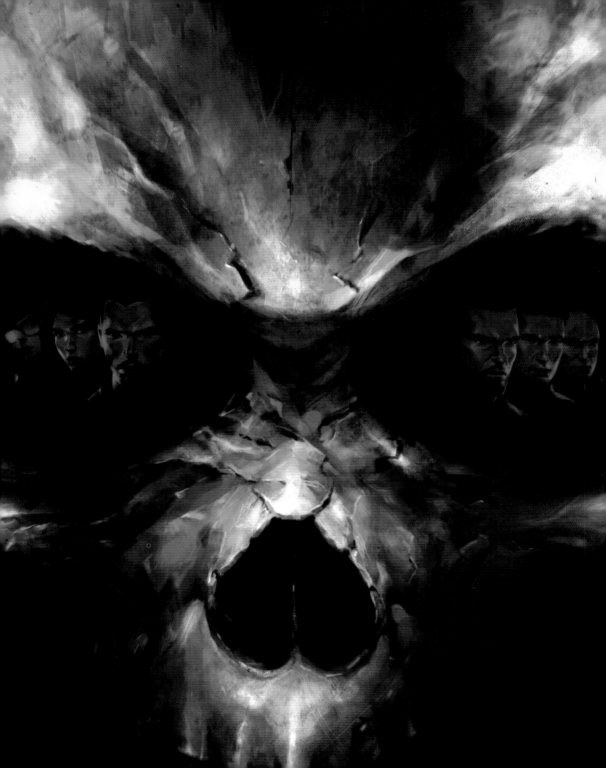

"Everyone move!
Get onboard as fast as you can."

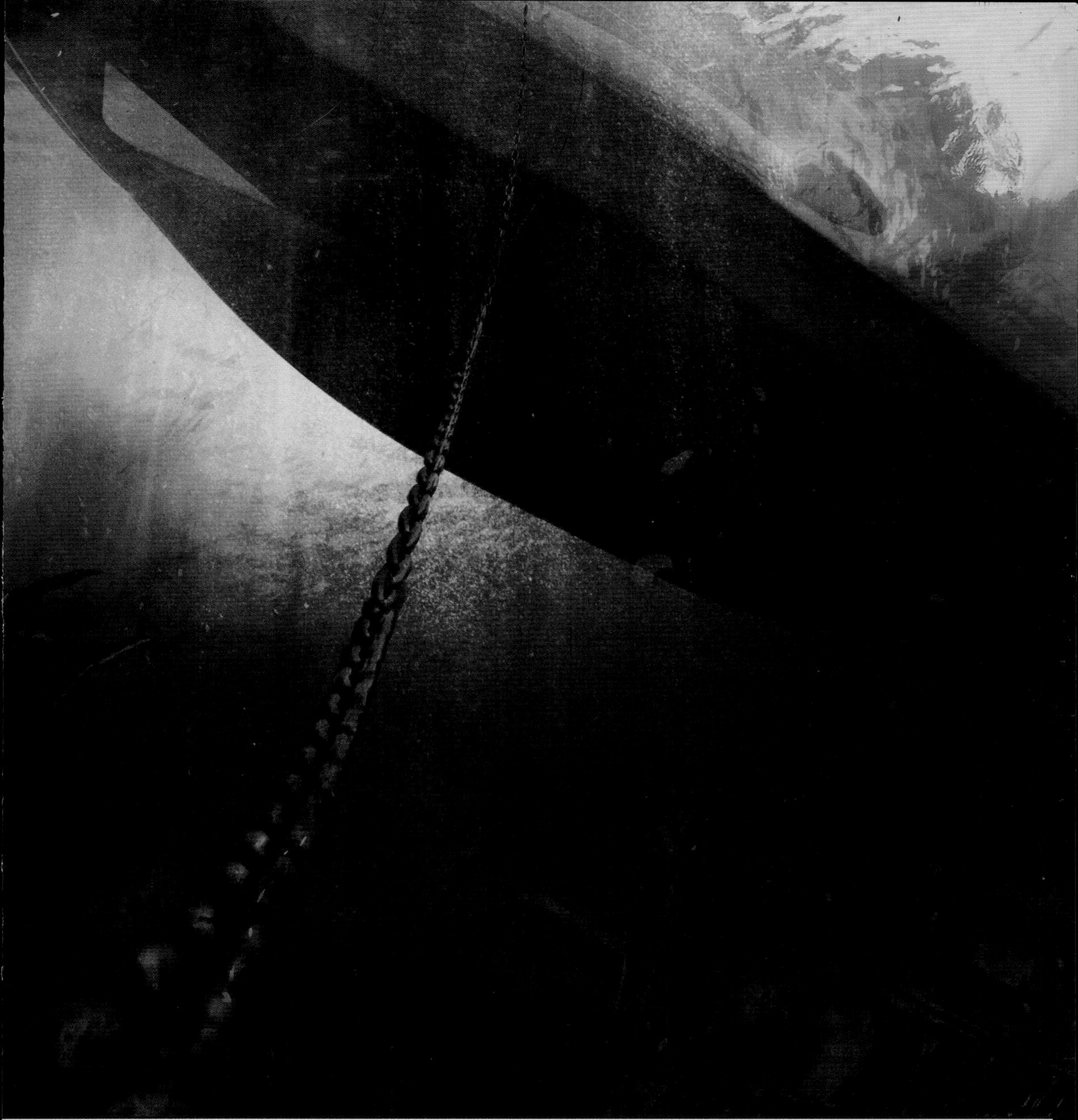

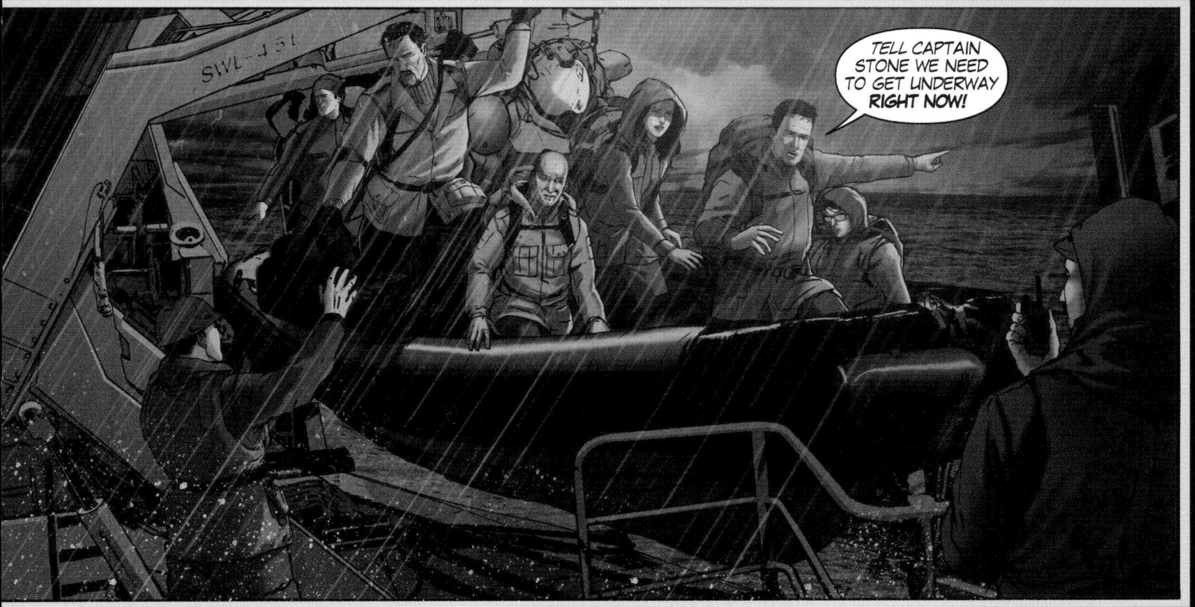
TELL CAPTAIN STONE WE NEED TO GET UNDERWAY RIGHT NOW!

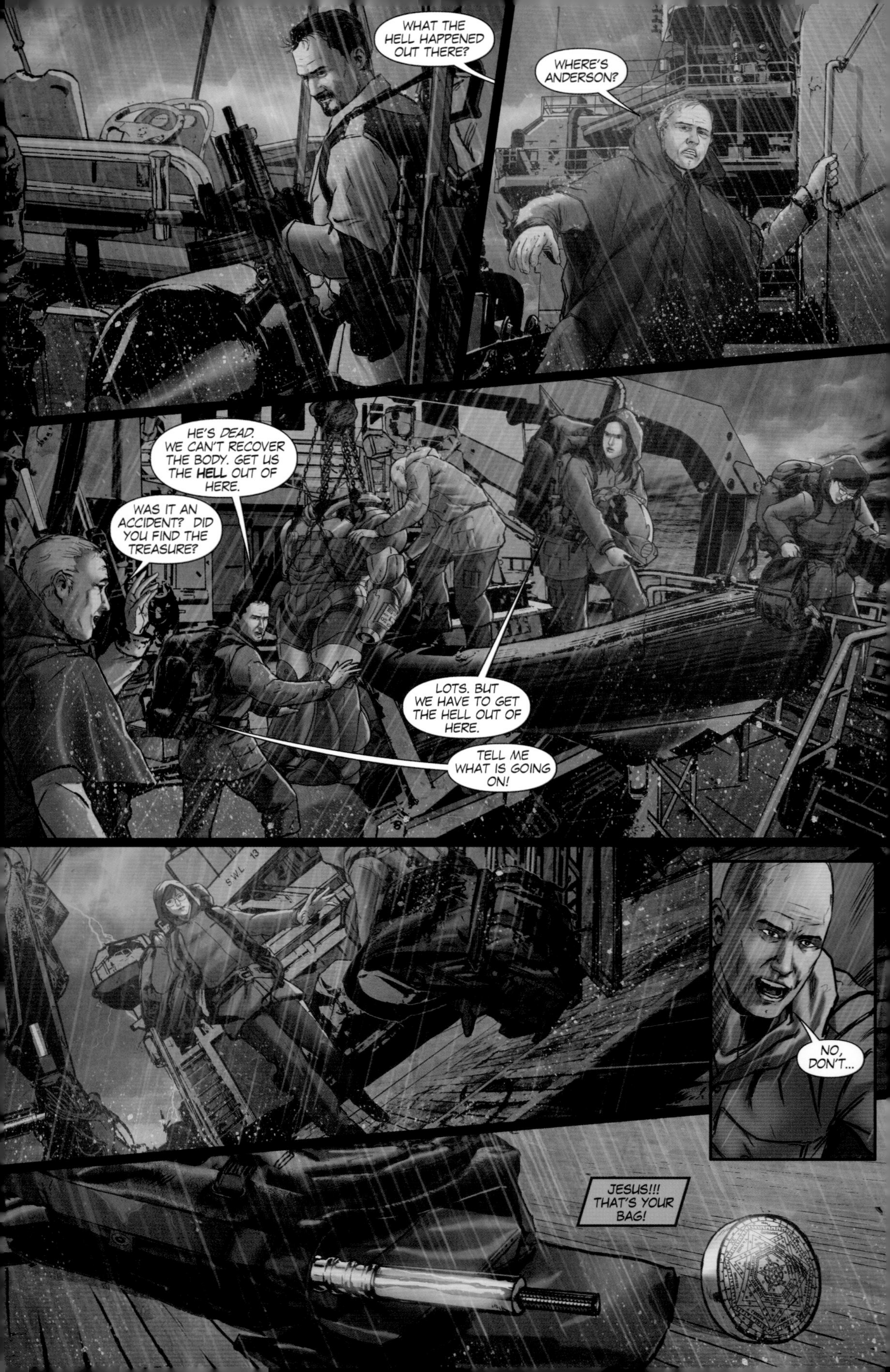

WHAT THE HELL HAPPENED OUT THERE?
WHERE'S ANDERSON?
HE'S *DEAD*. WE CAN'T RECOVER THE BODY. GET US THE **HELL** OUT OF HERE.
WAS IT AN ACCIDENT? DID YOU FIND THE TREASURE?
LOTS. BUT WE HAVE TO GET THE HELL OUT OF HERE.
TELL ME WHAT IS GOING ON!
SWL 13
NO, DON'T...
JESUS!!! THAT'S YOUR BAG!

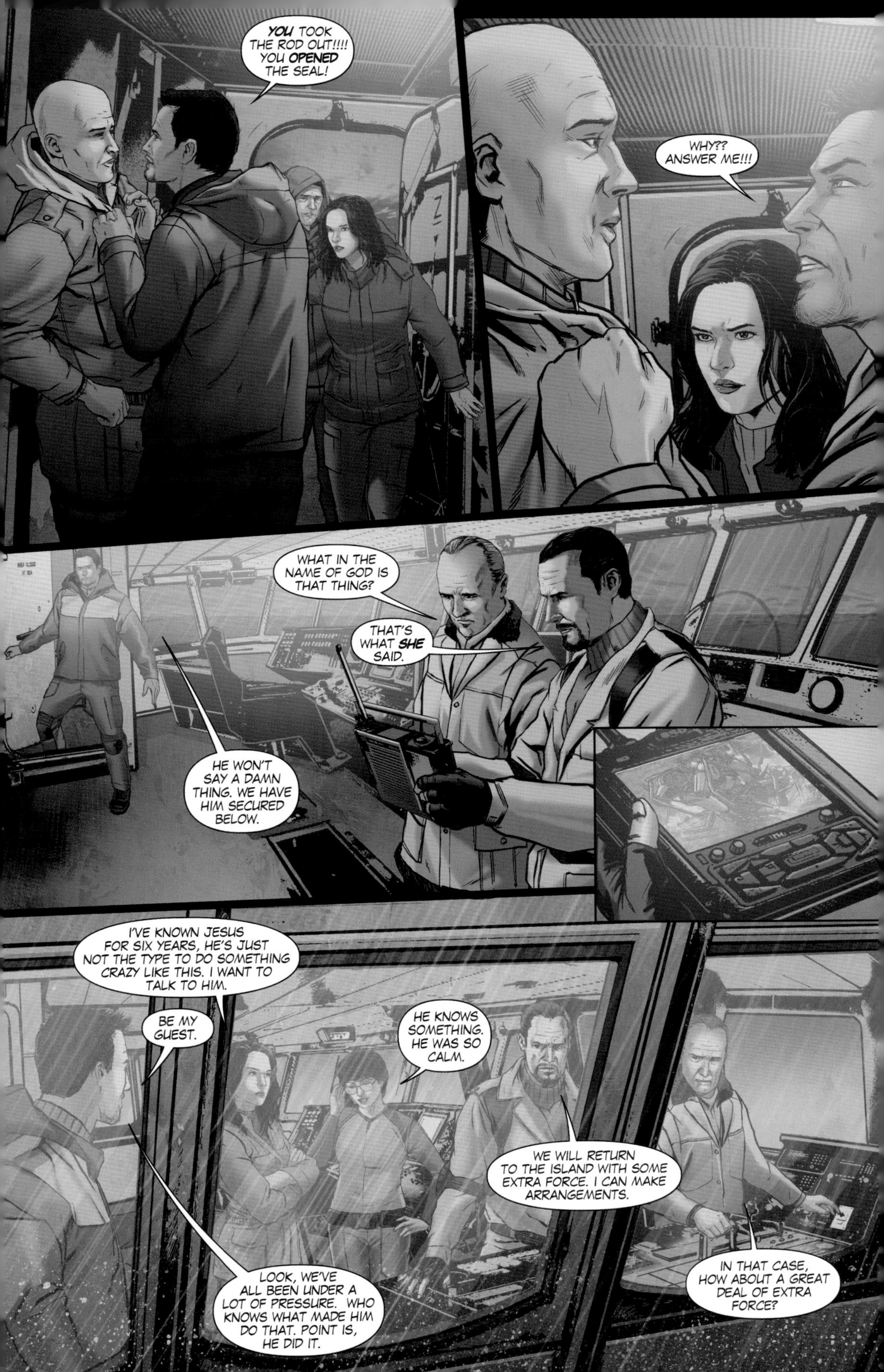
YOU TOOK THE ROD OUT!!!! YOU OPENED THE SEAL!
WHY?? ANSWER ME!!!
WHAT IN THE NAME OF GOD IS THAT THING?
THAT'S WHAT SHE SAID.
HE WON'T SAY A DAMN THING. WE HAVE HIM SECURED BELOW.
I'VE KNOWN JESUS FOR SIX YEARS, HE'S JUST NOT THE TYPE TO DO SOMETHING CRAZY LIKE THIS. I WANT TO TALK TO HIM.
BE MY GUEST.
HE KNOWS SOMETHING. HE WAS SO CALM.
WE WILL RETURN TO THE ISLAND WITH SOME EXTRA FORCE. I CAN MAKE ARRANGEMENTS.
LOOK, WE'VE ALL BEEN UNDER A LOT OF PRESSURE. WHO KNOWS WHAT MADE HIM DO THAT. POINT IS, HE DID IT.
IN THAT CASE, HOW ABOUT A GREAT DEAL OF EXTRA FORCE?

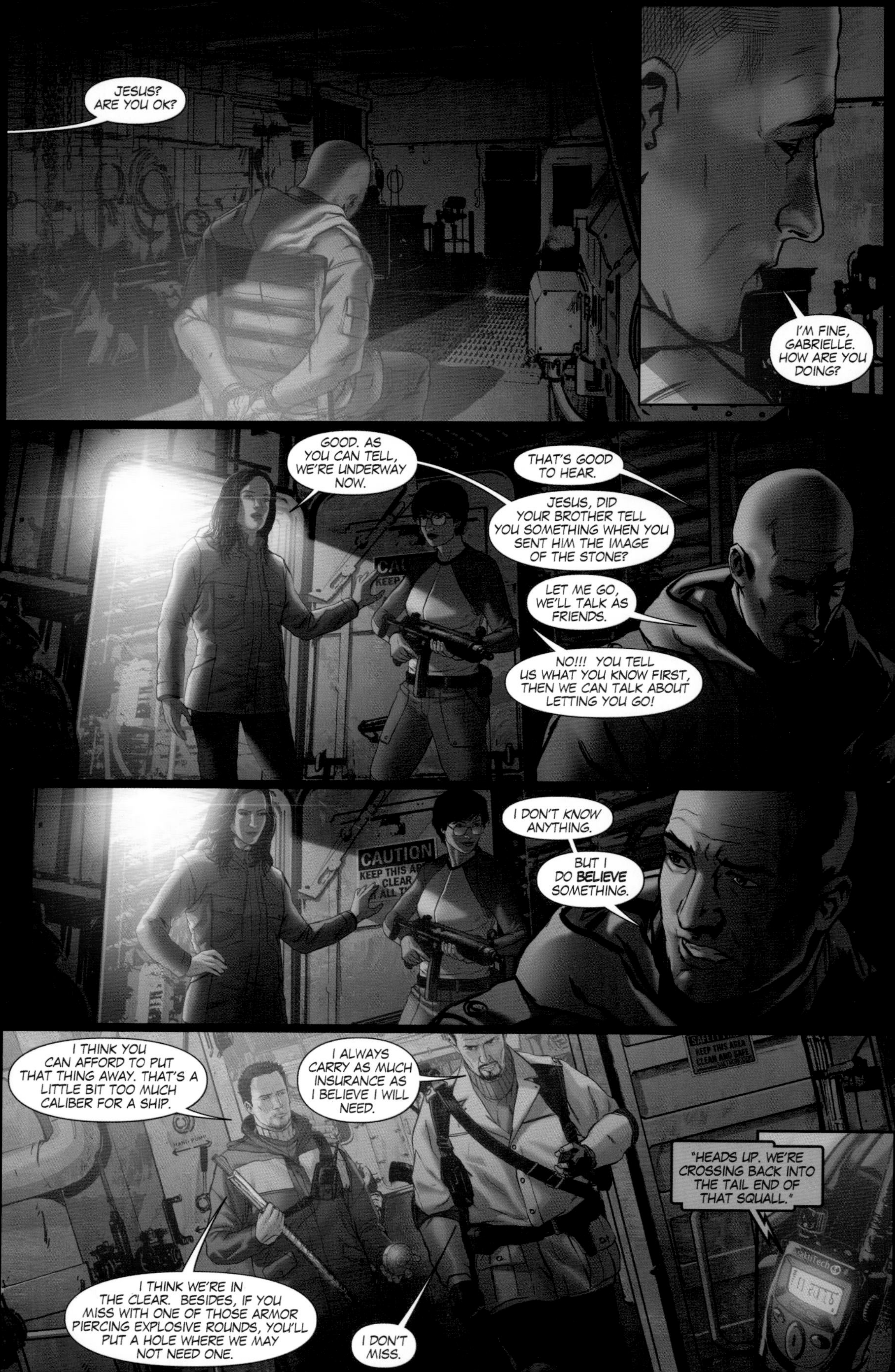
JESUS? ARE YOU OK?
I'M FINE, GABRIELLE. HOW ARE YOU DOING?
GOOD. AS YOU CAN TELL, WE'RE UNDERWAY NOW.
THAT'S GOOD TO HEAR.
JESUS, DID YOUR BROTHER TELL YOU SOMETHING WHEN YOU SENT HIM THE IMAGE OF THE STONE?
LET ME GO, WE'LL TALK AS FRIENDS.
NO!!! YOU TELL US WHAT YOU KNOW FIRST, THEN WE CAN TALK ABOUT LETTING YOU GO!
CAUTION
I DON'T KNOW ANYTHING.
BUT I DO **BELIEVE** SOMETHING.
I THINK YOU CAN AFFORD TO PUT THAT THING AWAY. THAT'S A LITTLE BIT TOO MUCH CALIBER FOR A SHIP.
I ALWAYS CARRY AS MUCH INSURANCE AS I BELIEVE I WILL NEED.
"HEADS UP. WE'RE CROSSING BACK INTO THE TAIL END OF THAT SQUALL."
I THINK WE'RE IN THE CLEAR. BESIDES, IF YOU MISS WITH ONE OF THOSE ARMOR PIERCING EXPLOSIVE ROUNDS, YOU'LL PUT A HOLE WHERE WE MAY NOT NEED ONE.
I DON'T MISS.

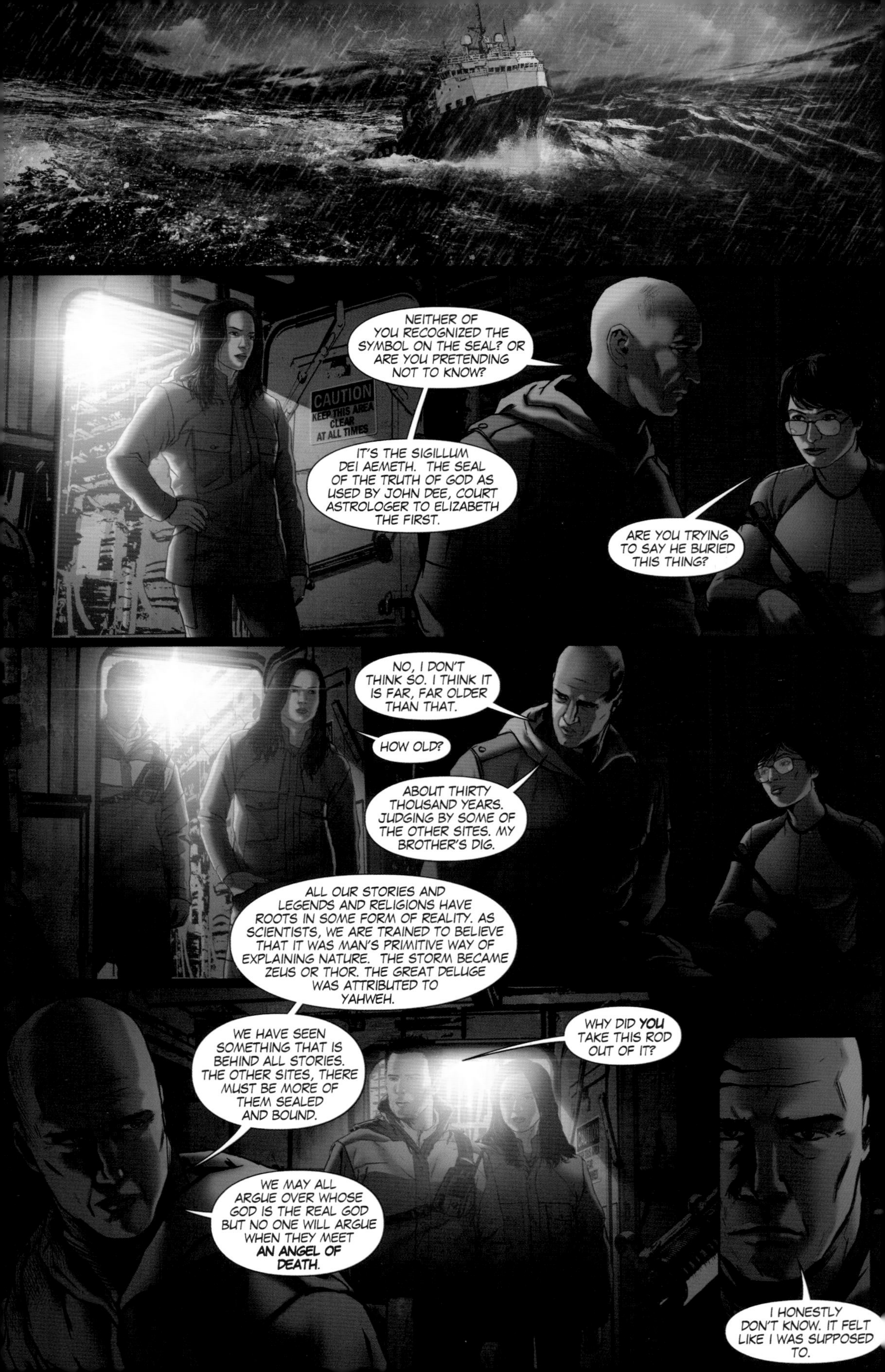
NEITHER OF YOU RECOGNIZED THE SYMBOL ON THE SEAL? OR ARE YOU PRETENDING NOT TO KNOW?
CAUTION KEEP THIS AREA CLEAR AT ALL TIMES
IT'S THE SIGILLUM DEI AEMETH. THE SEAL OF THE TRUTH OF GOD AS USED BY JOHN DEE, COURT ASTROLOGER TO ELIZABETH THE FIRST.
ARE YOU TRYING TO SAY HE BURIED THIS THING?
NO, I DON'T THINK SO. I THINK IT IS FAR, FAR OLDER THAN THAT.
HOW OLD?
ABOUT THIRTY THOUSAND YEARS. JUDGING BY SOME OF THE OTHER SITES. MY BROTHER'S DIG.
ALL OUR STORIES AND LEGENDS AND RELIGIONS HAVE ROOTS IN SOME FORM OF REALITY. AS SCIENTISTS, WE ARE TRAINED TO BELIEVE THAT IT WAS MAN'S PRIMITIVE WAY OF EXPLAINING NATURE. THE STORM BECAME ZEUS OR THOR. THE GREAT DELUGE WAS ATTRIBUTED TO YAHWEH.
WE HAVE SEEN SOMETHING THAT IS BEHIND ALL STORIES. THE OTHER SITES, THERE MUST BE MORE OF THEM SEALED AND BOUND.
WE MAY ALL ARGUE OVER WHOSE GOD IS THE REAL GOD BUT NO ONE WILL ARGUE WHEN THEY MEET **AN ANGEL OF DEATH**.
WHY DID **YOU** TAKE THIS ROD OUT OF IT?
I HONESTLY DON'T KNOW. IT FELT LIKE I WAS SUPPOSED TO.

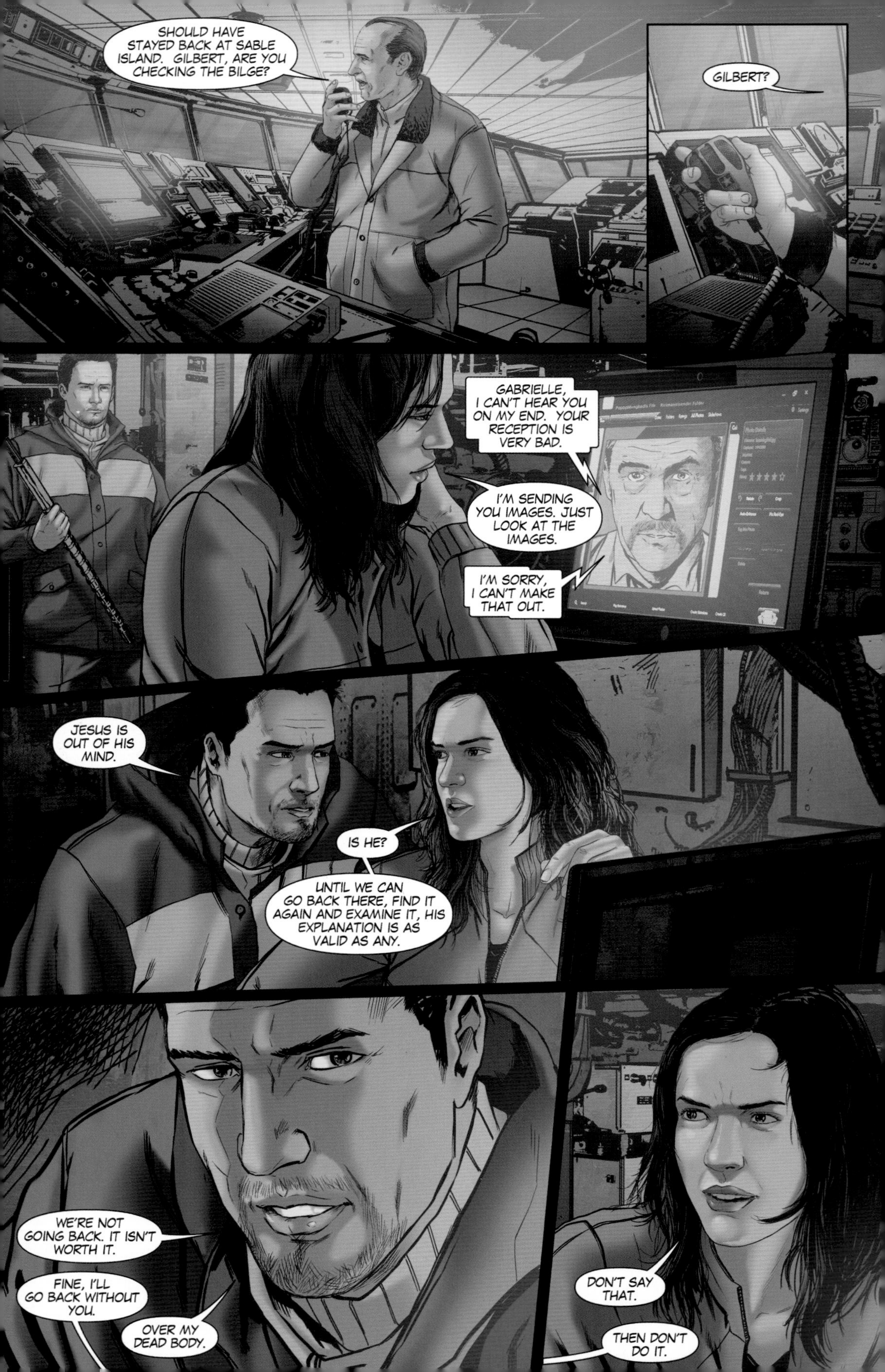
SHOULD HAVE STAYED BACK AT SABLE ISLAND. GILBERT, ARE YOU CHECKING THE BILGE?
GILBERT?
GABRIELLE, I CAN'T HEAR YOU ON MY END. YOUR RECEPTION IS VERY BAD.
I'M SENDING YOU IMAGES. JUST LOOK AT THE IMAGES.
I'M SORRY, I CAN'T MAKE THAT OUT.
JESUS IS OUT OF HIS MIND.
IS HE?
UNTIL WE CAN GO BACK THERE, FIND IT AGAIN AND EXAMINE IT, HIS EXPLANATION IS AS VALID AS ANY.
WE'RE NOT GOING BACK. IT ISN'T WORTH IT.
FINE, I'LL GO BACK WITHOUT YOU.
OVER MY DEAD BODY.
DON'T SAY THAT.
THEN DON'T DO IT.

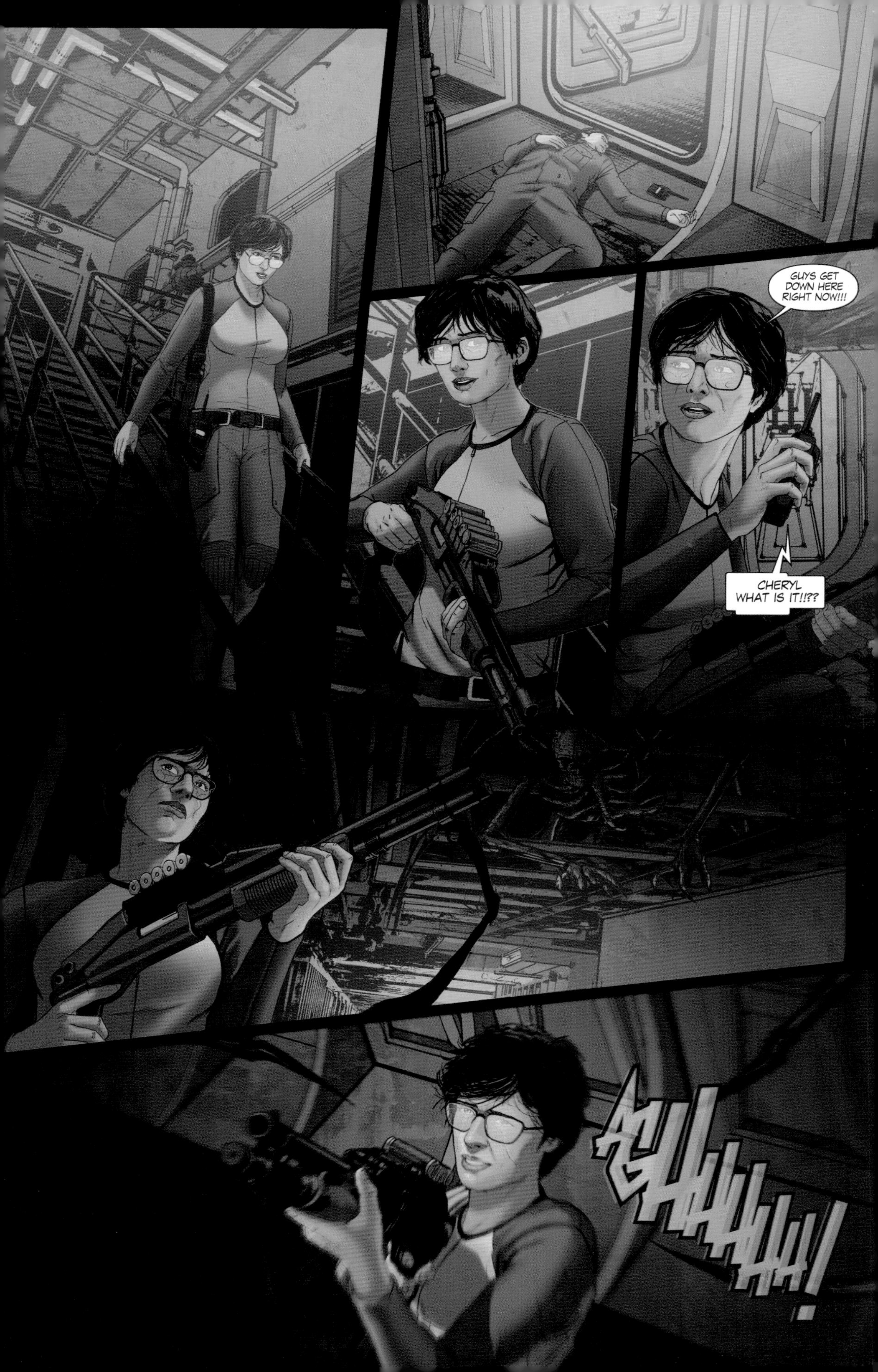
GUYS GET DOWN HERE RIGHT NOW!!!
CHERYL WHAT IS IT!!??
AGHHHHHH!

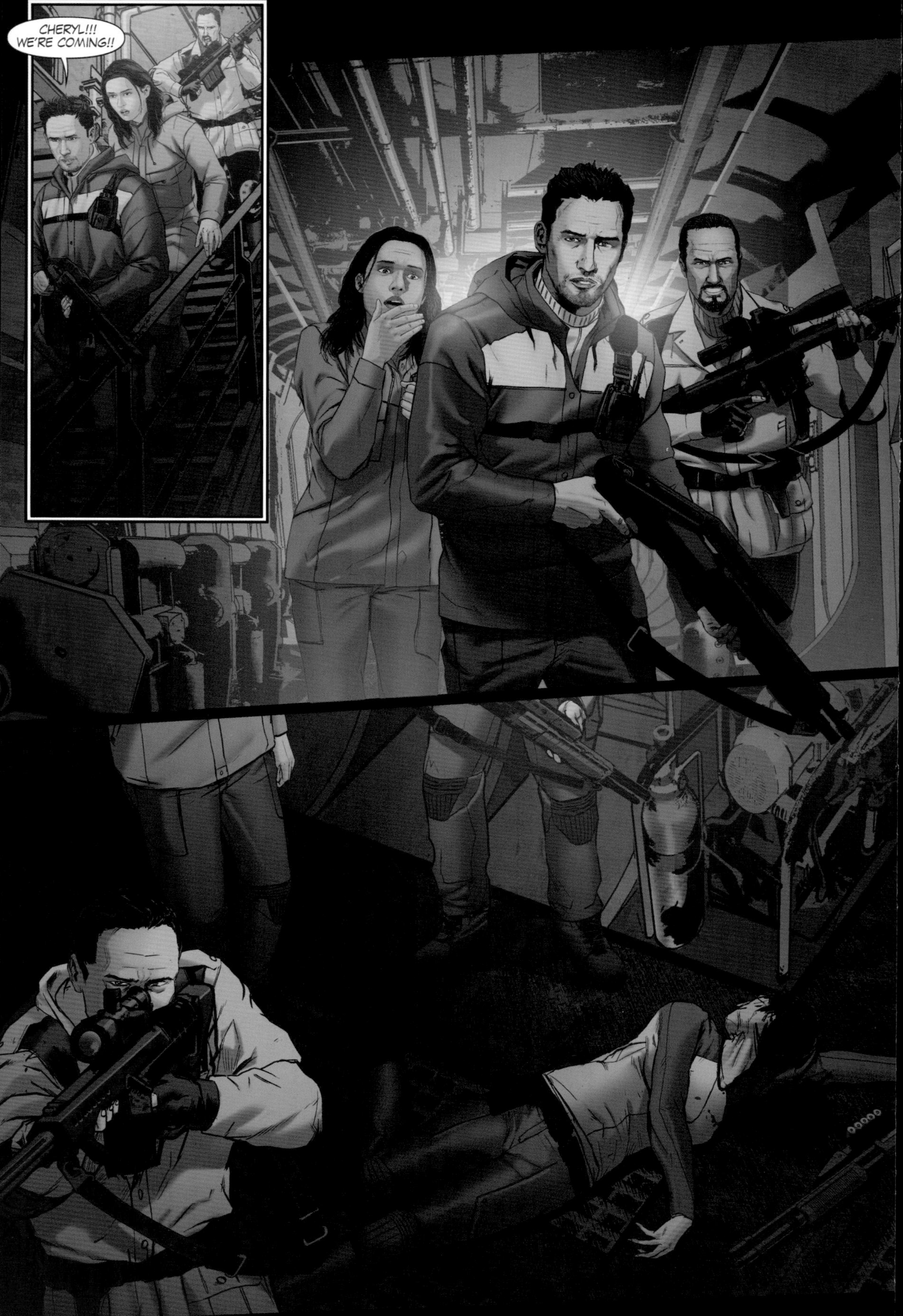
CHERYL!!! WE'RE COMING!!

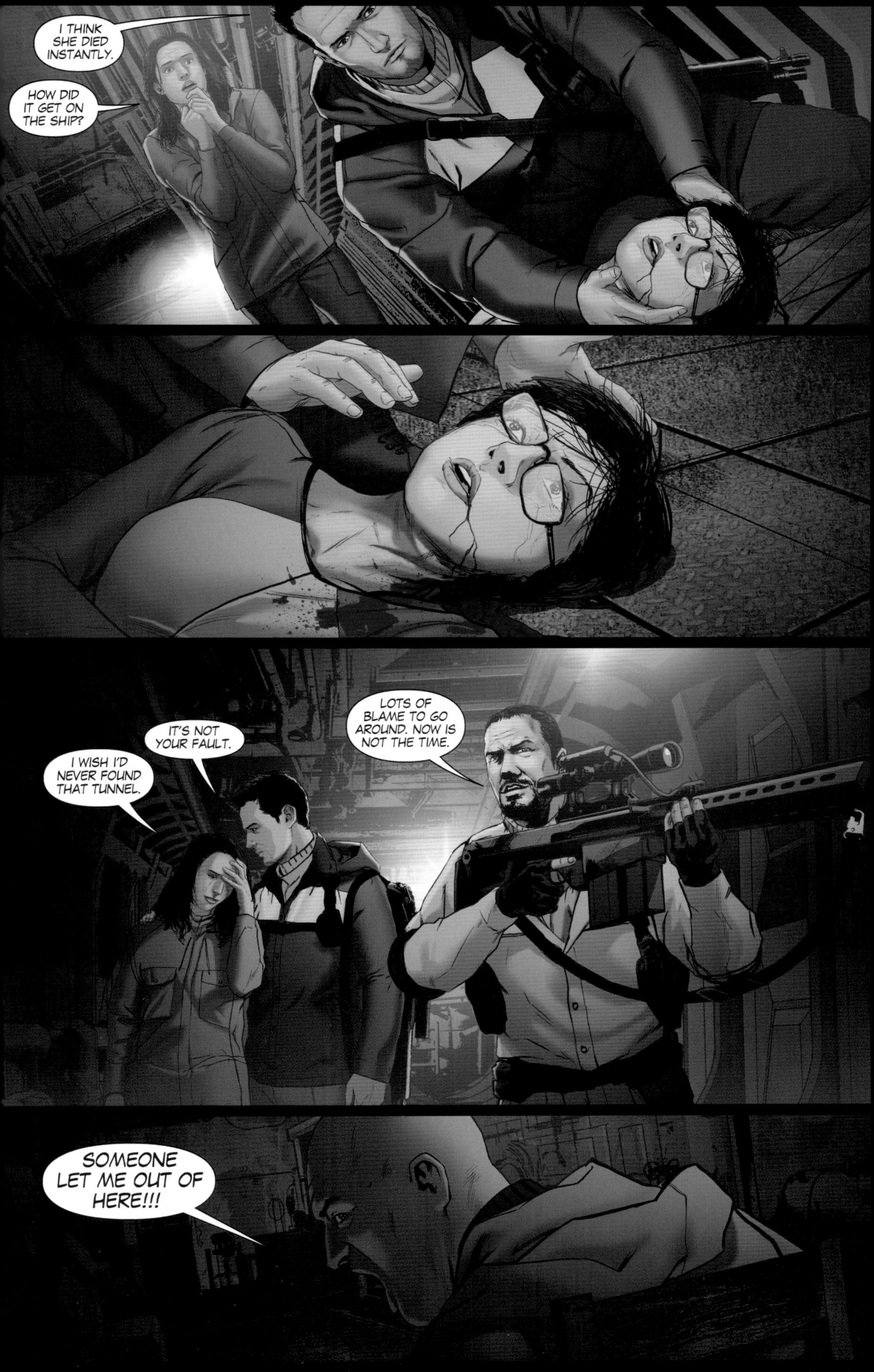
I THINK SHE DIED INSTANTLY.
HOW DID IT GET ON THE SHIP?
I WISH I'D NEVER FOUND THAT TUNNEL.
IT'S NOT YOUR FAULT.
LOTS OF BLAME TO GO AROUND. NOW IS NOT THE TIME.
SOMEONE LET ME OUT OF HERE!!!

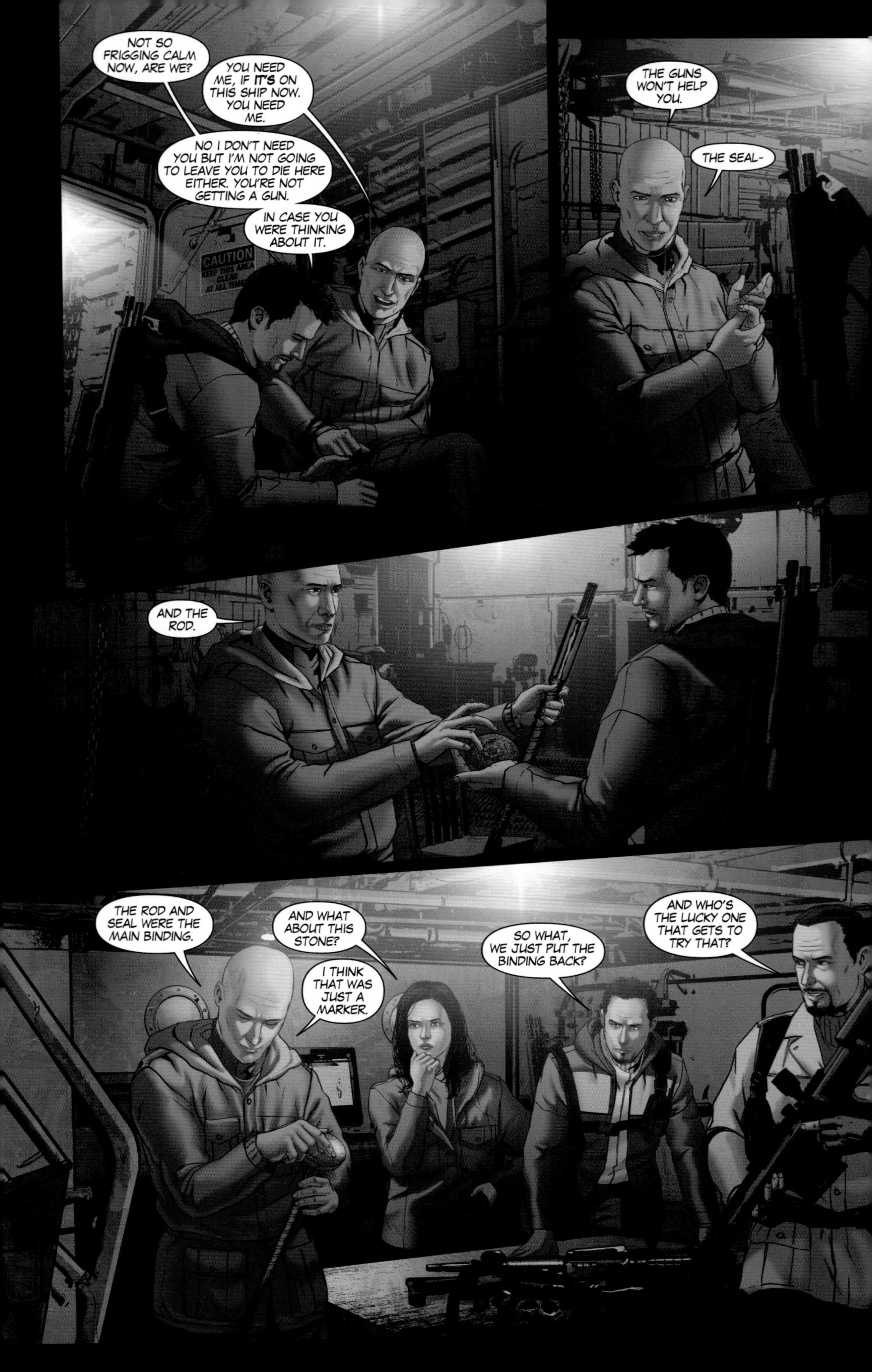
NOT SO FRIGGING CALM NOW, ARE WE?
YOU NEED ME, IF **IT'S** ON THIS SHIP NOW. YOU NEED ME.
NO I DON'T NEED YOU BUT I'M NOT GOING TO LEAVE YOU TO DIE HERE EITHER. YOU'RE NOT GETTING A GUN.
IN CASE YOU WERE THINKING ABOUT IT.
CAUTION KEEP THIS AREA CLEAR AT ALL TIMES
THE GUNS WON'T HELP YOU.
THE SEAL-
AND THE ROD.
THE ROD AND SEAL WERE THE MAIN BINDING.
AND WHAT ABOUT THIS STONE?
I THINK THAT WAS JUST A MARKER.
SO WHAT, WE JUST PUT THE BINDING BACK?
AND WHO'S THE LUCKY ONE THAT GETS TO TRY THAT?

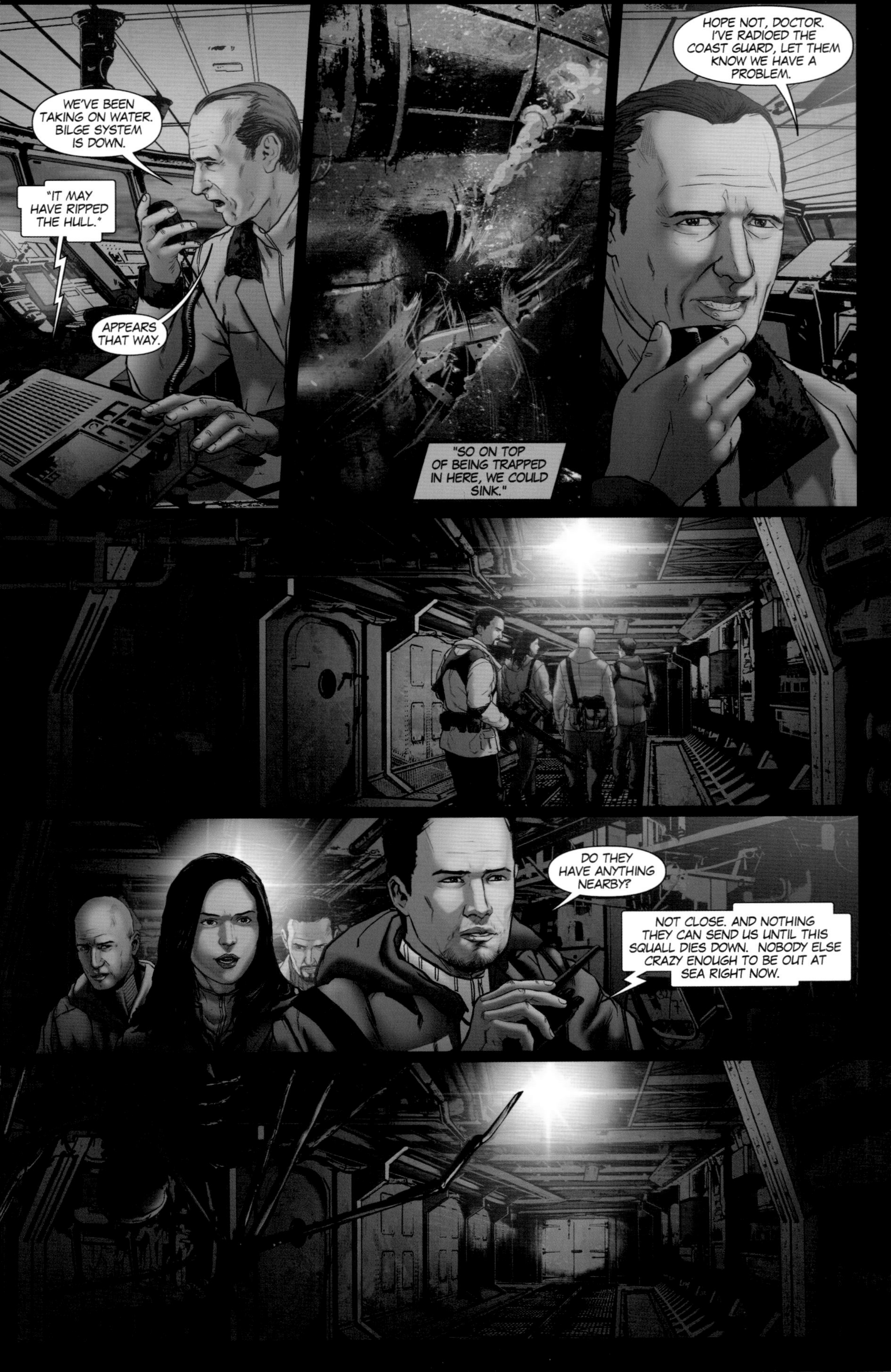
WE'VE BEEN TAKING ON WATER. BILGE SYSTEM IS DOWN.
"IT MAY HAVE RIPPED THE HULL."
APPEARS THAT WAY.
"SO ON TOP OF BEING TRAPPED IN HERE, WE COULD SINK."
HOPE NOT, DOCTOR. I'VE RADIOED THE COAST GUARD, LET THEM KNOW WE HAVE A PROBLEM.
DO THEY HAVE ANYTHING NEARBY?
NOT CLOSE. AND NOTHING THEY CAN SEND US UNTIL THIS SQUALL DIES DOWN. NOBODY ELSE CRAZY ENOUGH TO BE OUT AT SEA RIGHT NOW.

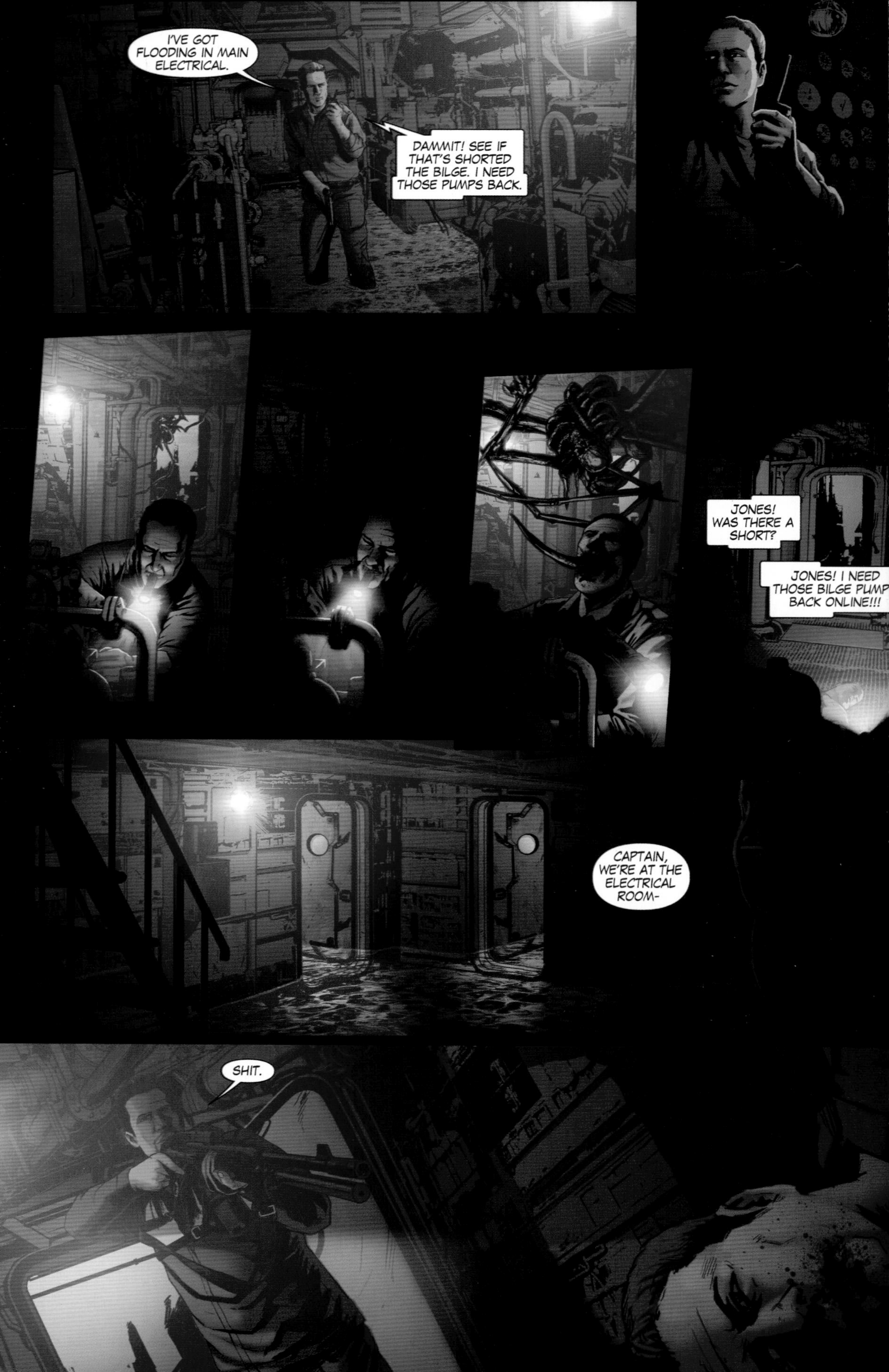

I'VE GOT FLOODING IN MAIN ELECTRICAL.
DAMMIT! SEE IF THAT'S SHORTED THE BILGE. I NEED THOSE PUMPS BACK.
JONES! WAS THERE A SHORT?
JONES! I NEED THOSE BILGE PUMP BACK ONLINE!!!
CAPTAIN, WE'RE AT THE ELECTRICAL ROOM-
SHIT.

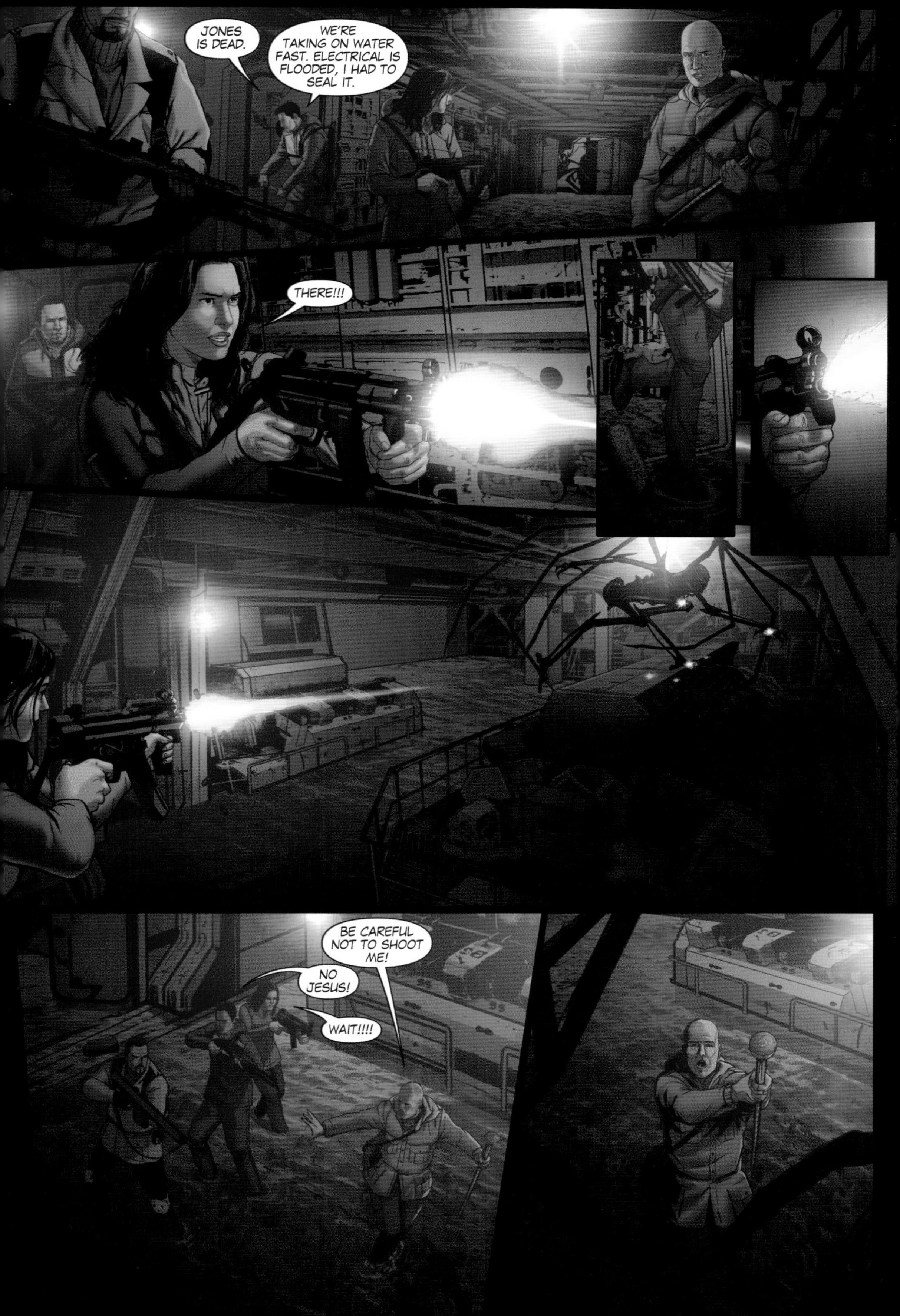
JONES IS DEAD.
WE'RE TAKING ON WATER FAST. ELECTRICAL IS FLOODED, I HAD TO SEAL IT.
THERE!!!
BE CAREFUL NOT TO SHOOT ME!
NO JESUS!
WAIT!!!!

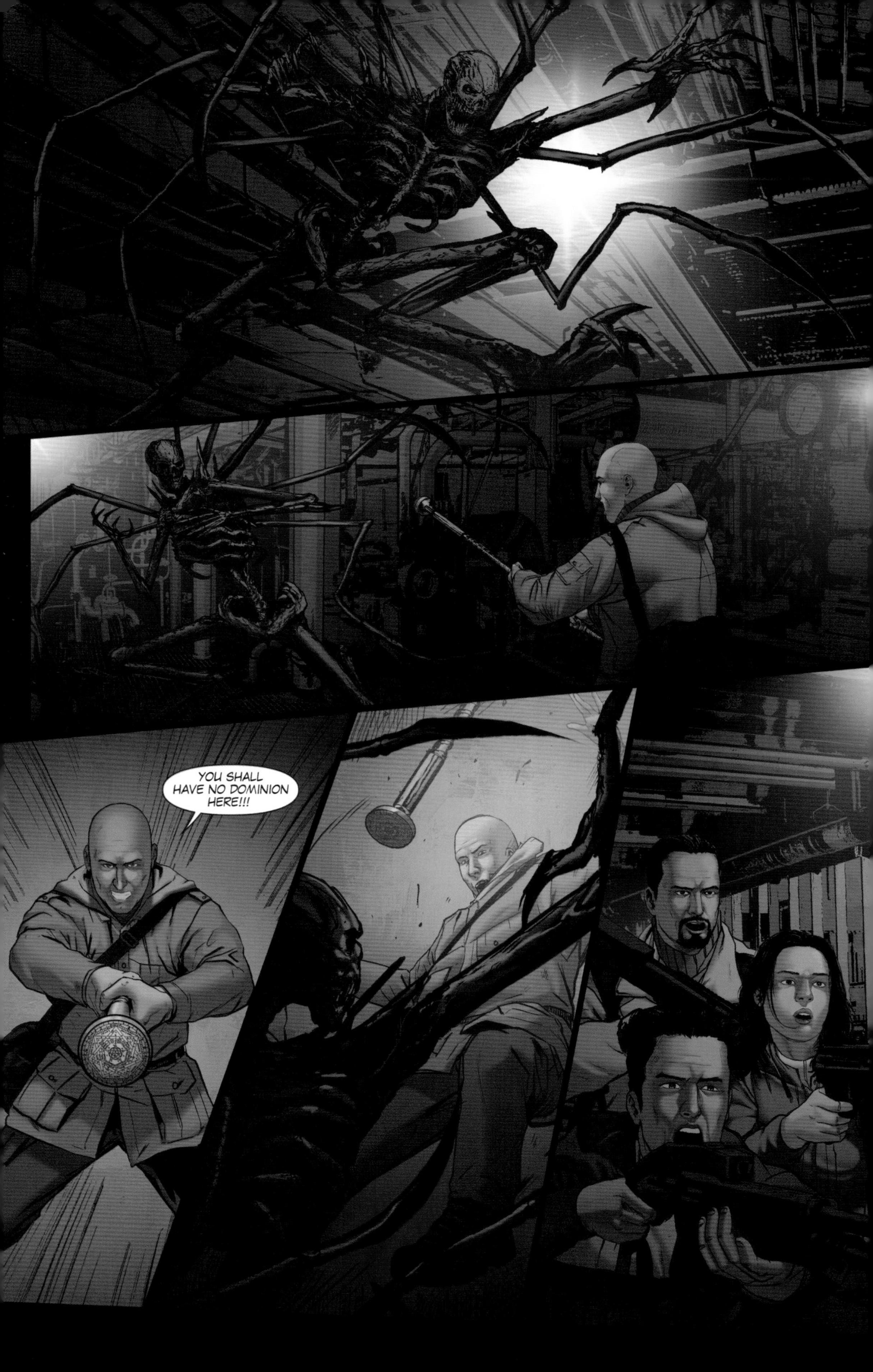
YOU SHALL HAVE NO DOMINION HERE!!!

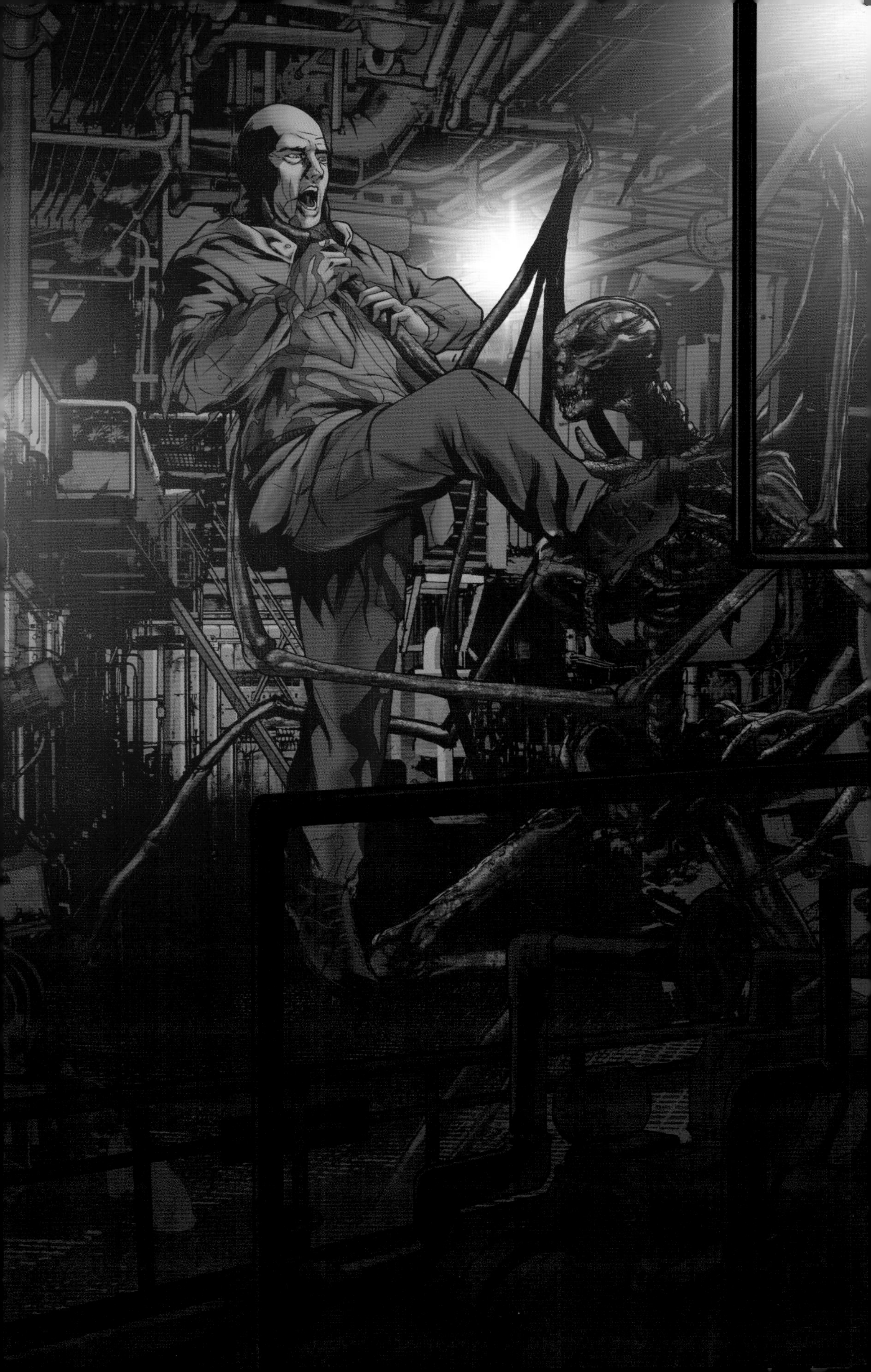

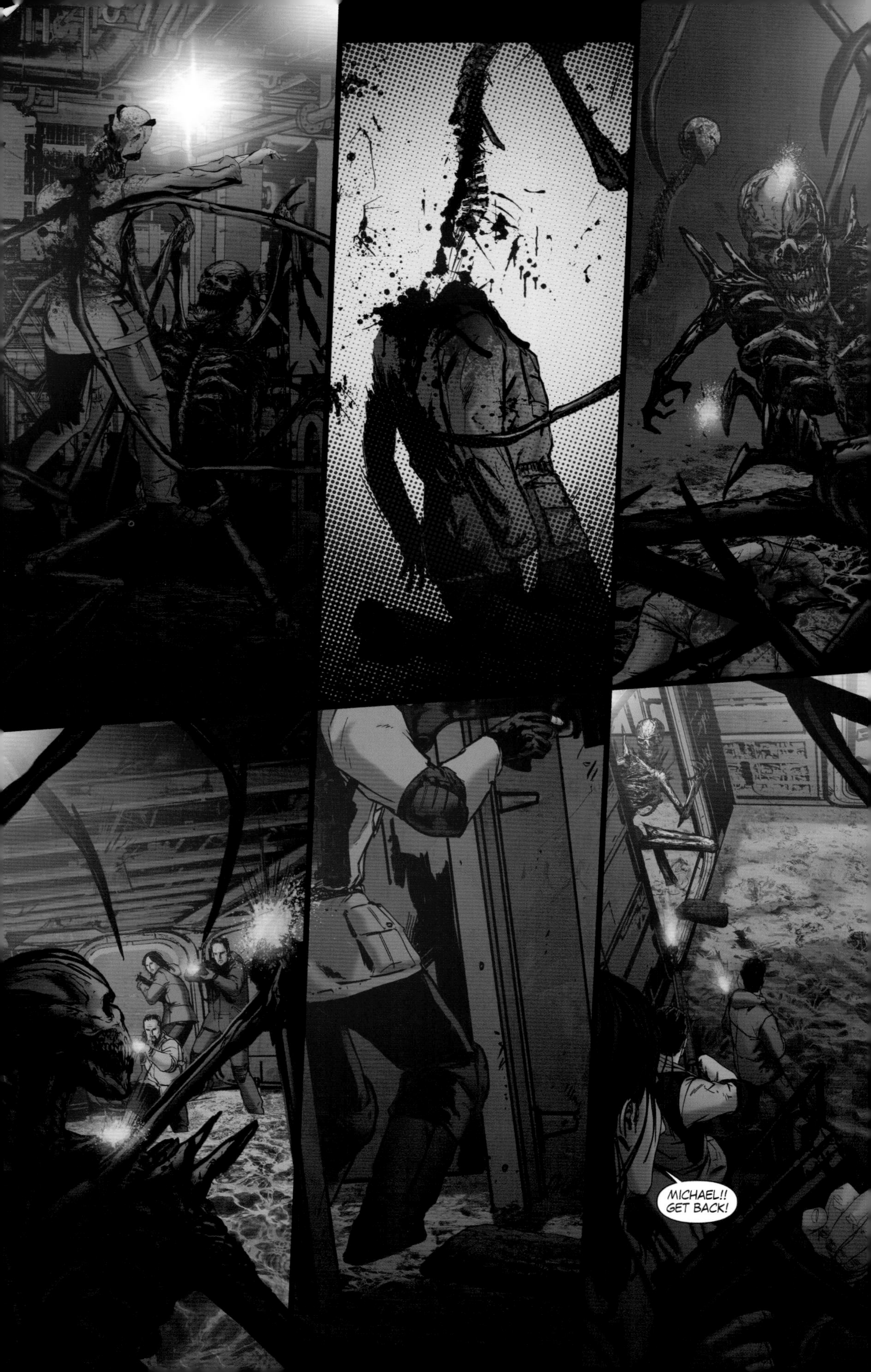
MICHAEL!! GET BACK!

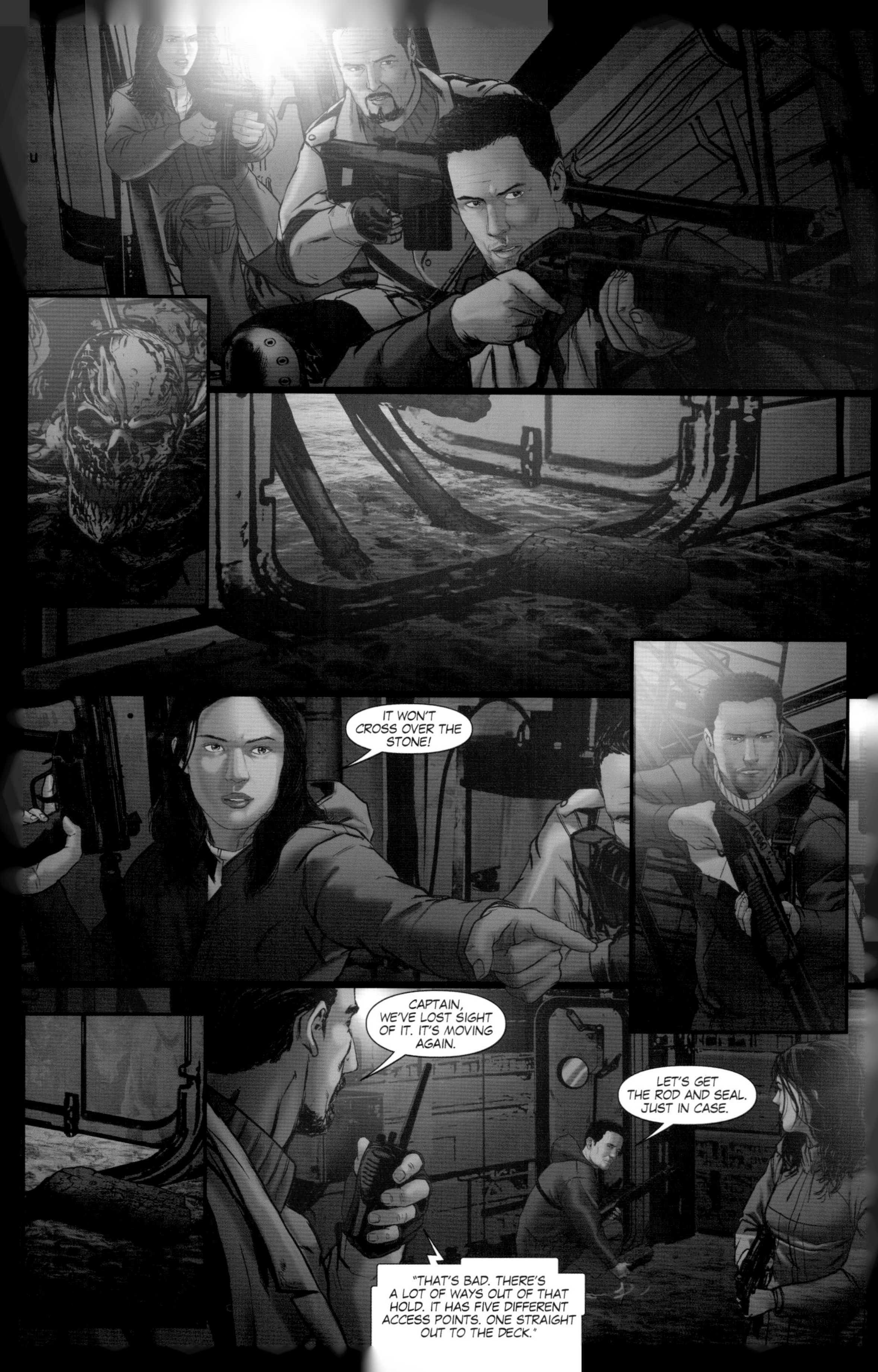
IT WON'T CROSS OVER THE STONE!
CAPTAIN, WE'VE LOST SIGHT OF IT. IT'S MOVING AGAIN.
"THAT'S BAD. THERE'S A LOT OF WAYS OUT OF THAT HOLD. IT HAS FIVE DIFFERENT ACCESS POINTS. ONE STRAIGHT OUT TO THE DECK."
LET'S GET THE ROD AND SEAL. JUST IN CASE.

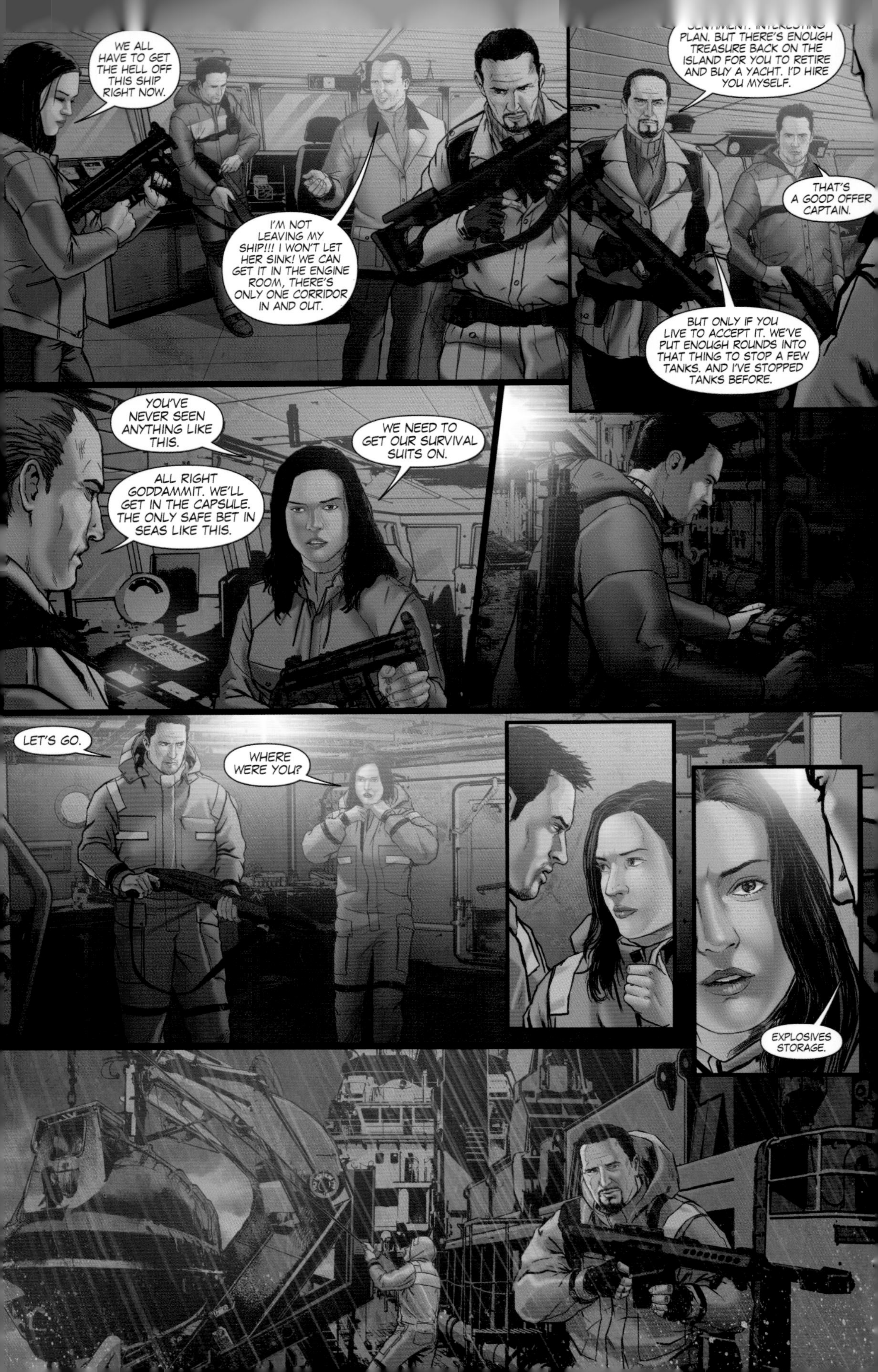
WE ALL HAVE TO GET THE HELL OFF THIS SHIP RIGHT NOW.
I'M NOT LEAVING MY SHIP!!! I WON'T LET HER SINK! WE CAN GET IT IN THE ENGINE ROOM, THERE'S ONLY ONE CORRIDOR IN AND OUT.
PLAN. BUT THERE'S ENOUGH TREASURE BACK ON THE ISLAND FOR YOU TO RETIRE AND BUY A YACHT. I'D HIRE YOU MYSELF.
THAT'S A GOOD OFFER CAPTAIN.
BUT ONLY IF YOU LIVE TO ACCEPT IT. WE'VE PUT ENOUGH ROUNDS INTO THAT THING TO STOP A FEW TANKS. AND I'VE STOPPED TANKS BEFORE.
YOU'VE NEVER SEEN ANYTHING LIKE THIS.
ALL RIGHT GODDAMMIT. WE'LL GET IN THE CAPSULE. THE ONLY SAFE BET IN SEAS LIKE THIS.
WE NEED TO GET OUR SURVIVAL SUITS ON.
LET'S GO.
WHERE WERE YOU?
EXPLOSIVES STORAGE.

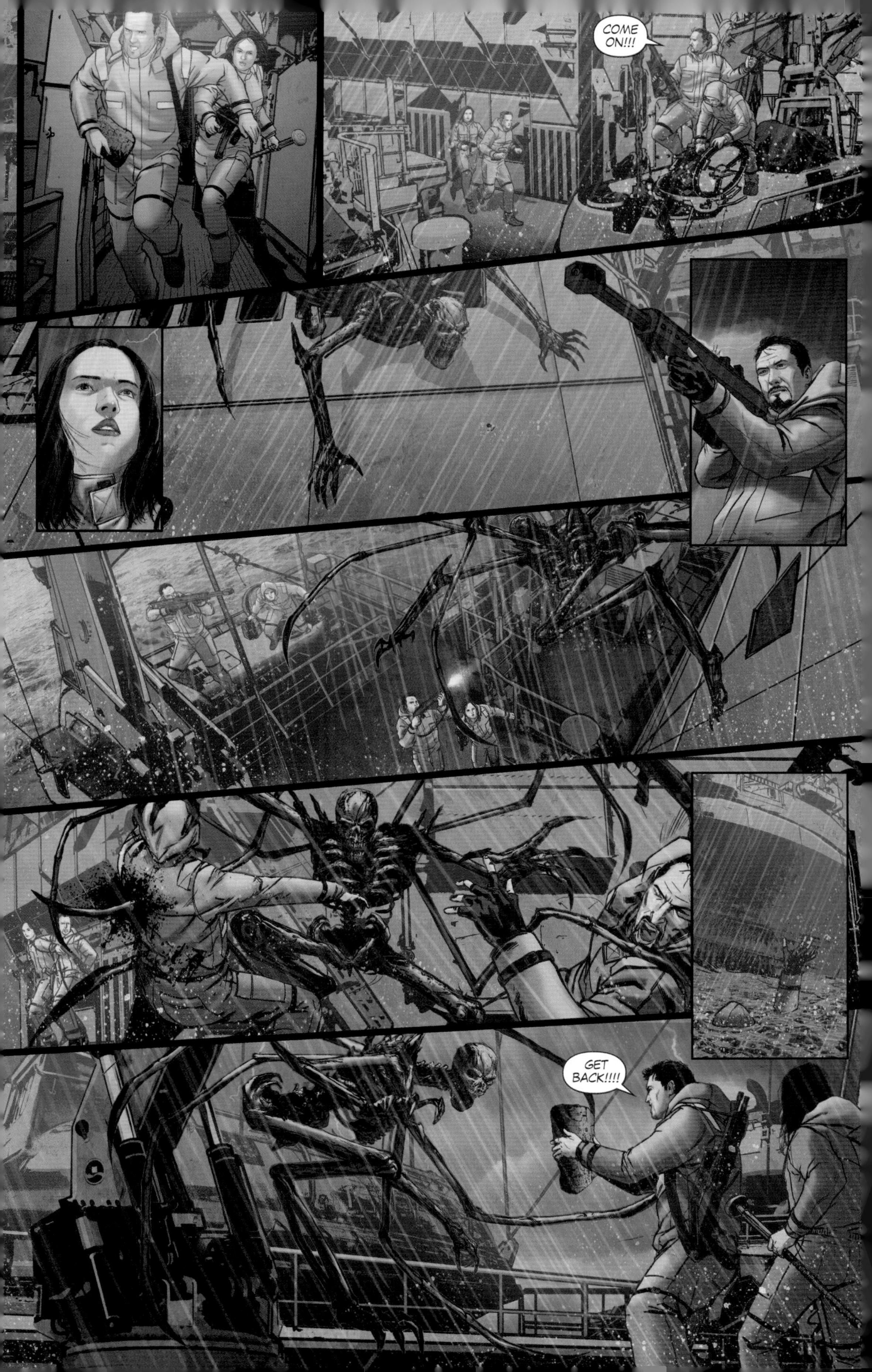
COME ON!!!
GET BACK!!!!

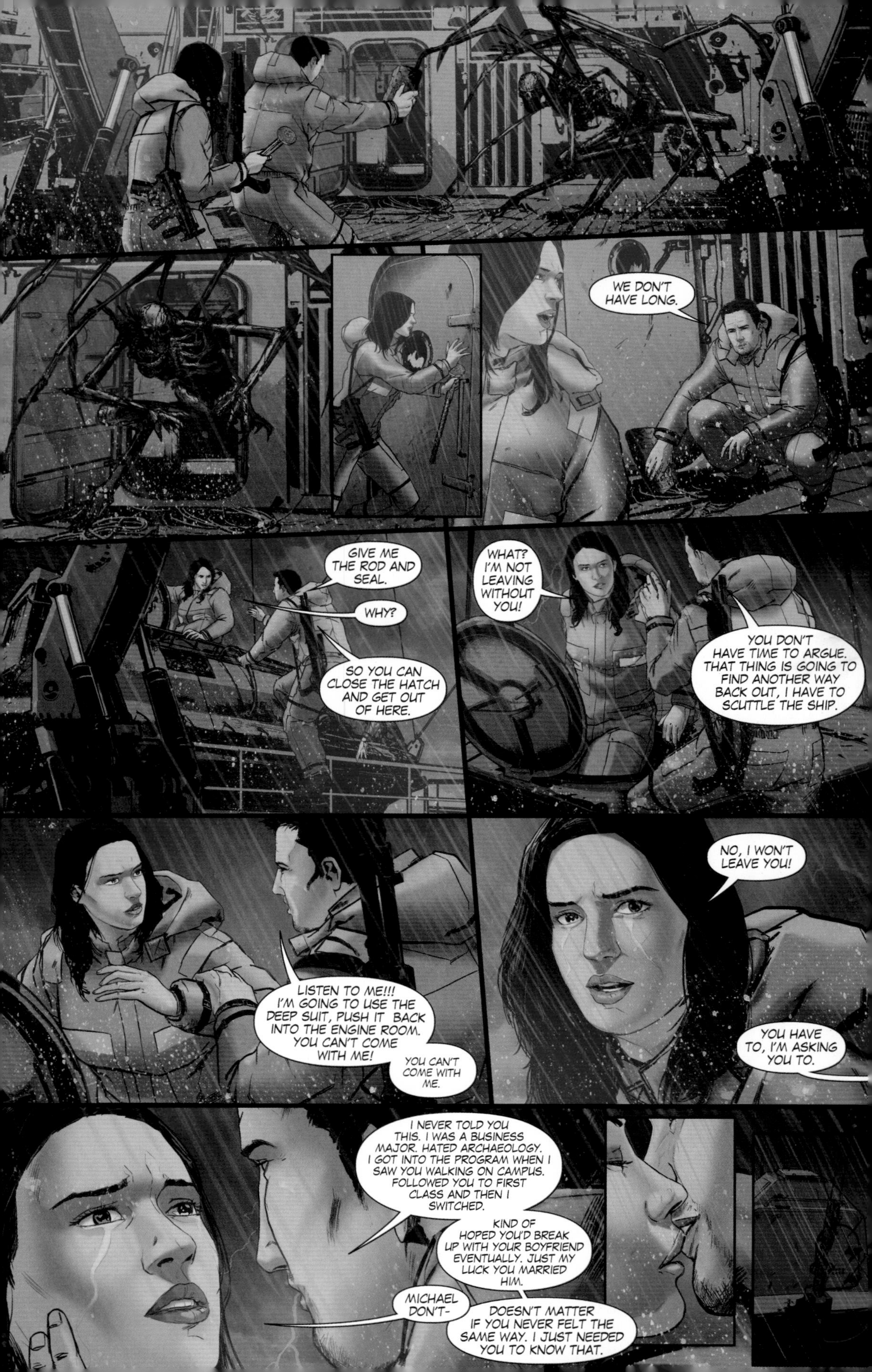
WE DON'T HAVE LONG.
GIVE ME THE ROD AND SEAL.
WHY?
SO YOU CAN CLOSE THE HATCH AND GET OUT OF HERE.
WHAT? I'M NOT LEAVING WITHOUT YOU!
YOU DON'T HAVE TIME TO ARGUE. THAT THING IS GOING TO FIND ANOTHER WAY BACK OUT, I HAVE TO SCUTTLE THE SHIP.
LISTEN TO ME!!! I'M GOING TO USE THE DEEP SUIT, PUSH IT BACK INTO THE ENGINE ROOM. YOU CAN'T COME WITH ME!
YOU CAN'T COME WITH ME.
NO, I WON'T LEAVE YOU!
YOU HAVE TO, I'M ASKING YOU TO.
I NEVER TOLD YOU THIS. I WAS A BUSINESS MAJOR. HATED ARCHAEOLOGY. I GOT INTO THE PROGRAM WHEN I SAW YOU WALKING ON CAMPUS. FOLLOWED YOU TO FIRST CLASS AND THEN I SWITCHED.
KIND OF HOPED YOU'D BREAK UP WITH YOUR BOYFRIEND EVENTUALLY. JUST MY LUCK YOU MARRIED HIM.
MICHAEL DON'T-
DOESN'T MATTER IF YOU NEVER FELT THE SAME WAY. I JUST NEEDED YOU TO KNOW THAT.

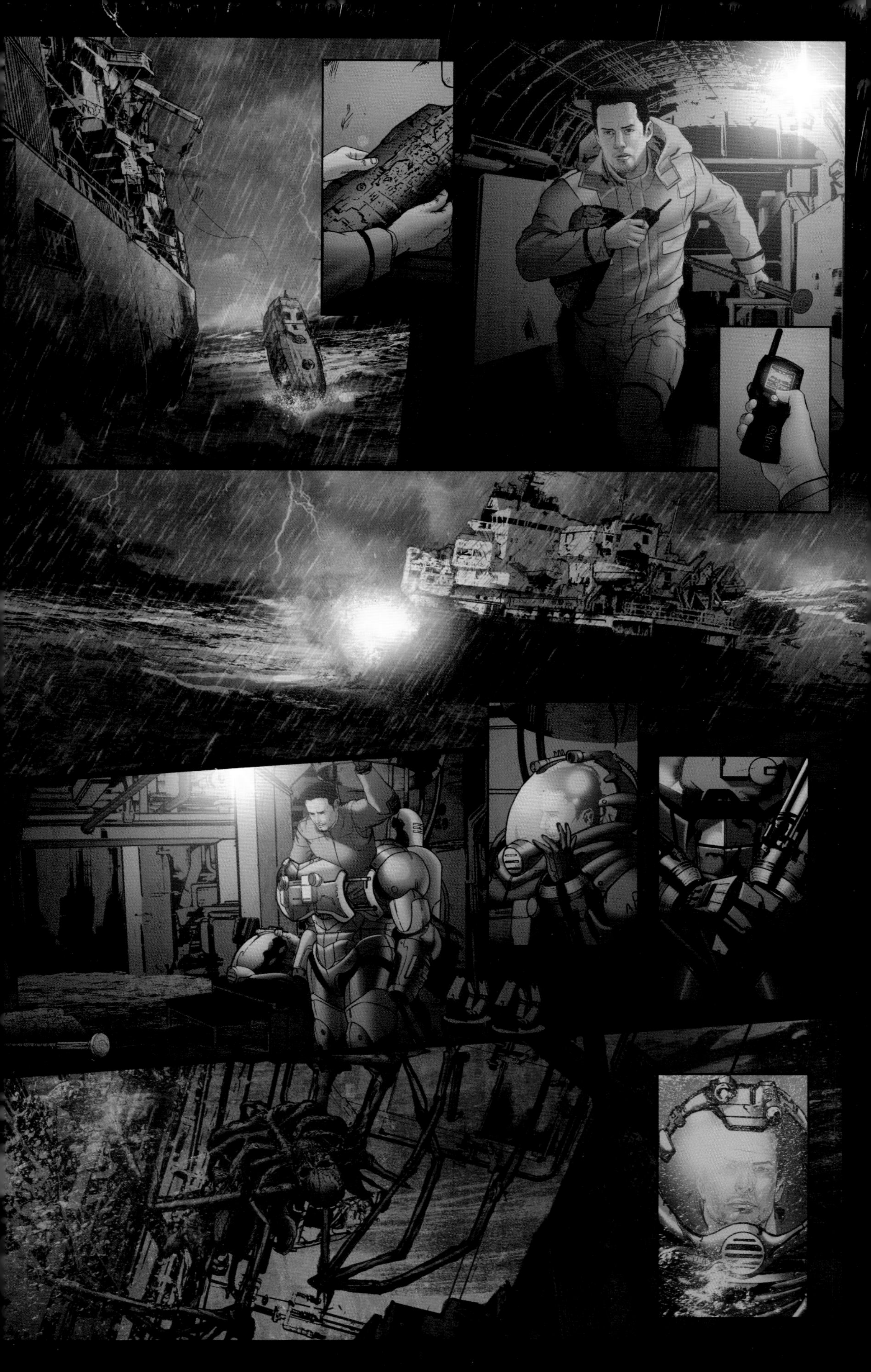

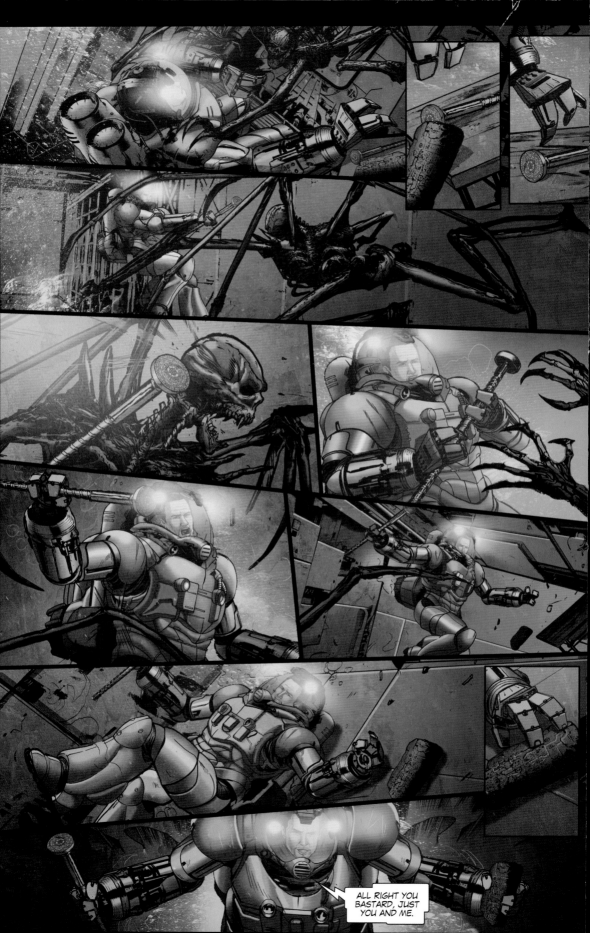

ALL RIGHT YOU BASTARD, JUST YOU AND ME.

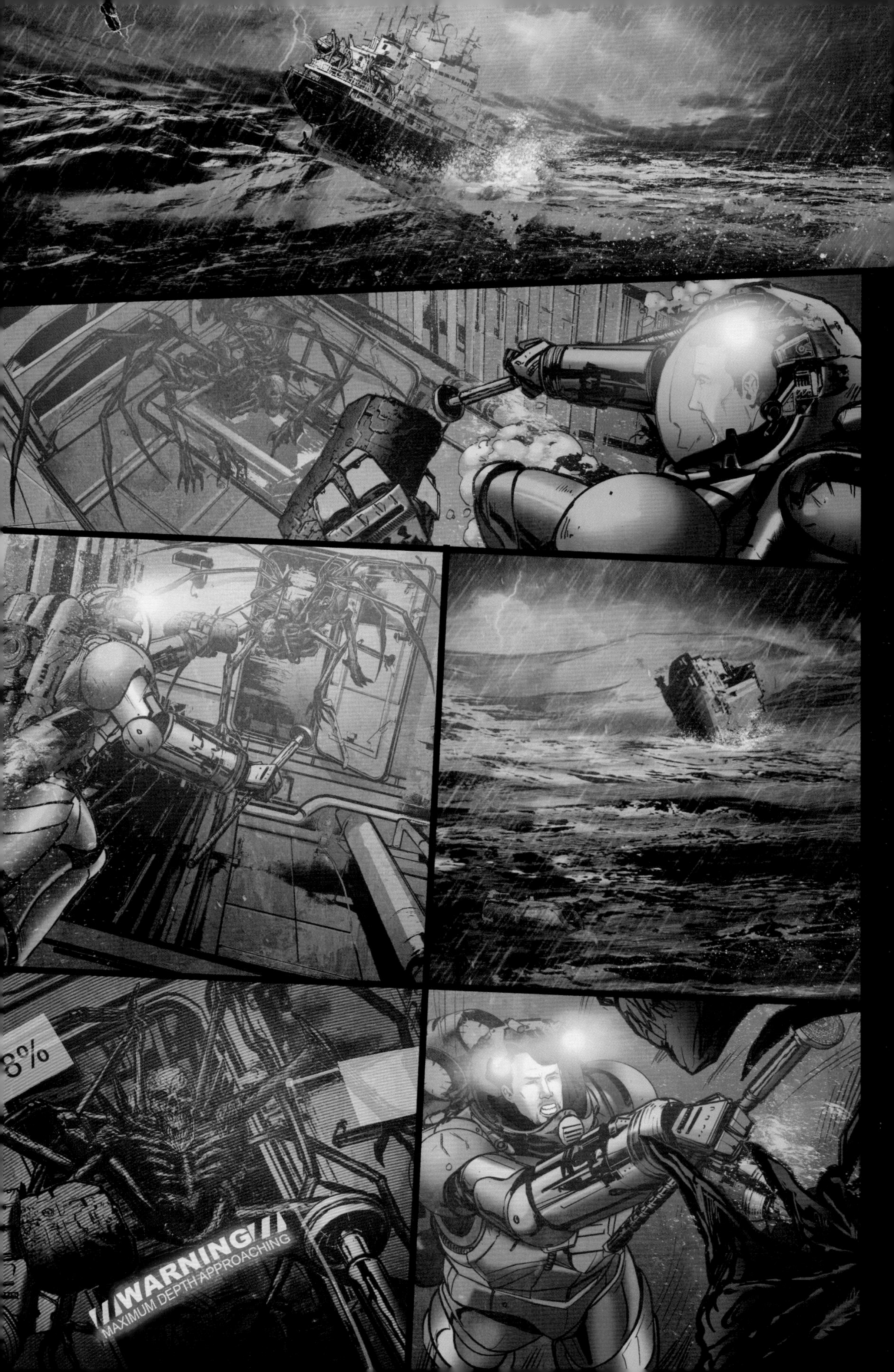
8%
//WARNING//
MAXIMUM DEPTH APPROACHING

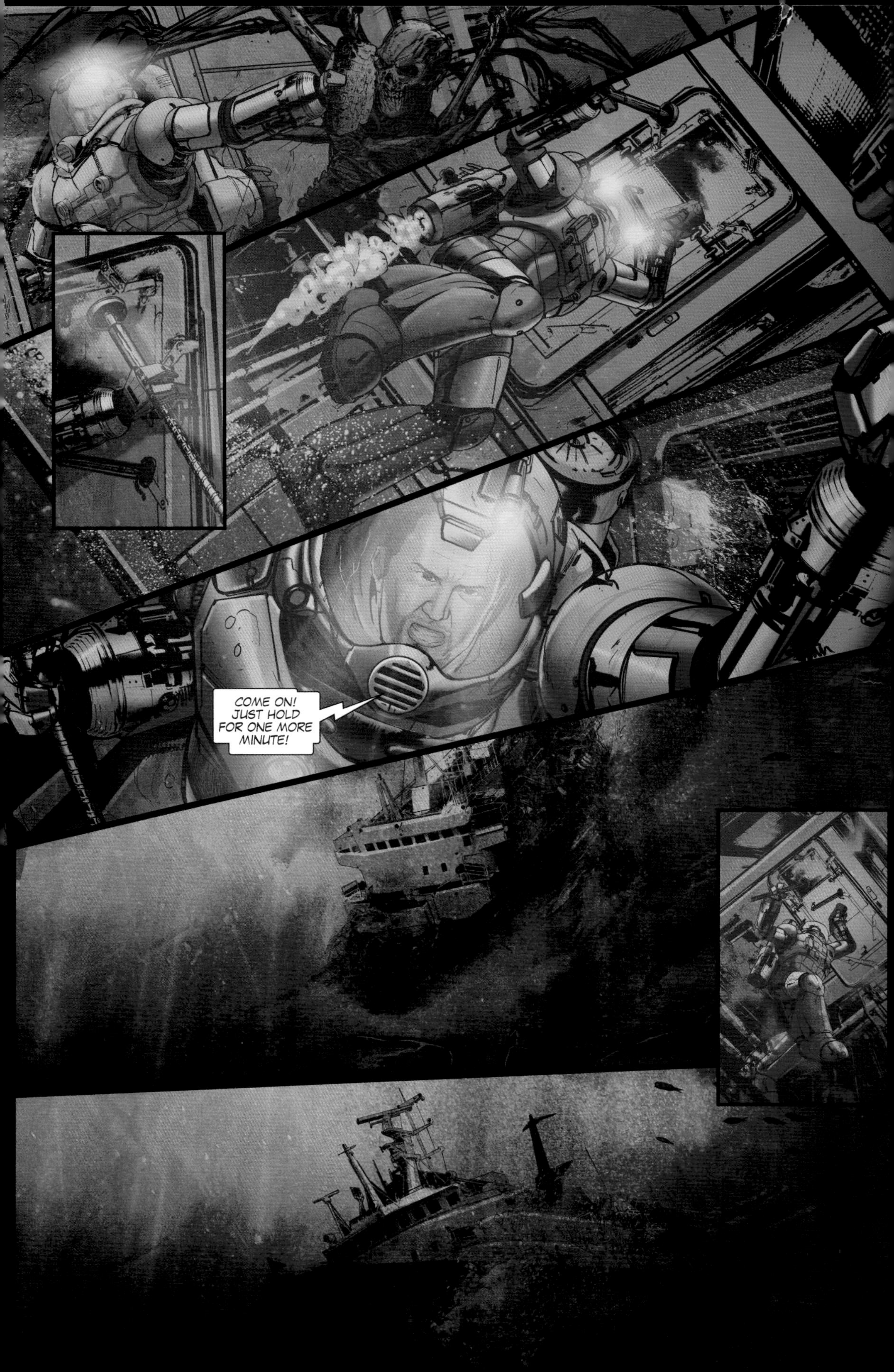
COME ON! JUST HOLD FOR ONE MORE MINUTE!

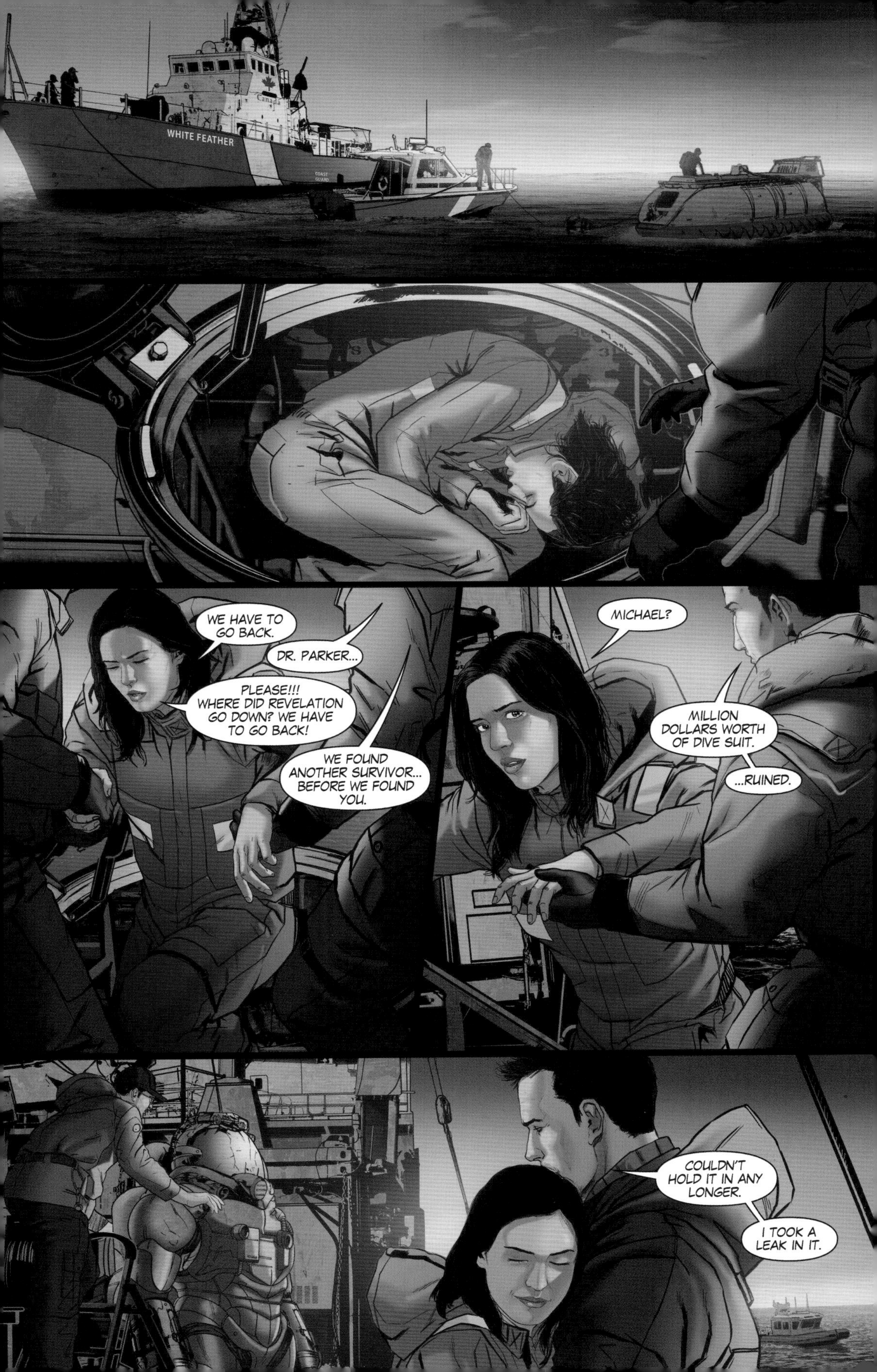
WHITE FEATHER
WE HAVE TO GO BACK.
DR. PARKER...
PLEASE!!! WHERE DID REVELATION GO DOWN? WE HAVE TO GO BACK!
WE FOUND ANOTHER SURVIVOR... BEFORE WE FOUND YOU.
MICHAEL?
MILLION DOLLARS WORTH OF DIVE SUIT.
...RUINED.
COULDN'T HOLD IT IN ANY LONGER.
I TOOK A LEAK IN IT.

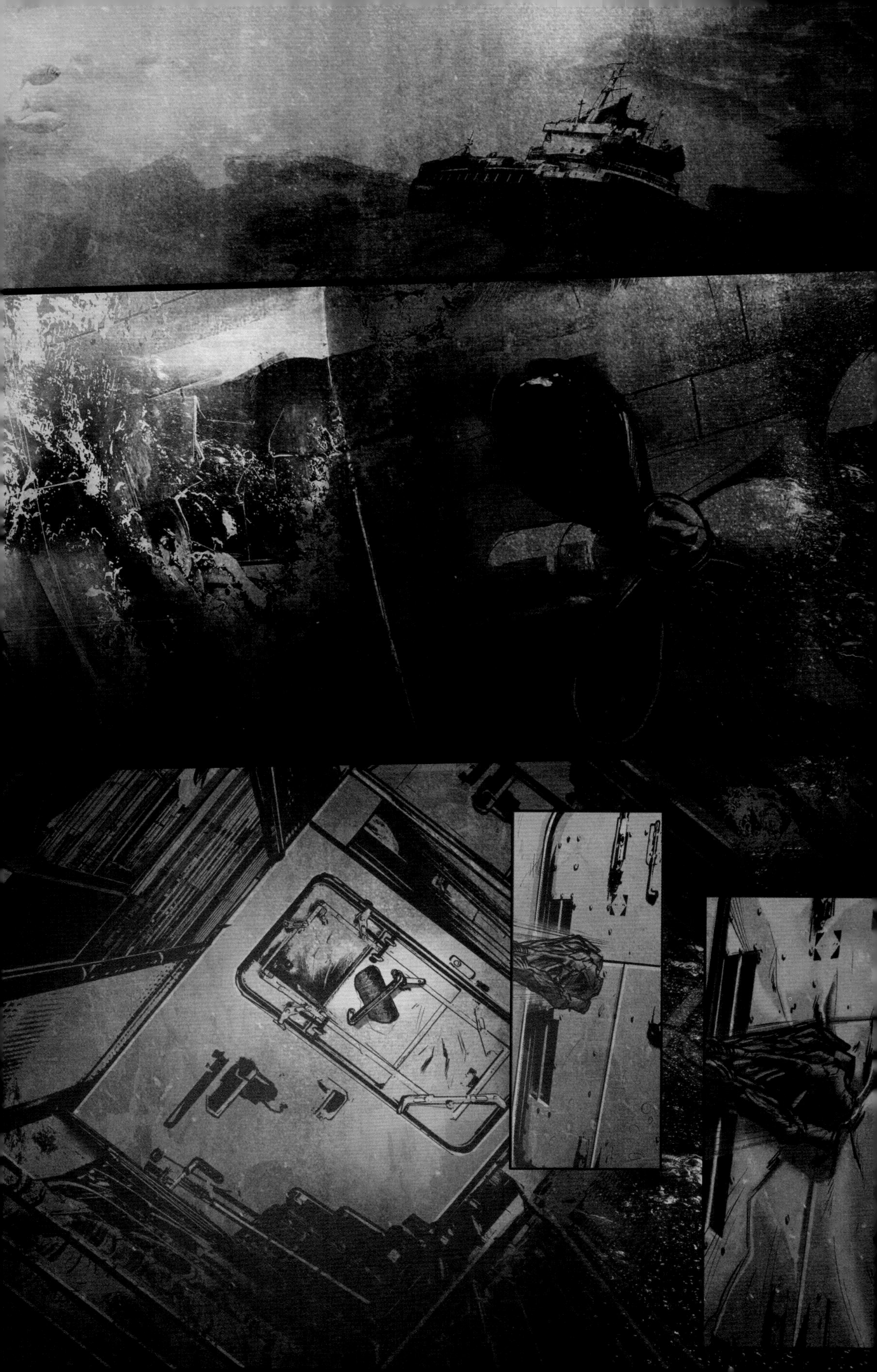

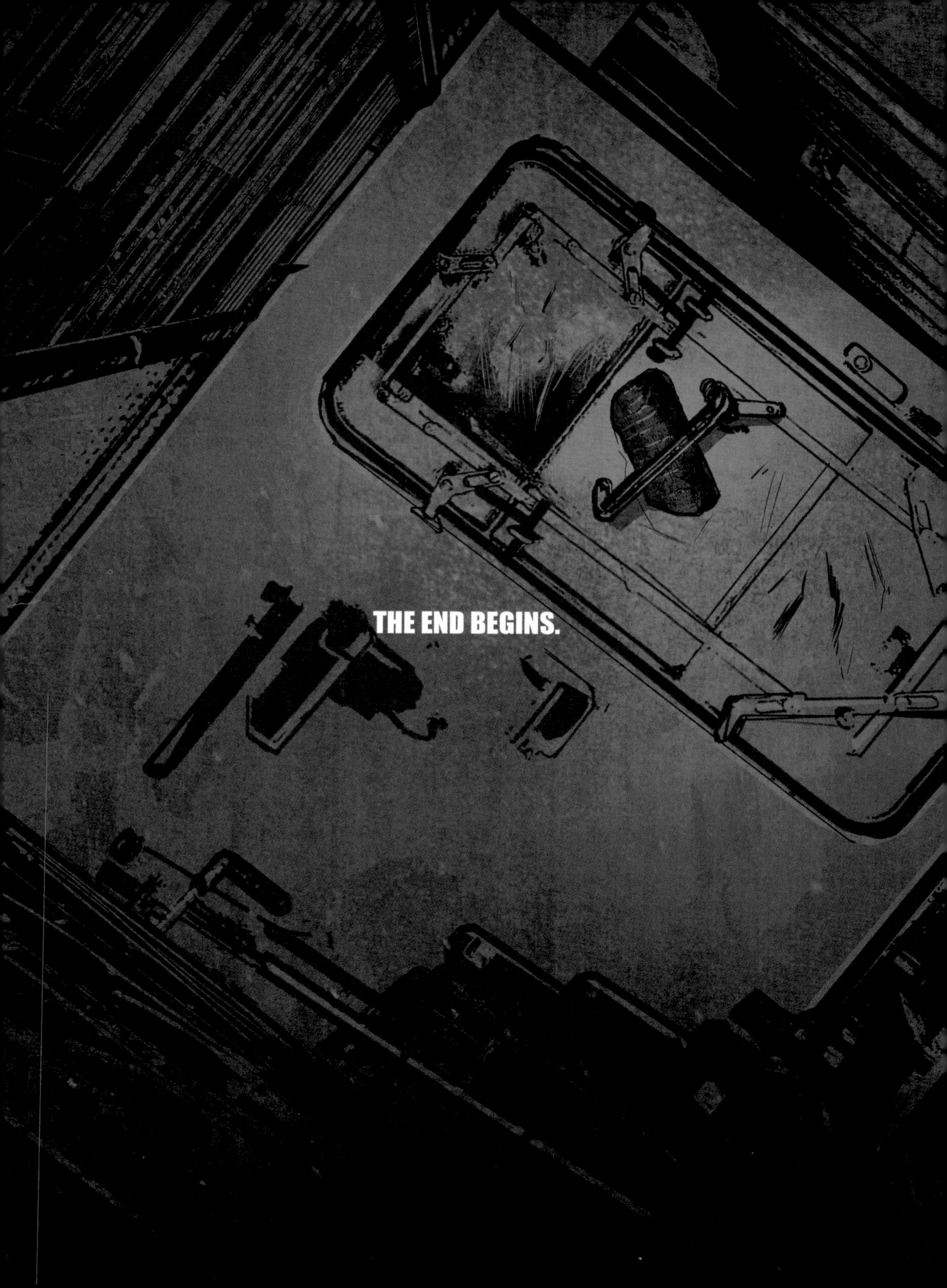
THE END BEGINS.

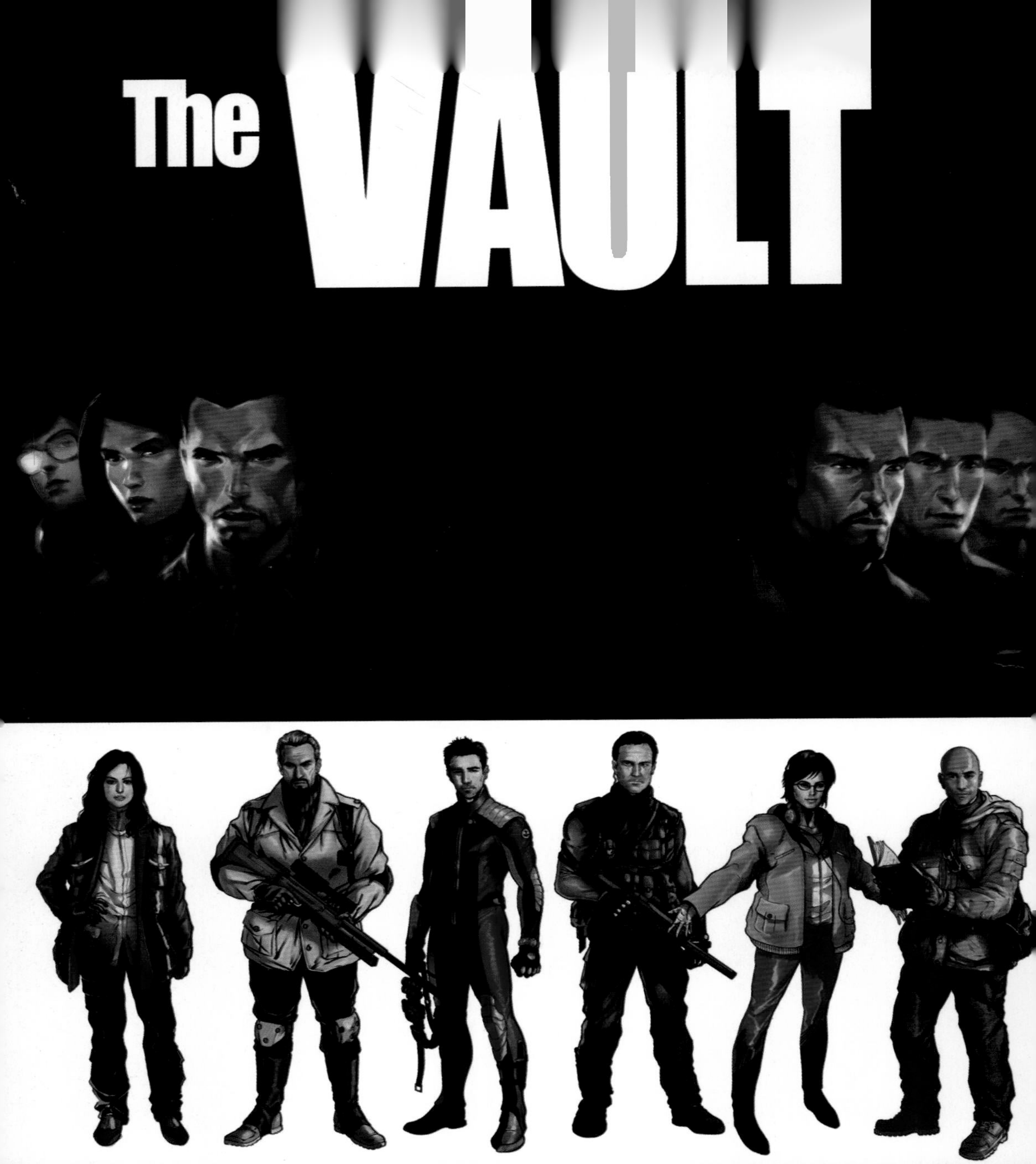
The VAULT

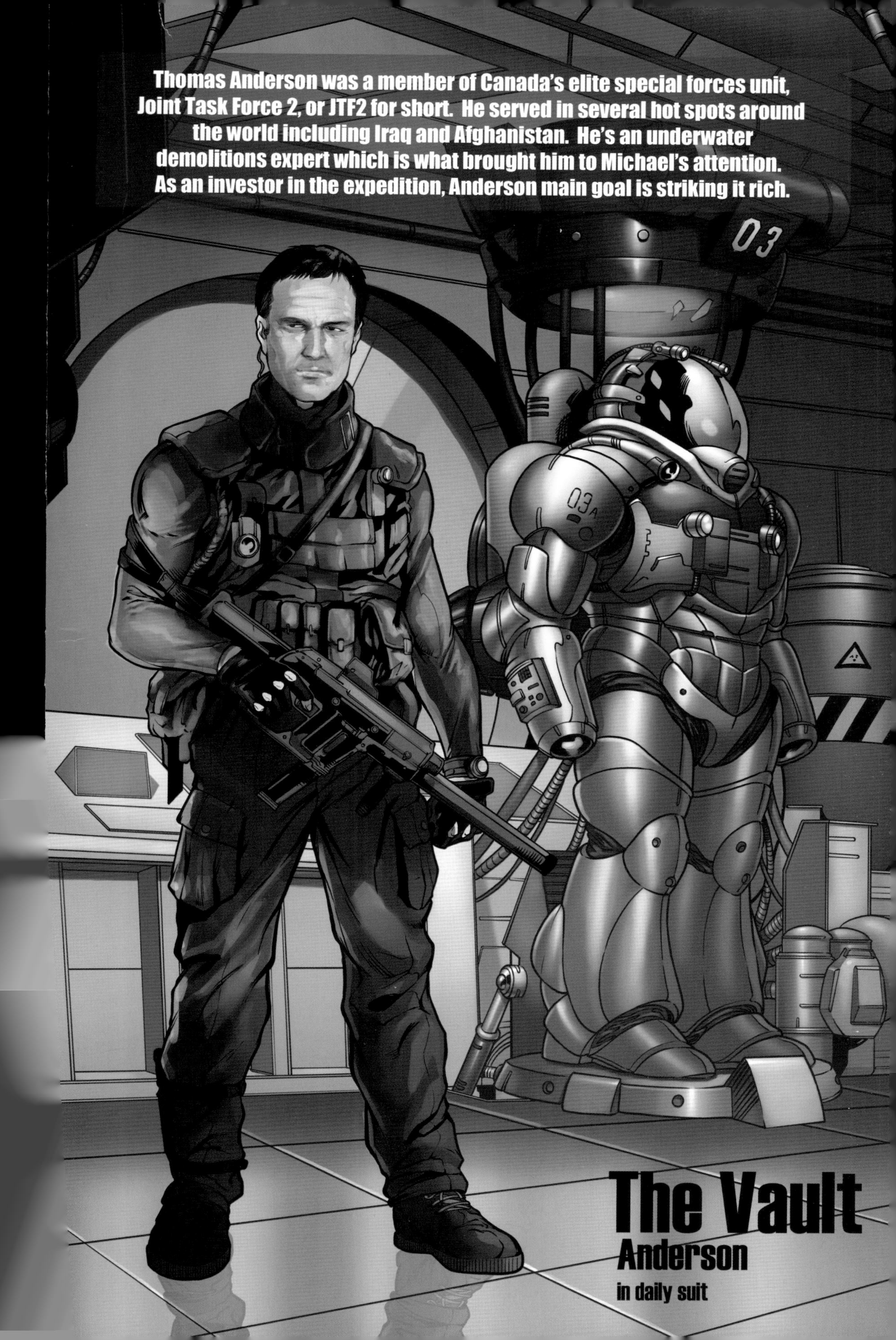
Thomas Anderson was a member of Canada's elite special forces unit, Joint Task Force 2, or JTF2 for short. He served in several hot spots around the world including Iraq and Afghanistan. He's an underwater demolitions expert which is what brought him to Michael's attention. As an investor in the expedition, Anderson main goal is striking it rich.
03
03A
The Vault
Anderson
in daily suit

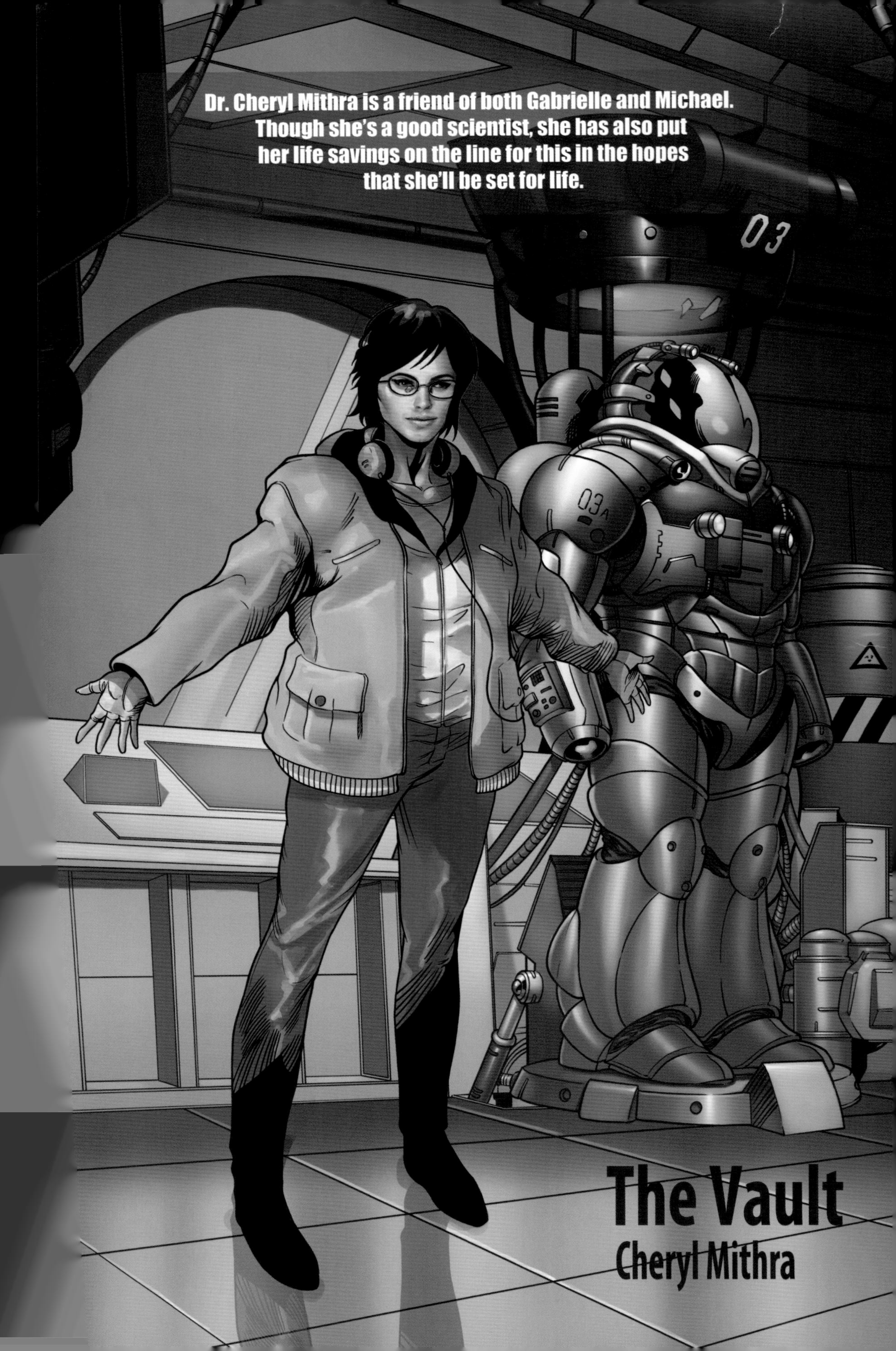
Dr. Cheryl Mithra is a friend of both Gabrielle and Michael. Though she's a good scientist, she has also put her life savings on the line for this in the hopes that she'll be set for life.
03
03A
The Vault
Cheryl Mithra

Jesus Mondragon and his brother have been working on pits similar to Oak Island and Sable Island for almost two decades. Like Gabrielle, Jesus has a background in linguistic archaeology. He worked on translating Mayan hieroglyphics.
Though he's a scientist, Jesus and his brother are both deeply spiritual and have been looking for links between the world's great religions.

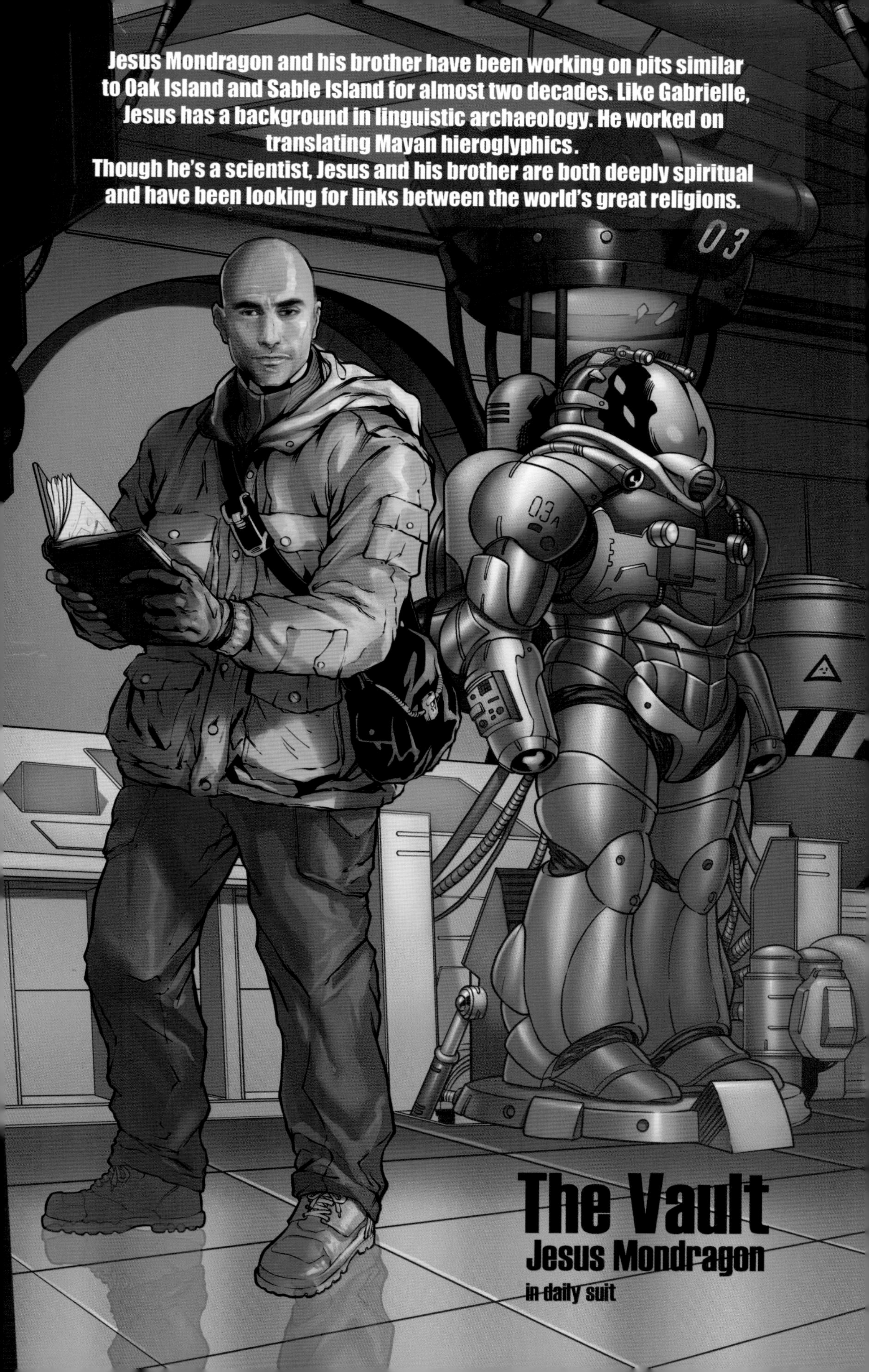
03
03A

The Vault

Jesus Mondragon

in daily suit

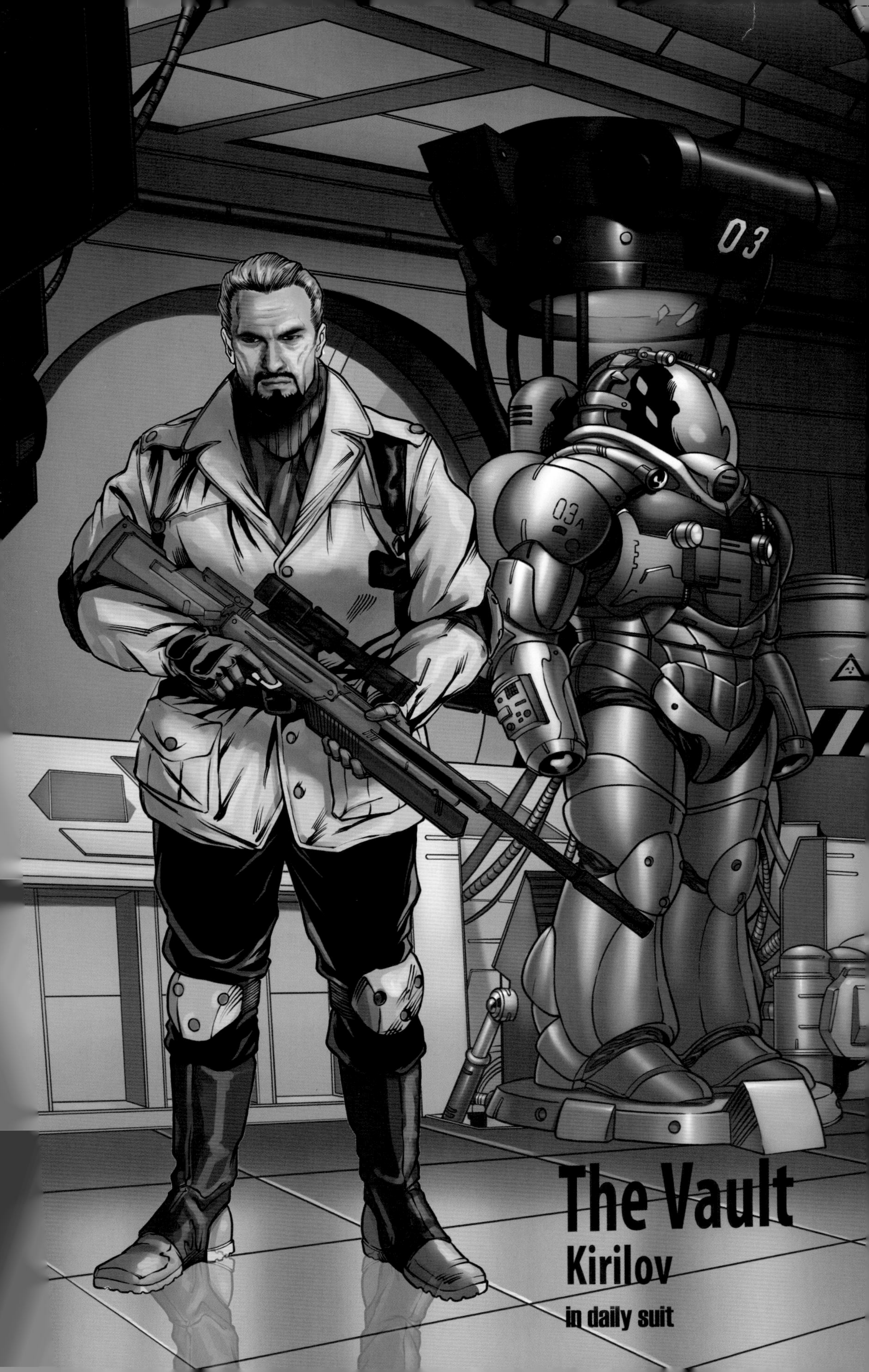
03
03A
The Vault
Kirilov
in daily suit

Kirilov's parents named him Alexei in honor of the nihilistic character in "Demons" by Fyodr Dostoevsky. A characteristic which he learned to embody growing up during the Cold War and the subsequent break up of the former Soviet Union. While it is known that Kirilov served in the Russian special forces, it remains unknown what role he had in the KGB and its successor, the FSB. As Russia came to its second phase in the post-Cold War, Kirilov rose to the top with his military and business connections in the West. Armed with cash, he co-founded a robotics company, Magnus Robotics with industrial and military contracts around the world. In his spare time, he is an avid treasure hunter, art collector, loves cross-country skiing, shooting, country music and likes to maintain his physique by swimming.

Macula is one of a series of the most advanced robots on the planet. Built by a joint Japanese-Russian consortium, headed by Kirilov, Macula was originally designed for interplanetary exploration but with obvious military applications as well.

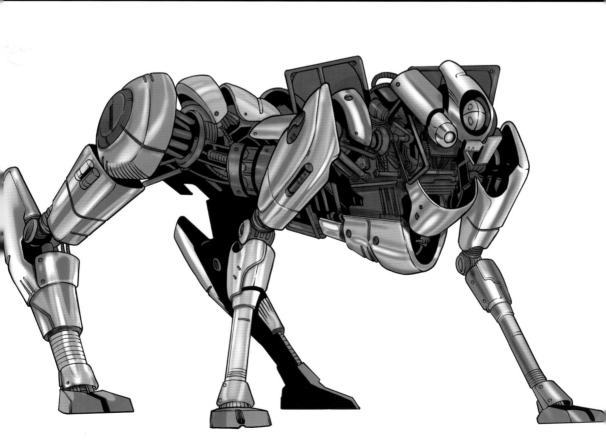

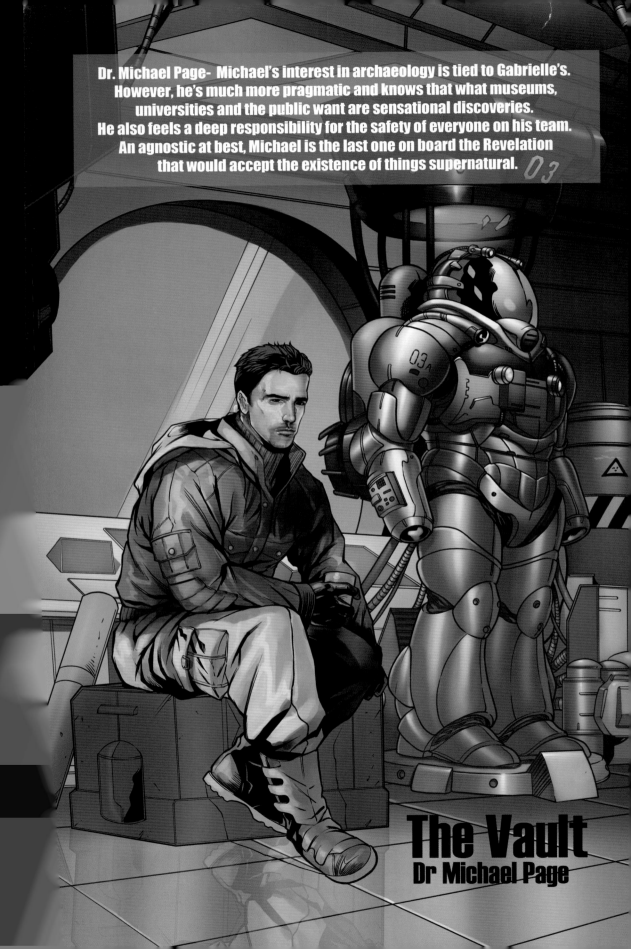

Dr. Michael Page- Michael's interest in archaeology is tied to Gabrielle's. However, he's much more pragmatic and knows that what museums, universities and the public want are sensational discoveries. He also feels a deep responsibility for the safety of everyone on his team. An agnostic at best, Michael is the last one on board the Revelation that would accept the existence of things supernatural.

The Vault
Dr Michael Page

Dr. Gabrielle Parker's main areas of focus are linguistic archaeology and early religious archeology. She married young and had a child but lost her child to an unfortunate accident. The Oak Island pit was one of her first major studies. Gabrielle is looking for things that have a radical impact on reshaping our understanding of history. In that sense, she searches for patterns and hidden meaning in small details.

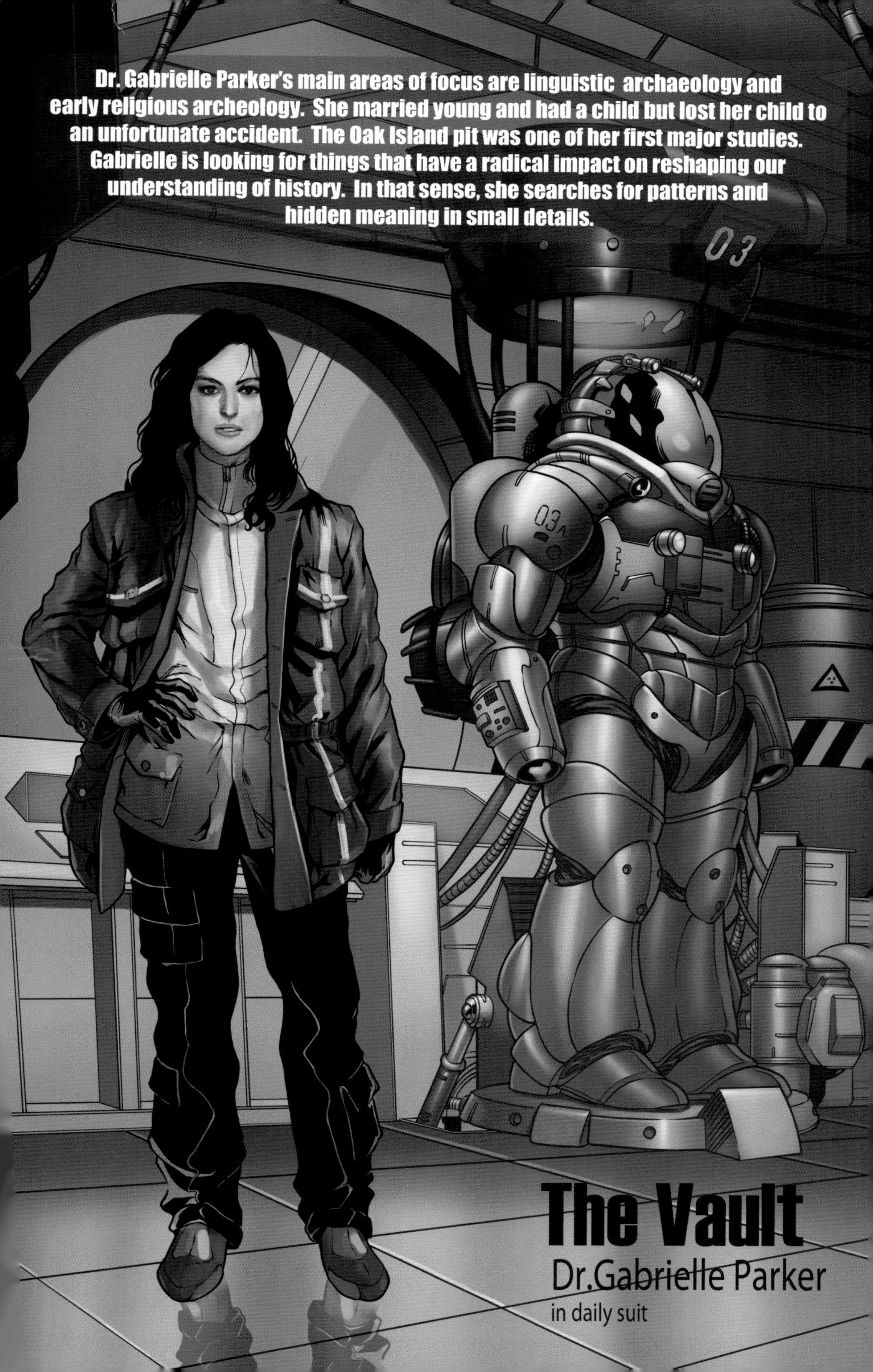
03
03A

The Vault

Dr.Gabrielle Parker

in daily suit

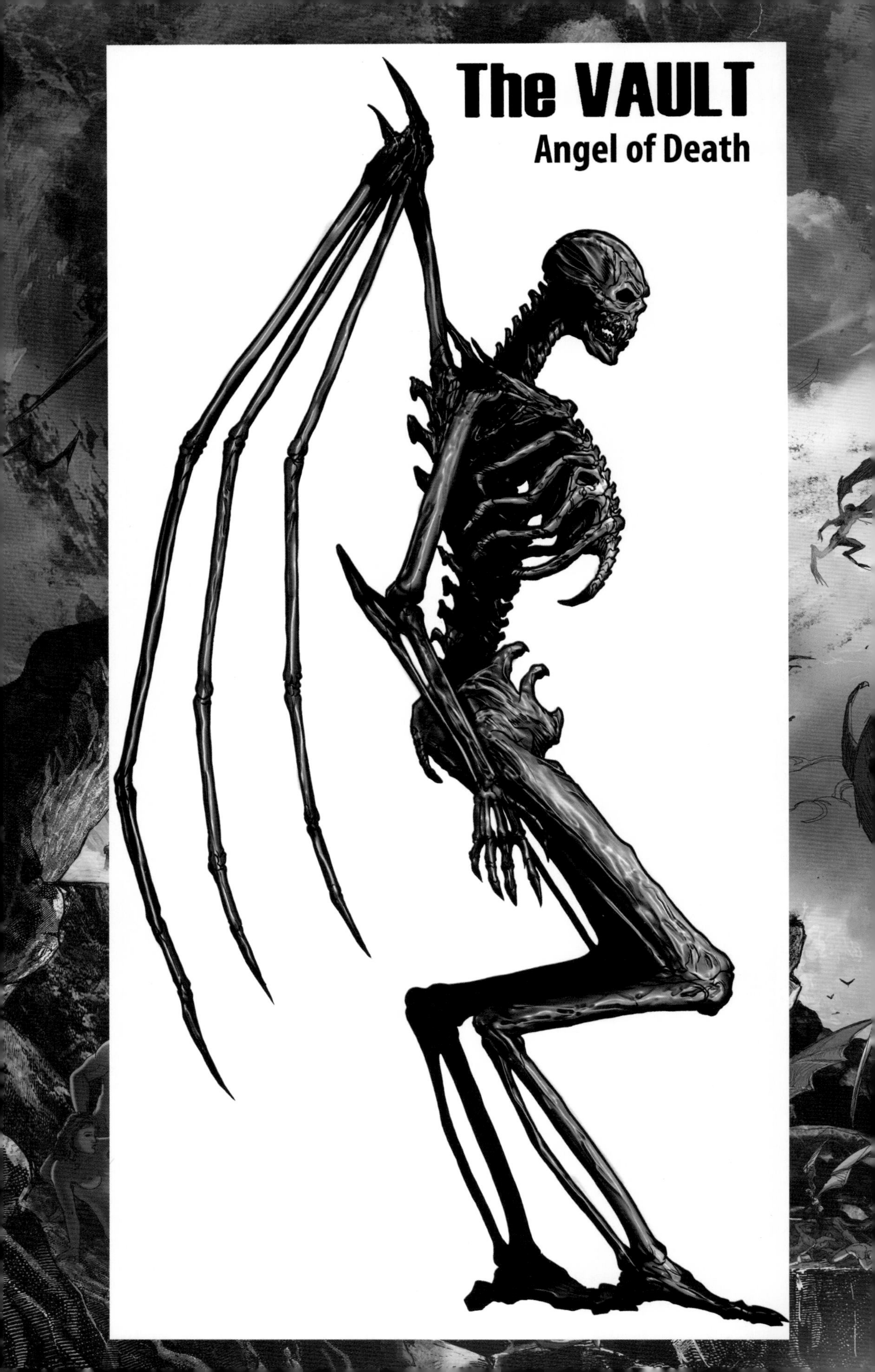
The VAULT
Angel of Death

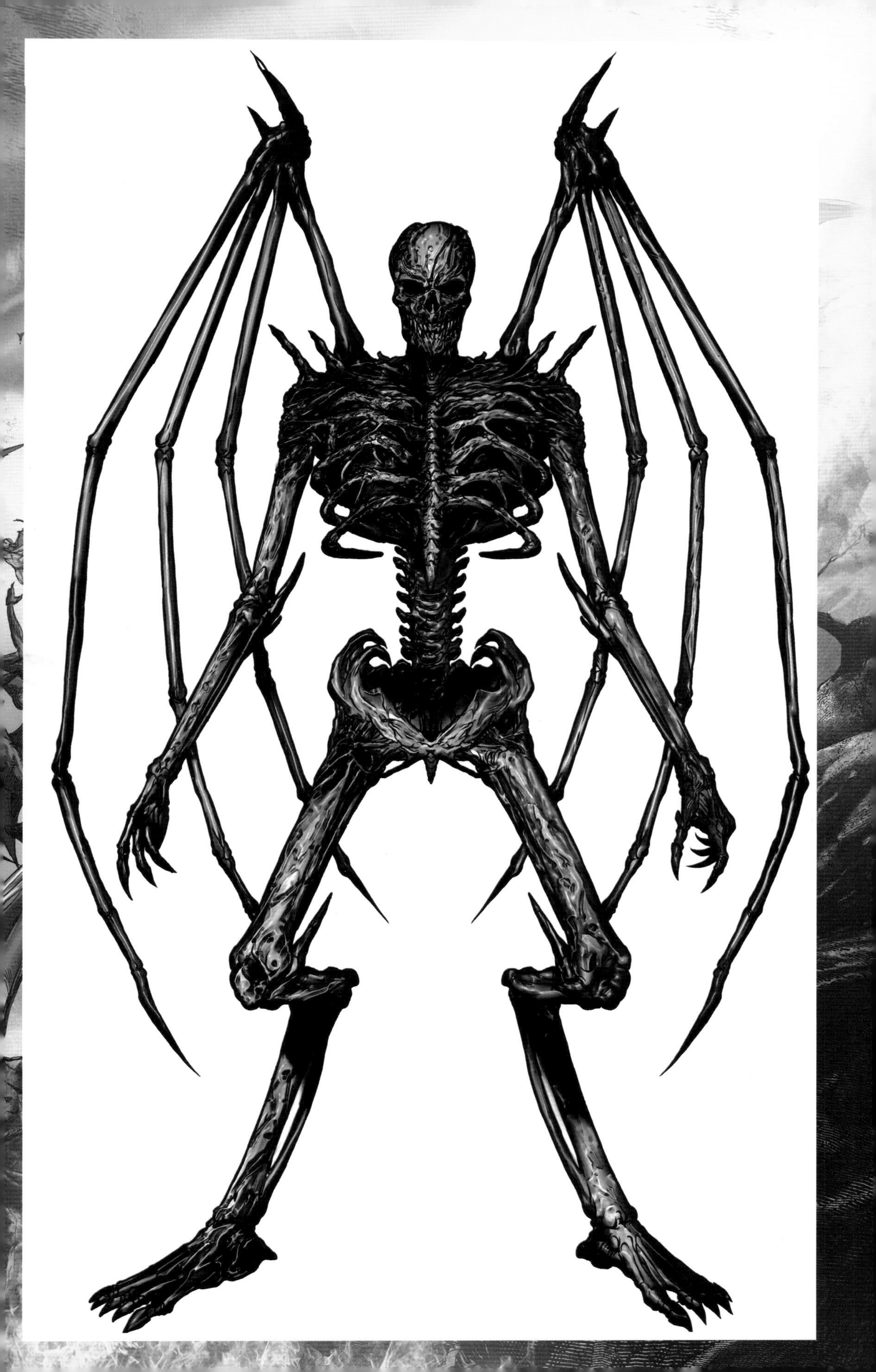

The VAULT

Production Art

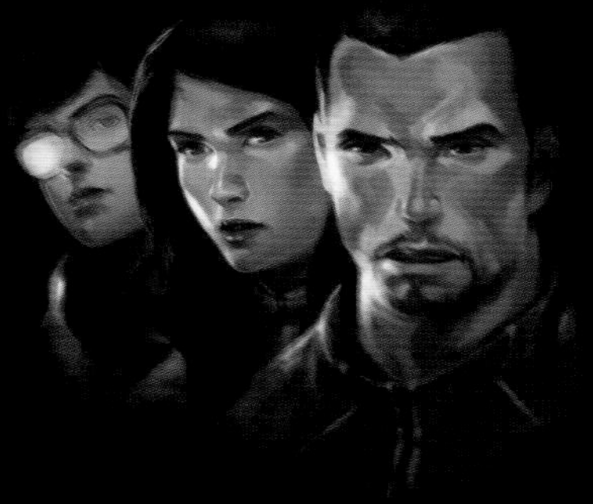

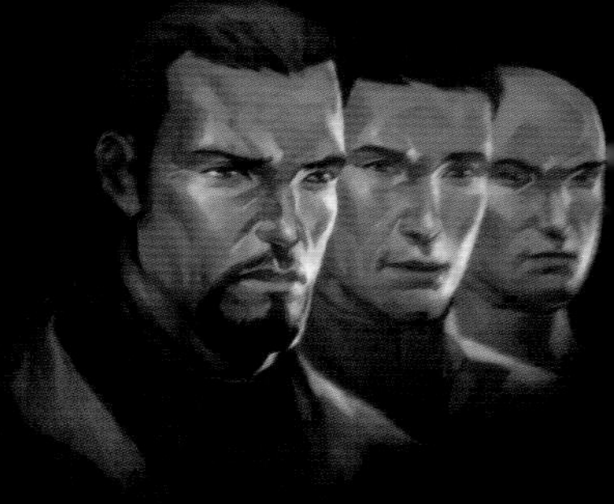

"Before starting any project it is always best to get some production art done for those key sequences in the story along with character designs. It saves a lot of time later on in the process."
- Dave Elliott

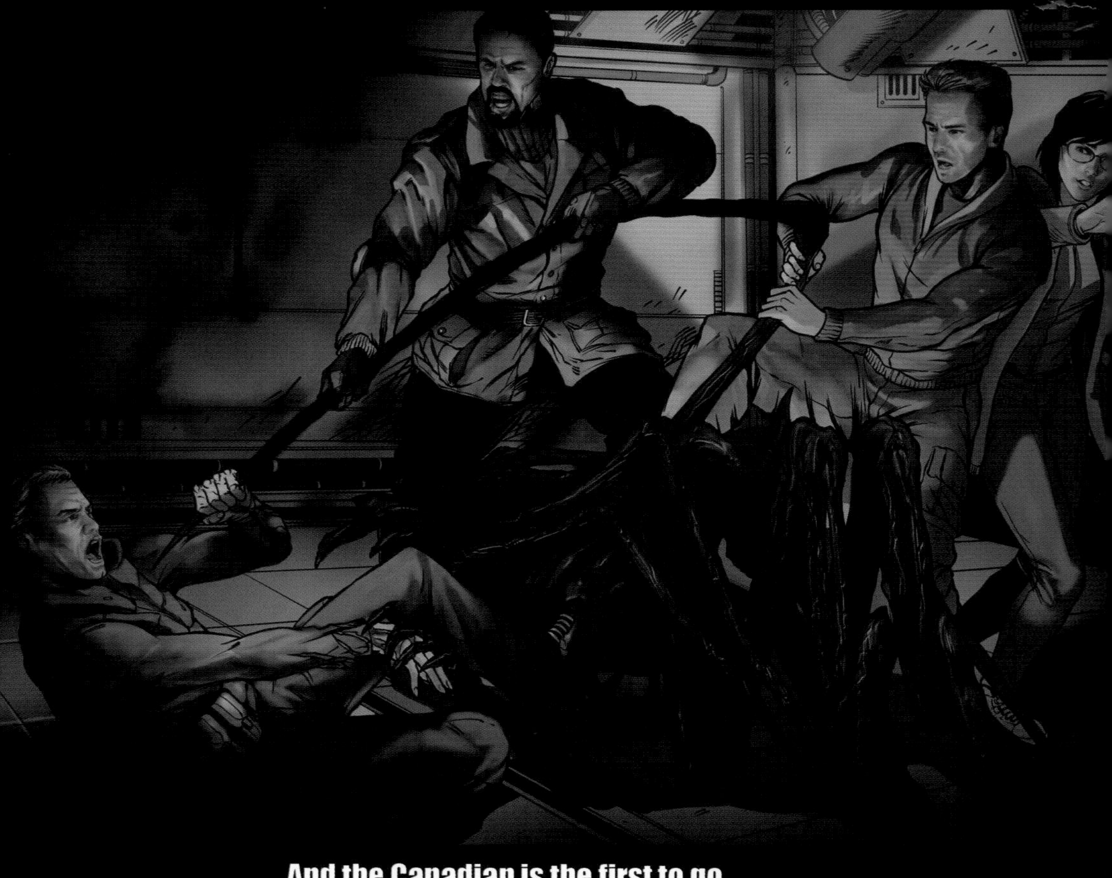

And the Canadian is the first to go . . .
When it first wakes up the Angel of Death is slow but there is no stopping it.

"It was our original idea that the MACULA would play a larger role in the story but space in just the three issues became a premium."
- Dave

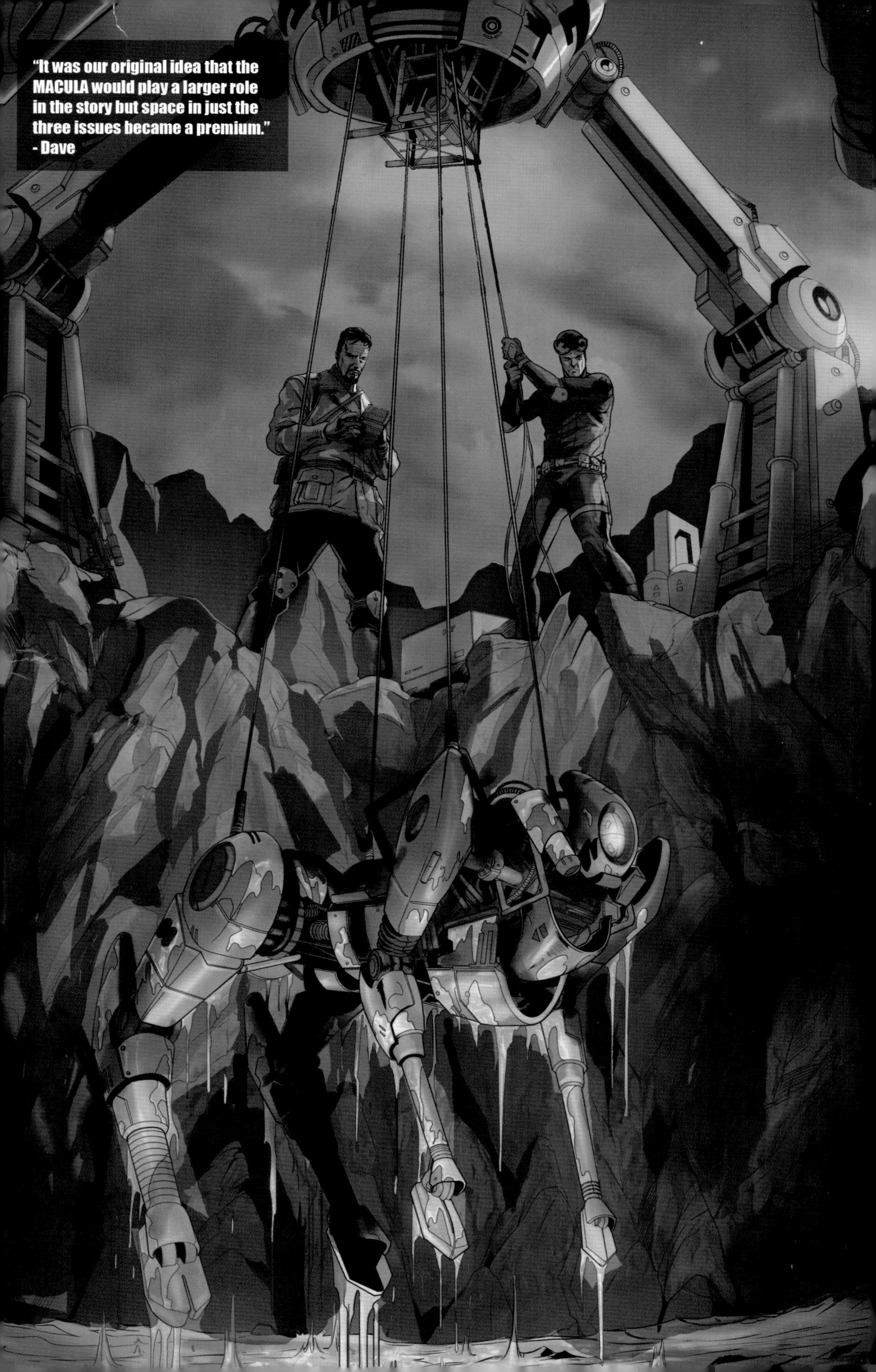

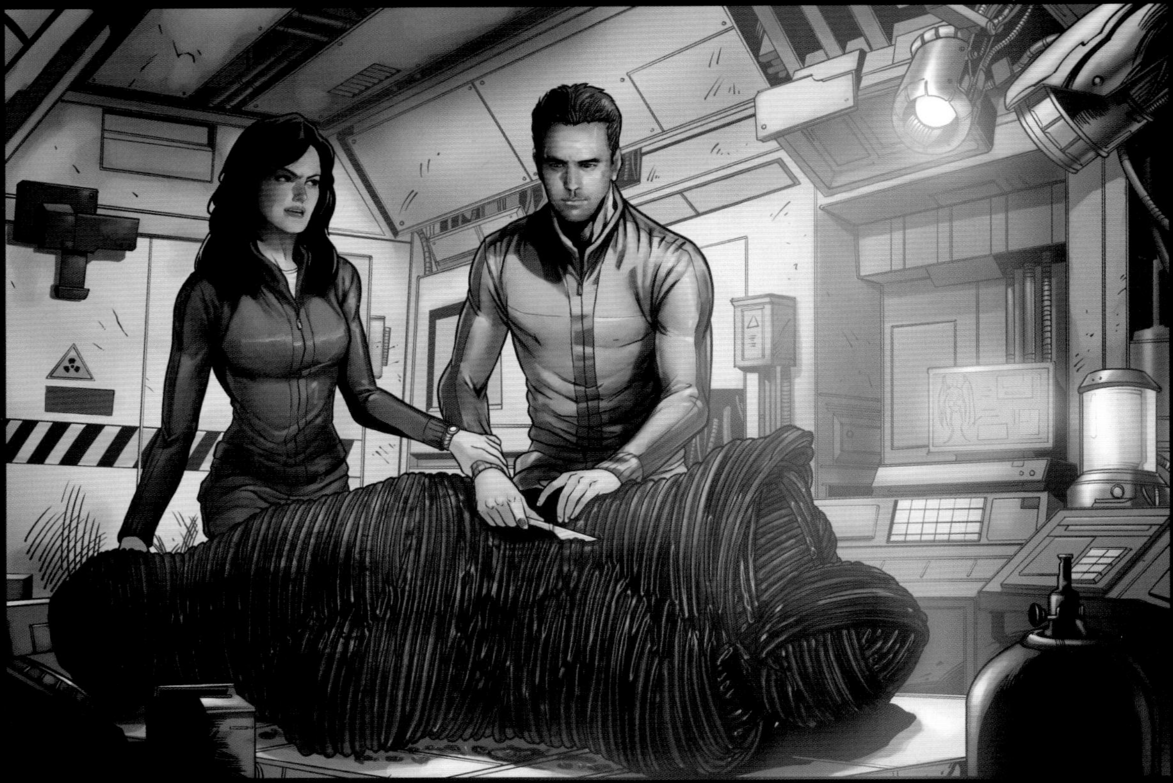

This scene highlights the relationship between the two leaders of the team; Gabrielle as the true scientist thinks about what is good for the world, while Michael's concerns are trying to make everybody happy. Michael knows the group wants to see what's inside the bindings but takes the risk of opening them upon himself.

The Angel of Death in Kirilov's sights. The crack shot industrialist, angry that this creature just killed his robot dog.

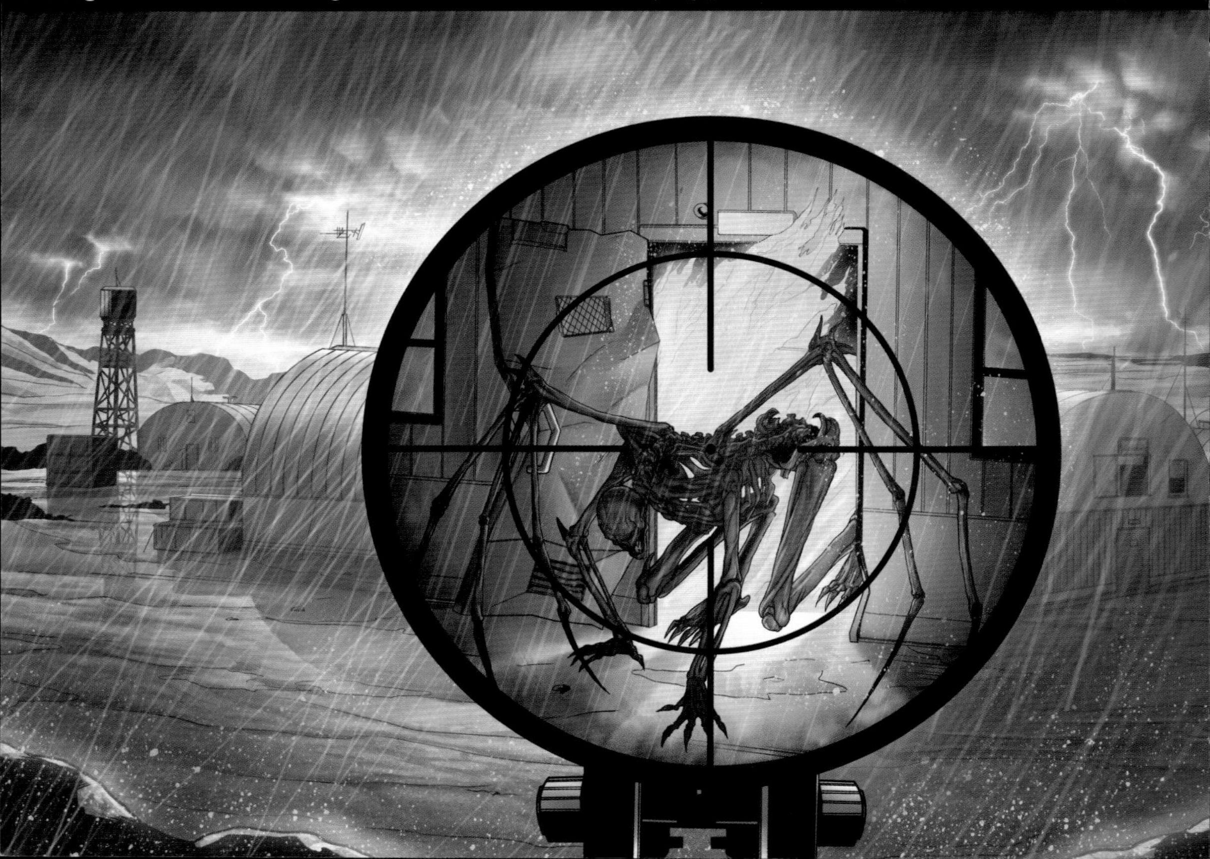

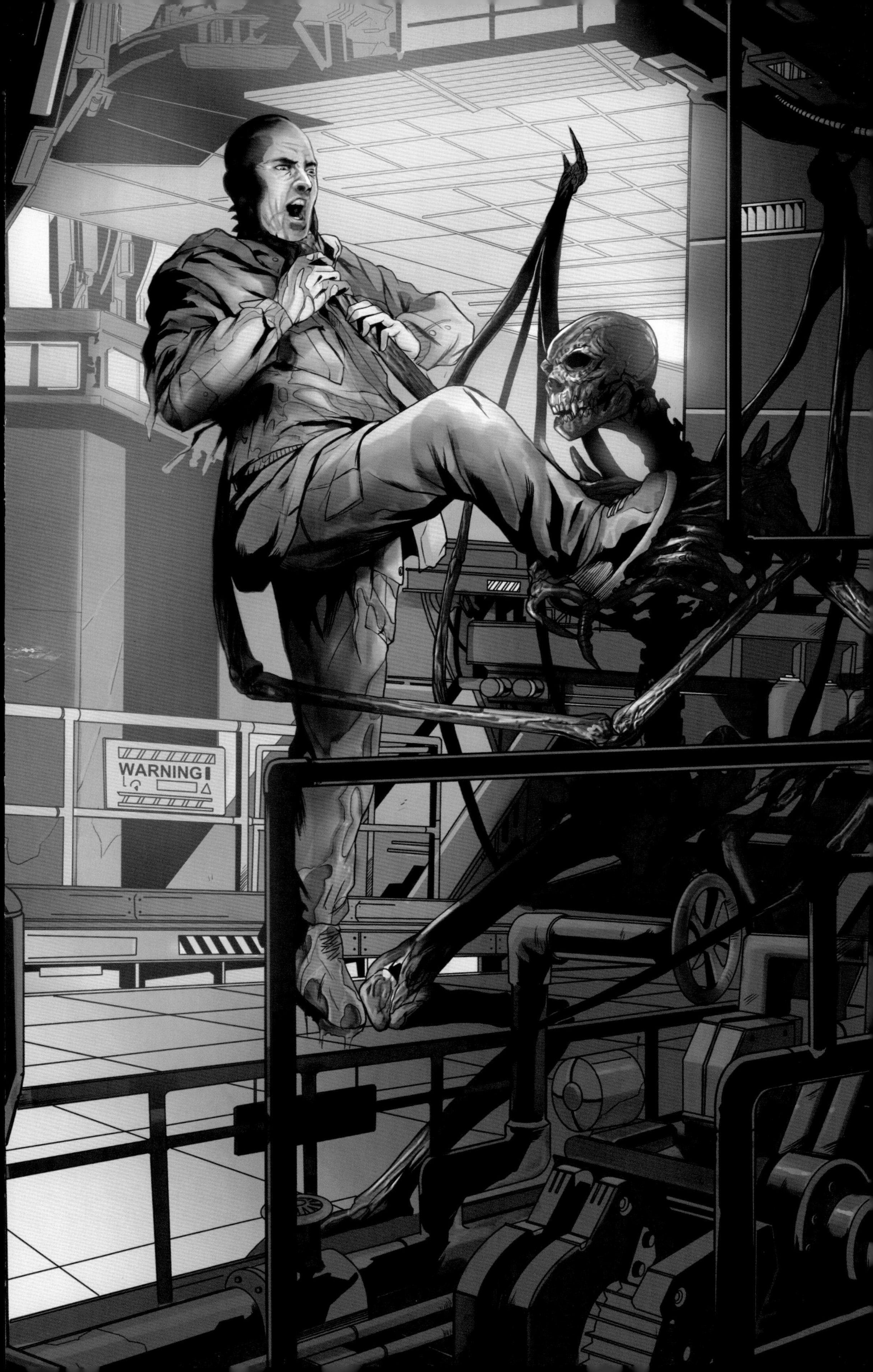
WARNING

REVELATIONS

CREW:

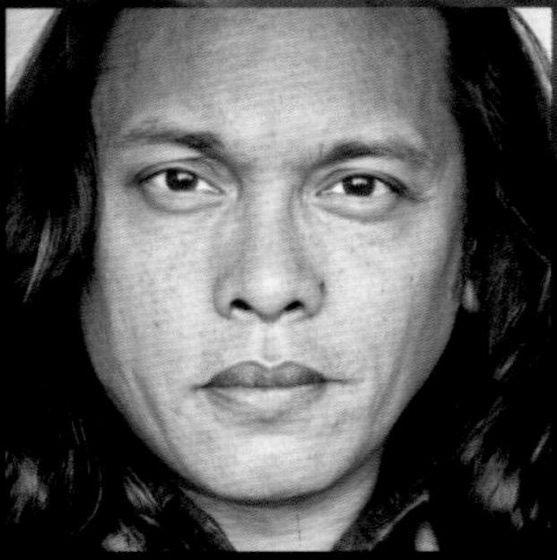

SAM SARKAR: Born in Halifax, Nova Scotia, Sam Sarkar is a 23-year veteran of the entertainment industry. He began his career as an actor and was one of the leads on the long-running, syndicated television series Neon Rider. Following the series, Sam decided to pursue writing and worked for the hit television series Beverly Hills 90210. Stemming from his work on the show, he also co-wrote a television pilot for Spelling Entertainment under the direct guidance of TV legend Aaron Spelling. Deciding then to embark on feature films, Sam took some chances, following a varied path of writing screenplays and working as a sound technician. In 2004, after working on several films with actor Johnny Depp, Sam was asked to help run Depp's production company, Infinitum Nihil, headed by Christi Dembrowski. As Senior VP at the company, he continues to serve the varied needs of Hollywood as an executive, producer and writer.

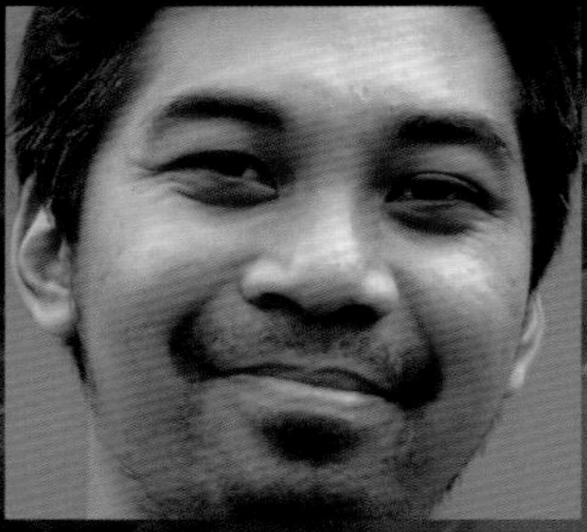

GARRIE GASTONNY: Having worked for several years as a comic book artist and illustration lecturer, Garrie Gastonny now mainly focuses on illustration to avoid getting beaten up. Garrie also serves as Senior Artist at Imaginary Friends Studios. His credits include Warren Ellis' Supergod, Caliber: First Canon of Justice and Lady Death. Garrie's next project is ODYSSEY with Dave Elliott .
For more information about the artist, please Watch his DeviantART page:
http://thegerjoos.deviantart.com/.

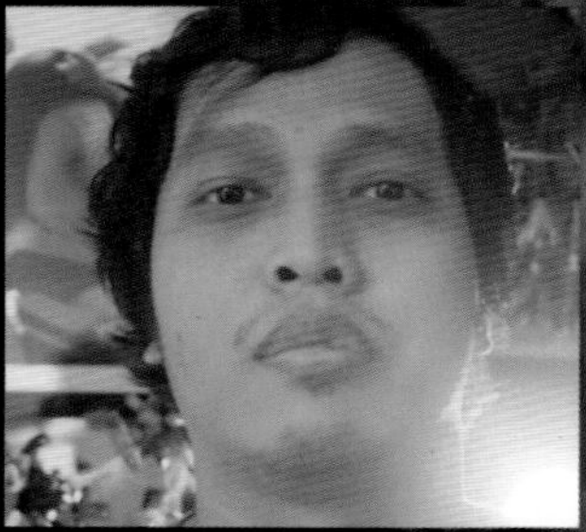

SAKTI YUWONO: As a shepherd from a distant land who tried his luck in the comic industry, it's understandable that he's very fond of the color green. Not to mention his love for lens flare and atmospheric settings. (J.J Abrams should be proud!). A hardworker. You can witness the proof when you see him late at the studio. But no, not for work. It's to cheer his favorite soccer club. (He's also a talented Right Wing player) Sakti works include projects from Image, Topcow, Ubisoft, Benaroya and more. Watch Sakti on DeviiantART at:
http://saktiisback.deviantart.com/

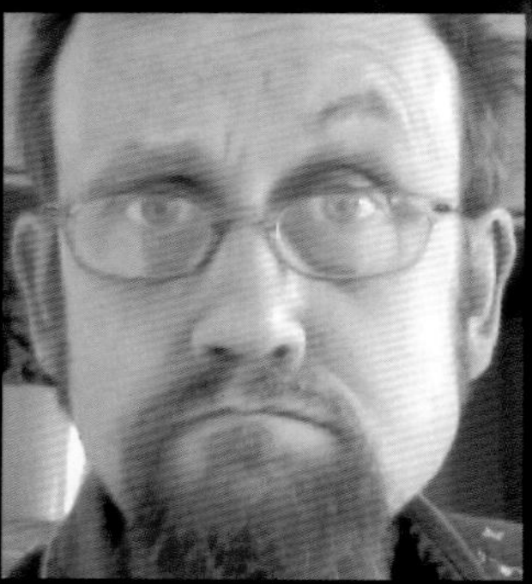

DAVE ELLIOTT: He has 25 years of experience working in every aspect of the comic industry from writer and artist to editor and publisher, working on diverse titles such as A1, Deadline, Viz, Heavy Metal, Penthouse Comix, 2000 AD, Justice League of America, Transformers, GI Joe and Doctor Who. Dave was the creator os SHARKY as well as co-founder of Radical Studios before developing several projects for Benaroya Publishing. Dave's next project's are ODYSSEY with Garrie Gastonny and ALIEN ARENA with the whole IFS crew for HEAVY METAL magazine. Dave welcomes all visitors to his DeviantART page;
DeevElliott.deviantart.com
Follow him on Twitter @DeevElliott

COMING SOON

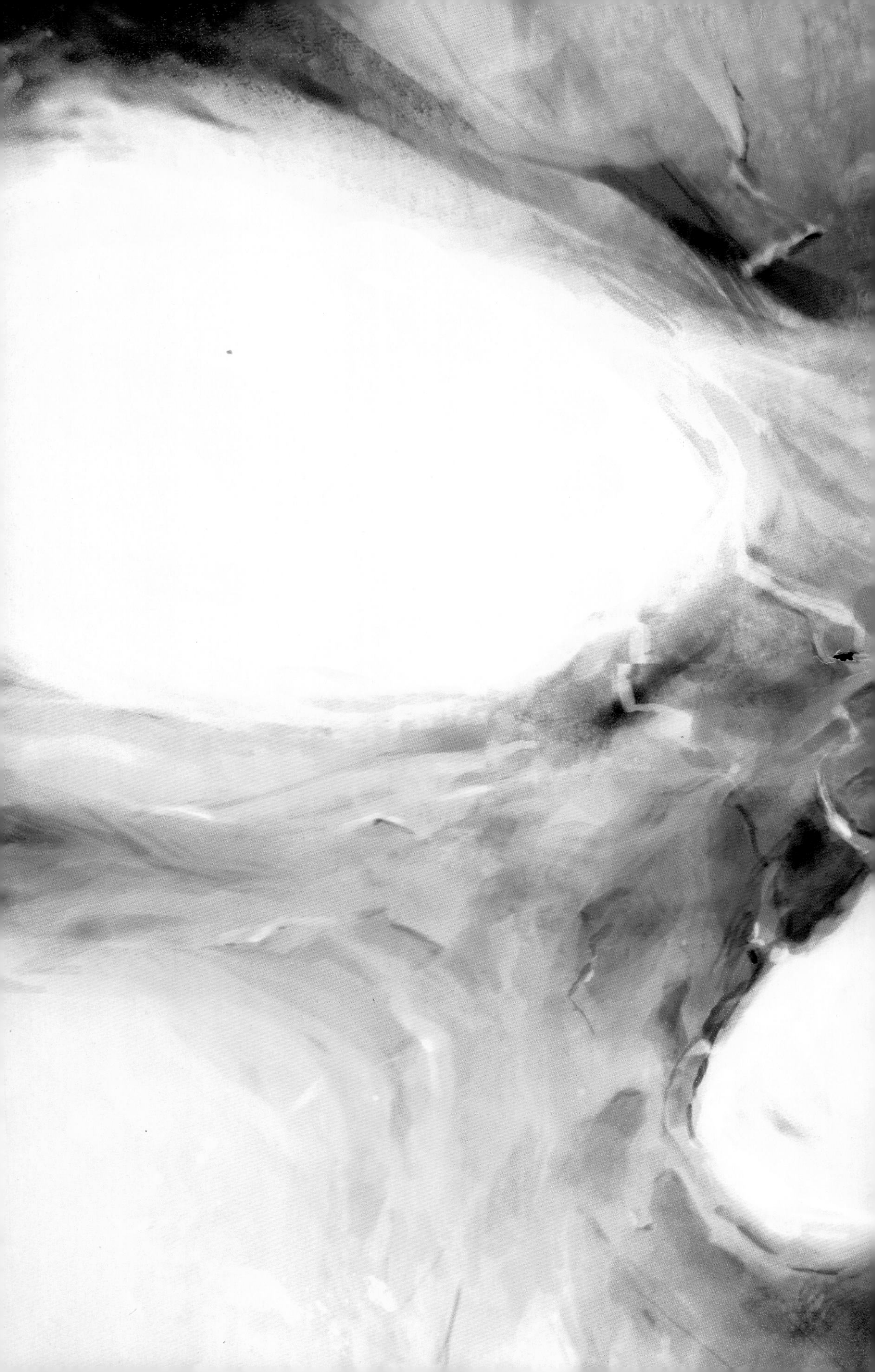